Praise for Linda Strader's *Summ*
Adventure, Love and Courage

"Linda Strader turns up the heat in *Summers of Fire*, a courageously honest memoir written by one of the first female wildland firefighters for the United States Forest Service." — Andrea Lankford, Ranger Confidential: Living, Working and Dying in the National Park

"This book needs to be read by all women who want to step into a man's world and see what it is like to give it your all and come away with much mental anguish and physical pain. We also can learn much about fighting forest fires, and many other parts of the National Forest world that we don't think about very much as visitors." — *For the Southwest by the Southwest Book Corner*

"Strader's writing is insightfully descriptive, from nature's wonders and brutality, to times when she survived only on sheer willpower, truly pushing herself physically to the brink, and the rewards she found working in the great Western outdoors. This well-written memoir will have readers caught up in the adventurous twists and turns to very end." — Karen Walenga, Review, *Green Valley News*

"Strader's story is an unsung part of the #MeToo movement . . . I found myself nodding and sympathizing as I read, and I thoroughly enjoyed her descriptions of working fires, building trail, and finding her way as a woman in what is tragically still a man's world." — Susan J. Tweit, Review, *Story Circle Book Reviews*

"It is a must read for anyone who wonders what it's like to run toward a towering wall of flames that everyone else is fleeing." — Laura Swan, *The Bisbee Observer*

"I must say I learned so much from reading this book, and this was what I enjoyed about it most. Altogether, I found this a great read on many levels and I would recommend it to anyone interested in memoirs about a different kind of life. It certainly opened my eyes!" — *Marvellous Memoirs: Reviews and links*

Uprooted

Uprooted

a new Life in the ARIZONA SUN

Linda Strader

Bink Books

Bedazzled Ink Publishing Company • Fairfield, California

978-1-949290-73-8 paperback

Cover background art
prettysleepy/Pixabay

Cover Drawing
by
Linda Strader

Cover Design
by

Bink Books
a division of
Bedazzled Ink Publishing Company
Fairfield, California
http://www.bedazzledink.com

For my dear friend, Gail,
who knows me better than anyone, even better than I know myself.

AUTHOR'S NOTE

This memoir is based on the journals I kept from 1972 to 1976.
Most of the names have been changed. Conversations in this book are
based on memory or from entries in my journals.

Acknowledgments

A heartfelt thank you to the following people for their help and support throughout the writing of this book: Joanne Burch (You are the best, Joanne!), Colin Treworgy, Cheryl Eriksen, Barbara Carter, Josiele Baron, and Keti Tamminga.

"You can't write a book in a day." But I'd sure like to try.
LMS December 31, 1974

Loneliness is a strange feeling one has inside. Sometimes one is glad to be alone. Free of all the worries that once inhibited one-self. But loneliness can also be a pain that aches constantly at one's heart, making you want to cry out, "Oh God, I need friendship to overcome this horrible feeling." But it can't always be so horrible. It just can't. Or can it? All I know is what I feel, that word, called loneliness.
LMS 1971

Chapter 1

Late summer, 1972

LIKE A WHIRLING dervish in jeans and a print jersey top, my mom danced around our living room to the song "Arizona" playing over the radio, singing along, swinging her arms, and grinning. I'd never seen her dance before, and she looked ridiculous. While that annoyed me, her joy over packing up our household and moving over two-thousand miles cross-country to Arizona proved more than I could take. I wanted to throw a sofa pillow at her and scream: *I don't want to move! My life is here. My friends are here!*

I ran into my room and slammed the door. *How could they do this to me?*

The talk of leaving cold and dreary Syracuse, New York to live in a warm sunny climate had started over a year ago. It now appeared that our family vacation to the west coast last summer had actually been to find the perfect place. After the trip, my mom had opened up the new issue of *Look* magazine. The "Ten Best Places in the U.S. to Live" article lay open on the kitchen table. Number three was circled in blue ink. Two weeks later, my mom announced we were moving to Prescott, Arizona.

Moving? I thought. *I won't go!*

In the months that followed, parental silence made me believe they wouldn't follow through. After all, I *couldn't* go. I'd be starting my senior year soon. Then, on June first, doom dropped from my mom's mouth: "Our house has been sold."

My stomach twisted. *You sold my home!* A stranger in my room? No! Would the new owners rip off the lovely blue and lavender floral wallpaper my mom and I had picked out? Would they cut down the fragrant lilac bushes where I picked bouquets? Would they tend my mom's rock garden, the one we planted with colorful tulips, violets, and hyacinths? Fourteen years of wonderful memories in this house threatened to drown me. This couldn't be happening.

The first week of August we again headed west, this time to rent a house in Prescott, and for my dad to finalize his new business plans: Prescott's first ambulance service. Once in Prescott, my parents and my younger sister, Elaine, looked at rentals. Uninterested, I sat in our camper at the KOA. After three long weeks, we returned to Syracuse to pack and be out of our home by the end of September.

I brooded over leaving my friends behind; I couldn't even finish my senior year at Nottingham High School. Elaine didn't appear to mind, maybe because she was only twelve and just starting junior high school. My older sister, Cindy, who was attending nursing school in Albany, would be unaffected. But for me, moving now would be the worst thing ever.

"Why can't I stay behind and finish school?" I asked my mom, thinking maybe I could stay with my friend Sheri, or my other good friend, Gail. Not that I'd checked with them to see if it would be possible.

"Because you are going with us," she said, firm.

The next day, my mom walked into my bedroom, and deposited several large boxes. "You need to start packing."

I glared at her and said nothing. I didn't want to pack, but after she left, I opened my closet to begin.

Later, she walked in to catch me filling a box with childhood stuffed animals.

"We are not taking old toys, Linda," she said, her arms crossed.

I clung to Doggie, his music box broken, whose patches of fur resembled a bad case of mange. Near tears, I demanded an explanation. "Why not?"

"Because I said so."

I knew that tone. She would not change her mind. I unloaded the box, tears now falling, as I handled each precious one. Then I came up with a devious plan. I waited until no one was home, and hid every single stuffed animal in moving boxes where they would not be noticed until we unpacked. A defiant smile formed on my face. *So there!*

As days passed, I accepted my fate. What choice did I have? But I began to wonder: If I lived in a new place, could I turn myself into a new me? Exactly how the "Arizona me" would differ from the "New York me," I wasn't sure, but I wished I could be more like my friend, Sheri. She flirted with ease, and had guys falling all over her, including handsome Ben. I wanted what my girlfriends had. I wanted to know and experience the love I saw in their starry-eyes when they were dating a boy. I wanted to experience the elation, the excitement, the clandestine, romantic moments . . . everything. But this didn't seem realistic in my sad world. The boys I liked never liked me. I always fell for boys who were not only out of my league, but who also didn't know I existed. Why would they? The current me was nobody special.

Sheri and I would often watch her brother's track races. At one time, I adored her cute long-legged and lean track-star brother, with dark shoulder-length hair, and a spray of freckles across his nose. After we'd barely spent any time together, Ted gave me his class ring to wear on a chain around my neck, a symbol of a serious relationship. But two days later, Sheri said he still had contact with his ex-girlfriend in another town. I gave it back. Next, I fell for his, sandy-haired, bearded, track-star friend. As usual, though, he had eyes for Sheri. In my junior year I went crazy over the drop-dead gorgeous French exchange student in my English class. I could've listened to his sexy accent all day long. No way would I even try to get past the gaggle of ogling girls surrounding him.

Maybe boys would like the new me better.

With three weeks to go until moving day, I attended classes even though I'd never finish anything I started. At lunchtime, as usual, I joined Ben and Sheri. I sat quietly while they talked and laughed, feeling awkward. I wished I could talk to Ben alone, but I could tell Sheri really liked Ben, and I didn't want to get between them. Once in a while Ben would give me a hug, or ask how it was going, but I figured he was just being polite because I was Sheri's friend.

Laden down with textbooks and focused on getting to my next class before the bell rang, I turned a corner to see Ben at the other end of the corridor. We both froze and grinned. I set my books on the floor. Drawing our finger "weapons," we pointed, and "shot" at each other, as though we were in a corny western movie. We dissolved into laughter, and then went on our way. For a brief moment I thought: *Is he interested in me?* But then I reminded myself: Why would he be? Sheri was far more fun, more slender, and prettier, than fat, boring me. That nasty roll of excess weight around my middle was embarrassing, especially in gymnastics, where we wore leotards. But embarrassment didn't stop me from raiding the fridge after team practice, smothering cookies with Reddi Whip—a sugary treat that helped fill the emptiness in my chest.

On an Indian Summer afternoon, a few days before moving, I sat on the school's lawn waiting for Sheri. She was late, yet again. She knew this drove me nuts. I kept my eyes lowered so I didn't have to notice classmates ignoring me, picking through the blades of cool, sweetly scented grass, looking for a four-leaf clover. I often did this, believing they could bring me good luck.

A figure threw a shadow across my search area. I raised my head. Instead of Sheri, I was looking into Ben's eyes through a veil of his shoulder-length blond hair. "Can I join you?" he asked.

Stomach flutters made their way into my throat, rendering me speechless. Instead of saying, "Oh, please do!", all I could manage was a smile and a nod.

He sat down, cross-legged, resting his arms on his thighs and his eyes on the ground. I studied the attractive sharp features of his face, his long eyelashes fringed against his cheeks, and the braided leather lace tied around his tanned neck.

"What're you looking for?" Ben asked, glancing up at me.

To my shock and surprise, he reached out and innocently straightened the silver and turquoise necklace I always wore. I could never let anyone else touch it, or me, like that. Hoping that he didn't notice my hands tremble, I coolly tucked a strand of my long hair behind one ear.

"A four-leaf clover. I need all the good luck I can get . . ." *Oh great, now he thinks I am silly, and superstitious.*

"Let me help you," he said.

Ben lay on his stomach, and began the search. "Found one!"

Grinning, he plucked the clover and placed it in my outstretched palm, touching me ever so slightly, sending tingles up my arm, and making my inner world spin. I placed the clover between the pages of a textbook. Just then, Sheri plopped her books between us and knelt close to Ben, who instantly sat upright, giving her his full attention, turning me invisible. All at once, the idea of moving did not seem quite so bad. I wanted to leave, right away, and abandon my invisible self on the school's front lawn.

IN LATE SEPTEMBER, my parents, Elaine, Peanuts—our beagle-mix, Tabitha—our calico cat, and I, climbed into our red Ford station wagon to head west. I dreaded the boring five-day drive. I stared out the window with a sedated Tabitha on my lap, oblivious to the state lines we crossed. Outside of some God-forsaken Midwestern town, our car broke down.

In a repair shop, I wrapped Tabitha in a blanket and stood by the car with my sister and my mom while my dad talked with the mechanic. My stomach hurt with the worry that my beloved Tabitha would die of fright from all of the loud shop noises, or somehow escape my arms and be lost forever. Thank goodness the repair was minor, and we were back on the road in a few hours.

Days later, on the first of October, we arrived in Prescott at our rental before the moving van. I stared at our new residence in disbelief. *This is it?* The plain house sat on a bare gravel lot with no landscaping whatsoever, unless the weeds were planned. Once inside, I hated the place even more. The teal shag carpet reeked of something stale and was probably infested with bugs. I'd have my own room, but the walls were dingy white, and the one window looked across bare dirt to the neighbor's wall. It was all I could do not to cry.

A couple hours later, the moving van arrived, and soon after that, a car pulled up. Out stepped an attractive guy with wavy chin-length hair who looked to be my age. I tried not to stare as I carried a box into the house. My dad greeted his new business partner's son, Richard, who'd been coerced into helping us unload.

Richard passed me carrying a large box, and smiled. This caught me off guard. *Was he smiling at me?* I lugged a heavy box labeled "Kitchen" up to the door. He set his box down on the porch.

"Here, let me give you a hand," he said, grinning.

Say something, stupid. Here's your chance to be the new you. I smiled back. "Gee, thanks!" *Gee, thanks. What a dumb response.*

Richard didn't think it was dumb, because we continued to smile at each other when we passed, back and forth from the truck to the house for the entire day.

At dusk, when everything was at last unloaded, Richard and I sat on the truck's tailgate sipping from glasses of lemonade. After a few awkward starts-and-stops of nonsense conversation, he asked, "Would you like to go grab something to eat?"

Despite every cell in my body screaming exhaustion, I lit up. Here was another chance to be the new me.

"Sure," I said, determined to be cool and calm, which I was not. Maybe this new place wouldn't be so bad after all.

Rich took me out for pizza, and my shyness melted away as we talked more. When he asked if I had been dating anyone back home, I lowered my eyes. "No . . ."

Why tell him I'd never had a real boyfriend?

Before dropping me off after midnight, he kissed me, sending my formerly aching heart soaring.

In the morning, I walked through the carpeted hallway of Prescott High School with my eyes lowered halfway, taking in my first impression of new classmates. Some boys wore buzz cuts, pointy cowboy boots, and cowboy hats; most of the girls wore skirts down to their knees—a good six inches longer than anything I owned—and button-front blouses secured at their throats. My bell bottoms, fringed belt, and peasant blouse, stylish at home, were the only ones in sight. I realized in horror that this was a cowboy town. To make it all worse, many of my course credits didn't transfer. Instead of two classes, I'd need seven. So much for an easy senior year. At least Rich had asked me out again, which helped make this new place less foreign.

Rich picked me up almost nightly to hang out with him and his friends—pot and beer always available. I drank the beer, but pot didn't interest me, and no one seemed to care when I passed it on. We'd been dating for a couple months the day Rich stopped me in the hallway between classes. Crowds swarmed around us while he stood a few feet away, staring at the floor, the clatter of lockers opening and slamming shut, kids laughing and talking as they moved on to the next class.

"I think it's best we don't see each other," Rich said, his voice straining to be heard over the din. That's when I noticed two of his pals hovering nervously behind him.

What? Did he mean we couldn't go out tonight?

"You don't fit in with my friends," he said, avoiding my eyes and catching those of his buddies.

All of the motion around us freeze-framed, sucking the air out of my lungs. *He is breaking up with me! Why?*

That's when he and his friends turned away and melded into the last of students dashing into classrooms. The bell rang. I stood there, unable to breathe, humiliated, devastated, and alone.

It took me a few moments to make a decision what to do next. In the principal's office, I asked to use the phone. Turning so no one could see my face, and speaking softly so no one could hear my voice cracking, I said, "Dad, I need a ride home."

"Are you sick?"

I stifled a sob. "No. I just want to go home."

Once outside, I sat on a cold concrete bench to wait, unable to contain my tears one second longer. I covered my face with my hands, and let them fall.

Silence filled the drive home. I stared out the car window, my face burning with shame, and my soul filled with rejection. As soon as we pulled into the driveway, I fled into my room, flung myself onto the bed, and sobbed for hours until I fell asleep from utter exhaustion. No one checked on me, which was fine. Heaven forbid I should have to explain how I'd been dumped. I wished I would die in my sleep.

Before school the next morning I told my mom that Richard and I had broken up.

"I'm sorry, Lin," she said, her brow furrowed as she spooned oatmeal into my bowl. "It'll be okay."

Okay? How can things be okay? All I wanted to do was get on a plane and go back to Syracuse. Either that or never show my face at that God-awful school again.

After another silent ride to school, my dad dropped me off at the entrance, saying, "Now, don't you go wearing your heart on your sleeve."

I wasn't sure what he meant, but I envisioned not only my heart on my sleeve, but blood dripping down my hand. Richard had humiliated me in front of the entire student body. I vowed to never, ever, let anyone hurt me like that again.

Within a week, I discovered that I'd associated myself with the *wrong* crowd—"The Dopers." How would I, or could I, ever live that down? I decided that I didn't care. I decided that I would never speak a word to another soul here. *Never*.

During study period I hid among the library bookshelves, sitting on the floor, poring over my music theory workbook. Not that I took music theory. It was bad enough that my parents could no longer afford my guitar lessons, but the school denied my one requested elective. Only band students needed music theory, or so the principal had said. No one paid any attention to me in this secluded spot, which was what I wanted.

One day, though, a guy moseyed into my private space.

"Hello," he said.

I glanced up, taking in his ruddy complexion and shaggy brown hair that touched the collar of a worn Levi jacket, annoyed that he had the nerve to speak to me and disturb my self-imposed exile. I acknowledged his gentle smile and greeting with a nod, and returned to my studies. *Please go away.*

This cursory acknowledgment didn't seem to faze him, and after a few minutes of inspecting book spines, he left.

A few days later, he returned, and again greeted me.

This time I decided not to be rude. I said, "Hi," but returned to my studies.

Again, after a few minutes of inspecting book spines, he left, this time waving goodbye.

After a few days of this, he came into my cubby, and squatted beside me. "Whatcha reading?"

Pleased that he would ask, I said, "I'm studying music theory."

Then I began to explain how and why, and he sat down, saying, "I'm Chuck, by the way."

Once I opened up, all of my pent-up loneliness made words spill out of me like a burst dam. Using a library voice, Chuck told me that he'd lived in Prescott (which he pronounced Pres-kit) all of his life. "I know some great places to go hiking. Would you like to join me some day?"

For the first time in ages, I didn't want to be alone and silent anymore. "Sure, sounds like fun."

Chuck became my first friend in Prescott. I soon decided that friendship was the ideal boy-girl relationship: no expectations, no stumbling around trying to impress, no pressure to make it anything more than friends, and, most importantly, *no* getting hurt. The other great part? I could be the real me. The Arizona me, or the New York me? With him, it didn't matter. Only one girl in that school made an effort to strike up a conversation, but I discounted her as friend material when she pressured me to convert to her religion. Besides, with the exception of Chuck, I didn't care if anyone else here gave me the time of day. I didn't care about the people, or the place.

One night, late, I went for a long walk by myself. Deep in thought, flashing lights behind me gave me a start. The police car pulled up to the curb, and the window rolled down. "What are you doing out so late?" the officer said.

Stunned, it took me a moment to reply. "Just going for a walk ..."

"Well," he said, "it's a half-hour past curfew. You need to go home."

Curfew? I'd never heard of a curfew. Trembling, I nodded, and briskly walked away, turning around to make sure the cop was leaving. A block later, my thoughts clouded. *What the hell was that all about?* I concluded that this town must hate teenagers as much as I hated this town.

LETTERS FROM MY Syracuse girlfriends were my lifeline, as were carefully timed long distance calls I made when I had enough money. "L.D." calls were all of five minutes and only once a month—all I could afford on my five-dollar allowance.

Right before Christmas, with kitchen timer in hand, I dragged the corded phone into my bedroom to talk in privacy with my dear friend, Gail.

"I miss you!" I said, my throat constricting. "What's new?"

"Nothing ... how's it going there?"

I could've sworn that was about all we could say before the timer went off and I had to hang up. Loneliness smothered me more after the call than before. Even though it was only seven o'clock, I stacked my favorite albums onto the record player and donned headphones to tune out the world. Tears flowed while I listened to the meaningful lyrics of Crosby, Stills and Nash, Buffalo Springfield, and Neil Young, wanting to go home to Syracuse, or die, until the oblivion of sleep ended my misery.

After school the next day, I checked the mail. Amidst assorted letters and bills, I found a small envelope addressed to me in unfamiliar handwriting. I glanced at the return address, and my eyes widened. *Ben?*

His note was brief, asking how I was doing in Arizona, and if I liked my new school. Thrilled to hear from him, I wanted to write back, but struggled with what to say. Should I keep it casual? *Yes, I'd better.* This was just a friendly "how are you doing" letter.

I wrote: *"Nice to hear from you! It's tough here ... I miss everyone ... what have you and Sheri been up to?"*

Two weeks later, there came another letter from him. Apparently, he and Sheri weren't an item after all—they were just friends. *"I used to look right through her to see you,"* he wrote.

Really? How much I wished I'd known that then. I wrote back to tell him how I'd always liked him, but respectfully stayed away because of

Sheri. Anticipation for his response chewed at my stomach. The letter took an eternal two weeks to arrive. I dashed into my room, shut the door, and tore into the letter like the lifesaver it was.

> *I always looked for you between classes, hoping to get a chance to talk to you,"* he wrote. *"Your smile made my day. Of all the girls at Nottingham, you were the one I should have asked out, but didn't. Now you're gone. I wish now I'd said something to you about how I felt . . . maybe we could've had something. Maybe it's not too late. I'd love to see you. Will you be coming back to Syracuse?*

I glowed. He'd noticed me when I hadn't been aware of it. The distance between us seemed like a cruel punishment. Why did it take me moving away to discover our feelings for each other? This was so unfair.

"I'll come after graduation," I wrote, determined to leave Prescott, find the love of my life in Ben, and live happily-ever-after. In order to do that, though, I'd have to save every dime I made at my after-school job.

I'd been slaving at Sandee's, a fast food joint, for a few months, despising the required matronly hairnet, my clothes reeking of grease. In early January of 1973, I quit to take a position answering the phone at a local print shop. Why the creepy owner thought he needed someone to answer the phone, I'd no clue. I usually fell asleep waiting for it to ring. Maybe he just wanted a young girl to leer at, because that's what he did.

I wrote Ben long letters several times a week, telling him how much I hated Prescott. How lonely it was here. He wrote twice a month, telling me that he was sad and lonely too, and wished he could make me feel better. When I heard from him, my heart would soar, but then stall mid-air. His letters were short—too short. Regardless, I lived for them—each misspelled word and missing comma serving to endear him to me more. On the backs of the envelopes he wrote in loopy cursive with tiny circles instead of dots over the "i"s: *It's just me!* And the little note cards he sometimes sent contained sweet, romantic sentiments. One of my favorites read:

*The postmark on this card ought to be a real collector's item . . .
it's from the loneliest place on earth. I miss you.
Love ya always, Ben*

I kept all of these romantic treasures tucked inside my personal journal, rereading each until I had them memorized. Also inside my journal, I had the four-leaf clover he'd given me, pressed between sheets of wax paper. I'd often stare at it, remembering that wonderful day in vivid detail.

In one letter, I told Ben about Rich, and how his doper friends pressured him to dump me because I didn't do drugs. Knowing that Ben smoked pot, I wasn't sure how he would react to this news. What a relief when he wrote to say he had nothing against people who chose not to smoke dope, and that, as a matter of fact, he thought they were the coolest of all. I could've danced around my bedroom . . . he loved me just the way I was! To have this two years older and incredibly good-looking man interested in plain, ten-pound overweight seventeen-year-old me, was way beyond anything I'd ever envisioned could happen.

Each day revolved around Ben, anticipating the next letter, daydreaming about being with him, holding him, talking with him. He would be the perfect boyfriend, attentive, loving, compassionate, and most importantly, he would rescue me from Arizona hell. While Ben did write that he loved me, I filled in between every line that he was madly in love with me; when I returned to Syracuse, we would be together forever. Late at night, though, awake, my brain worked overtime. Would our love be real in person? Would he still love me once we spent time together? Would I still love him? As it grew closer to my departure date, I fantasized about our reunion. Would we sleep with each other? I wanted to be ready for that. I wanted him to be "the first."

ON THE LAST day of school in warm and sunny May, I saw Chuck in front of the main entrance, talking with a guy I didn't recognize—which struck me as odd, because I thought I'd met all of Chuck's friends. I walked up to Chuck and said hello, offering a quick smile to the stranger.

"Hey, this is Roy. He plays guitar, too," Chuck said to me. "You two oughta get together."

Roy unnerved me when he grinned a bit too wide and scrutinized every inch of my body, as though he could see through my clothes. Self-conscious, I reached to make sure my shirt was not gaping open. I smiled a little, secretly hoping I'd never run into him again.

After Roy walked away, Chuck said, "Roy dropped out of school last year to get a job and help his mom pay the bills."

Dropped out of school? That was a first. Maybe that's what I should have done. It would have saved me from a year of torture.

Chuck asked me if I wanted to get together and celebrate after our graduation ceremony.

"I'm not going," I said, the same thing I'd told my mom. The day of the ceremony though, I changed my mind.

"Mom, I want to go."

She looked surprise, but pleased, and then, after a concerned glance at the clock, she said, "You'll need a dress."

In a panic, she took me shopping.

"What about this one?" she asked, holding up something that was fashionable ten years ago.

"Ugh. No. I don't see anything I like."

We ended up buying fabric and a pattern, and, having made most of my clothes for several years, I completed the garment in two hours, just in time to leave for the event.

Chuck waved at me from the crowd of students in graduation gowns, but we didn't get to talk or walk together to accept our diplomas. In less than two hours, it was over. Chuck picked me up about nine, and we stayed out the entire night, sitting in Sambo's, Prescott's only twenty-four-hour diner, talking. Although I refused to think of myself as a Prescott High School graduate, I was glad that I attended the ceremony to mark the end of an awful year, and later celebrated quietly by hanging out with a friend.

In the morning, the day before I'd fly to Syracuse, I decided to get some color on this girl who looked like she'd been living underwater for a year. My trip was all planned out: I would stay with Gail, a visit the length of which was never discussed. My ticket was one-way—a tidbit I hadn't divulged to my parents. Maybe my salvation wouldn't be in Syracuse, but at that point I decided that *anything* would be better than my life here.

After spreading a blanket in the gravelly, barren front yard of our rental home, I lay down on my back using a book for a sun shield. My arms tired, so I rolled onto my stomach to read. Soon I drifted off. After an hour, I awoke and went into the house.

When I sat down for dinner, I realized the backs of my legs hurt. Thirty minutes later they more than hurt, they raged. Turning in front of the hall mirror, I saw they were sunburned to a neon red. *Great.*

With my flight leaving at one a.m., and sunburn pain not remotely letting up, I endured the late night two hour drive to Sky Harbor International Airport in Phoenix. I'd packed a collection of albums into a carry-on, and paid extra to have my precious Guild guitar hand-placed into the cargo bay. There was no way I would travel without my music. My dad helped with the luggage and getting checked in, saying goodbye at the gate. Despite the promised special care of my guitar, what a relief to see a man tote it to the open hatch and pass it to the person inside.

This was my first plane trip, and I'd no idea what to expect. Stewardesses demonstrated safety procedures; I watched, wide-eyed, wondering if I would need to remember them later. At the Chicago airport, with far more people in one place than I'd seen in a very long time, friendly concierges helped guide me through the huge terminal. I didn't notice my guitar make the transfer, and prayed it would be okay.

The Syracuse airport was a hundred times less frantic than O'Hare, and I was greeted with heat and humidity I'd not experienced for eight months, making me regret my red, nylon body-suit, my bell-bottom corduroy pants, and my beloved hand-sewn navy blazer with red lining. I thought I'd look really nice, but instead my choices made me drip with sweat, which frizzed my long blond hair and created damp circles under my arms. My sunburned legs stuck to my pants, which amplified the pain. So much for making a good impression with Ben.

When I emerged from the gangplank, I knew Gail wouldn't be waiting for me because she was at work. Ben said he'd be there, and Sheri promised that she and another friend, Cheryl, would come. Three people waved wildly to get my attention, but my eyes focused on Ben. He took long strides and greeted me with a bear hug, lifting my feet off the ground. Pressing my body against his, I buried my face in his silky hair, clinging to him like he was a piece of driftwood in open sea.

I wanted to hug him longer, touch his face, make sure this was real, but I didn't get the chance: Sheri and Cheryl whisked us off and deposited me at Gail's house. It was hard to let Ben go, but we'd be spending every day together.

The next day, Ben came over and we went for a walk on the Lemoyne College campus near Gail's home. I couldn't get over how much greener it was here than Prescott. It even smelled green. Hand in hand, we walked on the freshly mowed grass, moist with dew.

"I want to take you on a trip to Canada," he said. "It's beautiful up there, and I think you'd love it."

I squeezed his hand and smiled. I'd love to go away with him.

After walking a while, we sat cross-legged opposite each other in the shade of a maple tree. I picked up a winged seed-pod, and twirled it between my fingers.

Ben smiled at me. "You know, I've never really gotten serious about a girl before you."

Really? I'd assumed he'd had many girlfriends.

Our conversation gradually turned to his home life.

"My dad left ages ago. It's been just my mom and me since then. She's great, and I want to make sure she's well taken care of."

No guy had ever shared such personal details with me. I felt privileged when he made it clear that even Sheri didn't know these things. I couldn't stop staring at the angles of his face, my heartbeat skipping every time his eyes met mine. When he held my head in his hands and kissed me, my body quivered, and my thoughts tumbled. *Don't stop, Ben.* That night, while we sat on Gail's front steps, I leaned into him, resting my head on his shoulder. "I love you," I said.

He squeezed me tight, and kissed the top of my head. "Oh, baby, I love you, too."

A couple of days passed, and even though I was busy catching up with friends, I found it odd that I'd not heard from Ben. He didn't call the next day, or the one after that. In fact, I didn't hear from him the entire week. I called his home and left a message with his mom, but still no return call. Ben had vanished from the planet. Numb, I didn't know what to think. My stomach hurt with the thought that we wouldn't work out. Wanting answers, I decided to go to his job at the YMCA, to confront him. I dropped a quarter into the fare box as I boarded the bus, and sat down on a cold, vinyl bench. With a hand clutching the metal armrest and my eyes focused on the seat in front of me, I mentally practiced what I would say when I found him.

Ben sat on a table in a large room, legs crossed, his hair hanging and nearly covering his face, attentive to the two teenage boys speaking to him. He glanced up, nodded, and left me standing there to wait. When the boys left, the questions I had planned to ask: "What's going on?" and "Why haven't you called?" disappeared from my vocabulary. So did my courage. I couldn't say more than a meek, "Um . . . are you mad at me?"

Ben shook his head. "No, no. It's just that I've got a lot of shit going on. I need to tell you something."

My breathing stopped as I waited for him to tell me what I'd done wrong. Instead, he said, "I've joined the Navy for four years."

The Navy? For four YEARS? I couldn't believe what he was saying. I didn't *want* to believe what he was saying. What about us? What about our life together? What about all the things I'd planned? To stay here with him—to not go back to Arizona. Forget the proverbial pulling-the-rug-out-from-under-you crap—my insides turned right-side-out. How could he do this without saying a word to me first? I wanted him to say more, to tell me everything would be okay, to tell me he still loved me, but instead, he brushed me off, saying, "I have to get back to work," and turned to engage another teen in conversation. Now invisible, I walked out.

Chapter 2

MY MINDSET: I would not let Ben ruin my summer. I channeled my energy into hating him. I mailed him a nasty letter, essentially telling him to go to hell. And who needed to move to become a new person? When a cute guy at Gail's graduation picnic asked me to go canoeing, I went, laughing loudly, flirting, even letting him kiss me that evening. My friend Cheryl invited me to a kegger, where, after I'd downed several beers, I made out with a guy whom I'd met an hour earlier. After that, flirting became my mission. At the music store, the attractive thirty-year-old man who'd sold me my guitar actually remembered me. Within a half hour, he invited me to his house to play music with him and his friends. It did cross my mind that this might not be a good idea, but I bravely took my first taxi ride to his house that night, anyway. I knew immediately that he hadn't invited me to play music. We kissed in his bedroom for an hour, and when he started to remove my shirt, I stopped him. I wasn't mentally prepared for this. I left with my virginity intact, and at midnight we parted as weird acquaintances. All the while, I justified my actions with: *Take that, Ben! I don't need you anymore.*

My wild behavior lasted almost two months. However, I eventually wore down, feeling directionless, hopeless, and, in a way, homeless. The whole time I'd lived in Prescott, despite my goal of finding a new me, all I'd wanted to do was go back to Syracuse. Now that I was here, I realized it wasn't the place I'd missed as much as the people. Most of my friends had college plans, and would be leaving soon. I had no plans to attend college because not only did I not have a clue what I would study, but my parents were by no means able to pay tuition. Feeling quite depressed, while Gail was at work at where she called "The Grease Pit" (aka Dunkin' Donuts), I sat in her dark kitchen, washing down frozen Hostess Twinkies with hot tea, until the caffeine and sugar made my hands shake, and guaranteed I wouldn't sleep all night.

Gail's mom came in and sat down. "What's wrong, dear?" she asked, resting her hand on mine.

That's all it took. I burst into tears, sobbing in her arms, missing my mom's arms, realizing it was time for me to return to my "real" home.

IN PRESCOTT, I toted suitcases into my new bedroom, inspecting my surroundings. I'd missed the hard work of moving into our newly built home. The house had been under construction when I left, but I'd not given it any consideration that I would be living there. I'd assumed that I would stay in Syracuse with Ben.

Kitty Tabitha was curled on the bed, and I picked her up and hugged her. She trilled a hello.

"Oh sweetie, I missed you," I said into her soft fur.

My mom had painted the walls my favorite shade of blue, and I appreciated the roomy closet and the two large sunny windows. Always frugal, but now for good reason as funds were tight, my mom had sewn-up curtains from new bed sheets. My bedroom was all set up, and I didn't even feel the need to rearrange. As much as I'd hated Prescott, it seemed oddly welcoming and familiar now. It was time to build a life here. Maybe get out on my own someday soon. I began a job hunt the next day.

Settled on the couch, I searched the want ads in the Prescott Courier. There wasn't much to choose from, which shouldn't have surprised me, considering the population topped out at about 12,000.

In the way of retail, we had one five-and-dime, a JC Penney, Sears, and a ranch supply and hardware store. We had a few locally-owned diners, the chain diner, Sambo's, the Third Base luncheonette, and three fast-food joints. A number of small professional offices, mostly real estate, attorneys, accounting, and the like, finished the list. Finding a good paying job would not be easy with only a high school education.

When the lecherous old man from the print shop—where I'd worked prior to graduation—called saying he needed some part-time help, I reluctantly agreed to a few hours a week. I'd have to put up with his leering and sexual innuendos, but I needed the money. Hopefully I'd find a better job soon.

The misery of the unsuccessful job search combined with missing my Syracuse friends improved when Chuck called on a warm Friday night around seven-thirty. We spent time at his house, and then went for a short walk, later meeting up with his friend Roy—the guy I'd met the last day of school and didn't much like. Chuck had things to do, and left Roy and me to play guitar together and talk. We had fun, and I really enjoyed myself, despite my earlier reservations about him.

In the morning, Chuck and I went for a hike in Sycamore Canyon with his pet raccoon, which attracted considerable attention from other hikers. "Is he yours?" "What's his name?" "Does he bite?" Chuck answered the questions every single time.

"I found him as a cub." "Rory." "No . . . not yet anyway."

I tired from all of the interruptions, which almost spoiled the enjoyment of this beautiful, lush canyon. With clear creeks and a blue sky above, the air clean, moist, and full of magical scents—how could this possibly be the Arizona I'd imagined as desolate as the Sahara before we moved here? At the edge of the water, Chuck reached in and plucked a handful of a green, leafy plant.

"Taste this," he said, offering me some.

Tentative, I ate a few of the tender watercress leaves, which left a pleasant, peppery flavor in my mouth. I never knew you could find something edible while out hiking.

"I'm thinking of moving to Alaska someday," he said, as we continued our walk. "Maybe even homesteading. Did you know that you can get free land up there if you set up a small farm? Free! I'd live off the land: hunt, fish, forage, grow some of my own food . . . I think that would be awesome!"

Free land? The thought of being self-sufficient intrigued me. I'd have to look into this.

Chuck and I fell into comfortable silence on the way back to his truck. I reflected: *What a great day . . . a beautiful place and a good friend to share it with.*

The next morning, though, I awoke to my current, depressing reality. I needed a job, but I still refused to face six months of greasy slavery for the measly price of a plane ticket. That was not my goal in life. What was my goal? For sure it was not making malted milkshakes at a buck-thirty an hour. And it certainly was not working at the print shop, where I grew more uncomfortable by the minute around the dirty old man and his creepy stares.

A week later, Chuck gave me a lead. "The U.S. Forest Service is hiring. You should go apply!"

They were temporary positions, but I didn't care. It was a job, and even better, it was a job working outdoors in the forest instead of in a stuffy office. I called the Prescott National Forest's office and left a message.

The phone rang a day later. The Forest Service. My heart started thumping.

"So, we've got a patrol position open," the man said. "It'll only last through wood-cutting season, but it may spill over to next year. No prior experience required. All you need is a driver's license."

My flying soul crashed. *Damn.* I had a learner's permit, but never saw the point of a license. I had no money or car to go anywhere, and if I wanted to go somewhere, my friends or parents gave me a ride. I hated how this ruined my chances of getting that job, but, lesson learned, I immediately started studying and practicing to take that driver's test. I felt optimistic. Maybe another Forest Service job would open up in the near future.

Still mulling over the idea of homesteading, I checked out a few books from the library. At home, I curled up on the couch, and turned the pages of the homesteading primer, fascinated by the idea that I could have my own Alaskan farm, complete with log cabin, chicken coop, vegetable garden . . . the works. *I'll have to cut down the trees . . . dig a well . . . firewood for heat . . . cold cellar for storage . . . can I do this? Why not?*

LATE AT NIGHT, snuggled under the covers and waiting for the oblivion of sleep with Tabitha curled at my feet, I mulled over Ben. Did I love him for who he was, who I thought he was, or for who he could have been? Maybe a little bit of all three. I turned onto my back. It was as though we were meant for each other, but it took my moving away for us to figure that out. Why had I believed he loved me? True, he had written about me being the right one for him, and how he wanted to be with me more than anything. All that time we wrote to each other, he didn't really say what he wanted to do with his life, and I hadn't thought to ask. Why did he decide to join the Navy without running it by me first? Although the day he told me I'd been angrier with him than I'd been at anyone in my life, it had faded. I missed him. Terribly. I wanted him back. But did he want me back?

I reviewed all I knew about Ben:

He stood about an inch short of six feet tall, with long light blond hair, brown eyes, and was a phenomenal two years older than me. An air of confidence, but not arrogance, followed him everywhere. I knew he smoked pot and cigarettes, but I thought that was no big deal. He wasn't a groupie; he never hung out just to be like the other cool kids.

But what I didn't understand were Ben's intentions with me. Well, actually, maybe I did. I concluded that he thought we would work out because I comforted him through bad and lonely times—just like he'd comforted me. But then he saw me. I wasn't pretty enough, that's for sure. I didn't know how to say the right things. Ben had much to offer, but he must have realized that I was not the one he was going to offer it to. I knew I'd never hear from Ben again, because if he'd wanted to contact me, he would have done so by now. I'd always love Ben.

THE NEXT TUESDAY, I made a gutsy move, and applied at the Prescott Music Center even though they hadn't advertised. I didn't have any sales experience, but maybe my love of music would help.

In the meantime, I'd passed the written driver's license exam. Next up: the dreaded road test.

Friday morning, I sat on my trembling hands in the waiting room. What if I screwed up and failed? Visions of accidentally running a stop sign were enough to make me queasy.

A grumpy, bald man called my name, giving me a look which translated in my world to: "Oh great, another female teenager on the road."

While sitting in my mom's Ford station wagon with the DMV test administrator, I tried to remember all of the things my dad had taught me: *Adjust the mirrors. Buckle in. Use the turn signal before leaving the curb. Always look to your right, then left, and then right again, before making a left turn.*

"Go straight, and turn left at the next light," Grumpy Bald Man said. And we were off.

Nervous as heck, I focused hard on the road, other drivers, checking all of my mirrors constantly. Thank goodness the test didn't include parallel parking, probably because Prescott had mostly angled parking spaces.

Back at the DMV, I put the car in park, and shut off the engine. Grumpy Bald Man mumbled, "Humpf. Unlike most teens, you passed the first time."

I guessed that was supposed to be a compliment.

In the morning, I proudly drove myself to the music store to check on my application. The owner was polite, and smiled kindly at me, but did not offer me a job. My bruised ego perked up when Chuck, Roy, and I went to the County Fair. We wandered around, played a few arcade games (where I proved I had no skills in those whatsoever), and people-watched. What a surprise to see Rich, the guy who dumped me at Prescott High School, and a group of his buddies. They must have been ripped, I decided, because they actually acknowledged that they knew me by saying, "Hey, hi." I nodded, but immediately turned my back. *Jerks.*

The next Saturday, I decided to set up "shop" at the Prescott Swap Meet. My family had boxes full of miscellaneous stuff from Syracuse that my mom gave me permission to sell. I hand appliqued pillows with scraps of felt, and hoped to sell those, too. I set boxes of items on the ground and wrote "25¢ each" on their sides, folded clothing into piles on the tailgate, and taped a "$1 each" sign next to them. I positioned the pillows next to the clothes, barely leaving enough room for me to sit.

After a couple hours in the hot sun, I had sold two blouses and a scarf. An hour later a woman bought a skirt. I added the dollar to the three in my shoe box.

Just as I looked up, there stood Roy.

"How's sales?" he asked, smiling.

I laughed. "I made four dollars so far . . . and probably got sunburned."

He eyed my handiwork, picking up one of the pillows decorated with a mountain scene. "You made this?"

I lowered my eyes and nodded.

"I'll buy it."

Thrilled, I added two more dollars to my stash. Maybe I could buy some sheet music tomorrow. "I'm done here for the day. Want to play guitar?"

"Sure," he said. "I'll meet you at your house."

Roy and I played for a few hours until we decided to go for a drive. I hopped into his Chevy pickup, sitting on vinyl seats cracked wide open, exposing the foam inside. The tang of oil and gasoline accompanied the roar of his turning over the engine; a puff of blue smoke spewed from the tailpipe.

A short time later, we parked on the shore of Granite Basin Lake. Although not a swimming lake—in fact, none of the lakes in Prescott were anything I'd get into because they were shallow, weedy, and, well, had questionable bottoms—this was one of my favorites. Nestled among house sized granite boulders tossed every-which-way, its deep blue water reflected the massive shapes, creating a perfect mirror image.

Roy and I climbed through the intricate maze. He scrambled atop a huge one, extending his hand to me. I didn't really need his help, but accepted the sweet caring gesture. We took turns giving each other a hand while leaping from rock to rock, laughing and joking, talking about Science Fiction movies and TV shows we'd seen and liked, leading to a discussion about life on other planets, and the possibility of aliens visiting Earth. When we reached a predominant perch, we sat to take in the view and catch our breaths.

"Remember when we went out with Chuck the other night? Maybe you noticed," he said, "I just couldn't stop staring at you. I really dig that smile of yours."

In fact, I had noticed and had wondered what that was all about. But why would he like my smile? Just his mentioning it made me cringe. Years ago a childhood friend had made fun of my smile, saying it was too wide and showed too much of my gums. From then on, I hated it with a passion. Sometimes I tried to hide it with my hand, or force my lips closed. But still, I thought Roy was a really nice kid—and I considered him a kid at only sixteen years old—someone I'd love to have as a friend, but nothing more. I thought he had other ideas. But after the heartbreak with Ben, I decided I would not let any guy cause me that kind of anguish again. Staying just friends seemed like a safe plan, one that would prevent either of us from getting hurt.

"Oh, look," Roy said, pointing. "A red-tailed hawk!"

The beautiful bird soared overhead, showing me red-tinged tail feathers from underneath.

After talking some more, we climbed down, and he drove me home.

On Sunday, I decided to return to the swap meet. The activity and crowds were fun, and encouraged by the sales yesterday, I hoped to make more money. This time I raked in $3.45, and that, along with the eleven I had saved from yesterday and what I'd earned working at the print shop, meant that I would have some spending money for our upcoming Phoenix trip.

Monday, I woke up with a nasty sore throat. *Rats.* I hated being sick. I also preferred to stay home when sick rather than infect everyone I met. I called the print shop to say I wouldn't be in. Not that I cared about missing work. My very part time job with that jerk needed to end. Not only did he creep me out with the way he leered at me, but lately he'd started asking prying questions about boyfriends. Even creepier. I had to find another job.

When Roy called that night to see how I was feeling, we talked for a while, or rather he did the talking because it hurt for me to do so. After we hung up, I thought, *How sweet of him to call*, but I also sensed that his concern tip-toed into more than friendly checking-up on me.

Next day, I felt better. Roy and I decided to play guitar at his house. We did more talking than playing. After three solid hours, it was pretty apparent that he was getting serious about us, based on the way he looked at me and the things that he said. I decided to make it clear that we could be friends, but nothing more.

"It's a long story," I said, "but Ben really hurt me last summer. He's out of the picture, but I'm not over him yet. So, I'd rather not get too serious right now. But we can be friends. Okay?"

Roy listened, nodded, and seemed to understand my pitch that we could be friends, which I found a tremendous relief.

"Let's get out of here and go for a drive," Roy said.

I saw no harm in it, and off we went.

A Bob Dylan tape playing, our conversation interspersed with laughter—we were having a genuinely good time cruising Prescott's narrow, winding mountain streets. At one point, Roy's forehead creased, and he turned down the music.

"It's fine with me to leave it as friends," he said. Locking his eyes with mine, he added, "But if you ever want to change things, I can certainly make arrangements."

Arrangements? I smiled at his formality, but I had no intention of changing my mind. "Um . . . okay."

Driving down another dark and twisting road, our speed barely requiring a shift into third gear, his voice turned animated.

"I'd planned on seeing the country this summer and would like to have you come with me," he said. "I want to take you to see all of these great places I know in Colorado, Idaho, maybe even to Missouri, where I plan on hitting up some farm sales to buy antiques for resale here. I want you to come." He turned to smile at me, then back to the road. "It'll be fun. Will you?"

Glowing with pleasure, I still had no idea what to say to all of this. Travel with him as "friends only"? How could I pull that off with my parents? They would never let me travel alone with a boy. Did I want to go with him? In truth, everything he said made me feel important and, well, special. I didn't say yes or no. "I'll think about it."

For the rest of the ride, Roy elaborated about all of the places we could go if only I would go with him. Then he said, "I don't know how guys can resist you."

He hit a sore spot. My mood plummeted; darkly I thought, *Didn't take much for Ben.*

Home again, Roy shifted his truck into neutral, and enclosed my right hand with both of his. "You know what they say . . . cold hands, warm heart."

I'd not heard that before, but let him continue to warm my icy fingers. I enjoyed the feeling of his strong hands wrapped around mine.

With eyes wide and locked onto me, he said, "Goodbye, friend."

He reached out and touched my hair. "You have beautiful hair, Linda."

My breathing halted while he fingered the strands draped across my shoulder, making my scalp tingle. God if "the look" wasn't in his eyes then my name is not Linda. What to do? For sure, his fascination with me electrified my soul. Even though I didn't see what he did, Roy made me *feel* beautiful. Stunningly beautiful—all by the way he looked at me, smiled at me, and laughed with me . . . but the only thing he didn't make me feel was romantic towards him. Why didn't it matter? Well, for one thing, I *knew* I was not pretty.

I'd never forgotten the day in the fifth grade, when a group of boys literally *barked* at me like a pack of dogs, pointing and laughing. Humiliated that they thought I was an ugly "dog," I hated every imperfect square inch of myself. To compensate, I took offense to compliments, believing they were insincere, believing the guys delivering these were dismissing me as a person with no mind, heart, and most important of all, no personality.

The longer Roy stared at me, the more nervous I became. To break the awkward silence, I sat up straight, and with my finger, wrote in the dust on the dashboard, *"Remember tonight."* Roy leaned over to read what I wrote. With his finger, he added beneath it, *"Remember yesterday."*

I'd no idea what he meant, but that didn't matter. I enjoyed Roy's company, reveled in the feeling that he thought I actually *was* pretty, while not feeling the same way that I was now darned sure he felt about me.

Chapter 3

EXCITING NEWS: A job I'd applied for at a travel agency actually generated a return call. I'd have to train in Kansas City for a week if I got it. What an adventure that would be! All of my fingers were crossed that this would actually happen.

Two days later, they called to tell me I didn't get the job.

What is wrong with me? Why is life just one disappointment after another?

I couldn't help but wonder if the world would be better off without me.

Later, Roy telephoned, and I shared the disappointing news first.

"I'm sorry to hear that," he said.

"Yeah, thanks."

We chatted about nonsense stuff, what we'd been up to, etc. The whole time I dreaded saying what needed to be said, but knew I had to be honest—clear the air about where our relationship was *not* going. When there was a lull in our conversation, I dove in before I chickened-out: "I've been thinking—hard. We really need to keep this just friends, Roy."

When he didn't say much other than "Okay," I figured we were good. What a relief.

WITH NEARLY FIFTEEN dollars burning a hole in my wallet, I joined my family headed to Metrocenter on Saturday, a shopping mall in Phoenix that probably matched the entire size of Prescott. On this trip, with a little financial help from my mom, I made out like a bandit. I bought two albums: Jackson Browne's *For Everyman,* and Neil Young's, *Time Fades Away,* two 45s of songs I loved, a stylish suede coat with cool zipper accents, new shoes, and both a chambray and flannel shirt. Because this kind of shopping event rarely happened, it almost felt like Christmas.

Even though we'd gotten home late that night from Phoenix, early Sunday I decided to try again at the swap meet. This time, a little more organized, I again used the tailgate to display some items, but hung clothes on a rack, and tagged everything with what I thought were reasonable prices. All set up, instead of frying in the sun like last week, I waited for customers while sitting cross-legged inside the station wagon, where I'd folded the seats down. I smiled politely at people funneling by, and then lit up when I saw a familiar face.

"Fancy seeing you here," Roy said, grinning.

Whenever he gave me his rapt attention, his eyes locked on mine, his smile and laughter as he talked to me, inexplicably, the world stopped, just as the world stopped for that guy in Rod Serling's *Twilight Zone* episode when he found a watch that froze time. By two-thirty, the crowds had thinned enough to make staying any longer a waste of time. I accepted Roy's offer to go somewhere. After closing up shop, I locked the station wagon, and climbed into Roy's Chevy pickup.

"Want to go to Sambo's? Or we could head out to Groom Creek," Roy said, smiling his Bob Dylan smile at me.

Cruising the streets, hiking, sitting in the woods talking, or, if we had any money, drinking tea in Sambo's: this was the way of life Chuck and Roy had introduced me to. Chuck had a decent job. Roy did too. At any rate, I wasn't working, and had no money to do things, so I followed their lead.

"Groom Creek!" I said.

Mid-October had transformed the forest . . . golden aspens, a touch of red and orange here and there, almost rivaling Syracuse's autumnal showcase. A wave of homesickness for the sugar-maple-lined street where I grew up threatened to swallow me whole. Last fall, before we moved, I collected the prettiest leaves I could find, mottled with a palette of orange, red, pink, and green, and dipped them into paraffin as a preservative. They were in an old stationary box on my upper closet shelf.

Soon Roy eased along an old mining road carpeted yellow with fallen aspen leaves. It had rained a few days prior, and the air was rich with the heavenly scent of leaf decay and damp pine needles. We parked amidst a grove of tall quaking aspens next to an old, weathered cabin with a tin roof. Peeking through dirty windows, I glimpsed a set of rusty bedsprings, and a small wood cook-stove.

"It's an old miner's shack," Roy said. "I used to come here and spend the night, until someone locked it up." He tugged on a sturdy padlock. "Follow me."

I shadowed Roy as he made his way through the grove. A stiff breeze rustled the yellow leaves far above our heads; a few floated down, seesawing through the air like golden feathers. Clueless teenagers, inspired by the aspen's smooth white bark, had carved hearts, initials, and "love forever" into some of the trees. Sacrilege. Whenever I saw this, I wanted to track down the culprits and make them erase what they'd done, but there was no undoing the permanent damage.

Roy stopped abruptly, sat down on the ground, stretched out on his back, and stared straight up. "Come look."

Lying at his side, I realized why he liked this: Glorious, lemon yellow leaves, dancing and twittering with the breeze, sunlit and shimmering, contrasted against the deepest of blue sky. Roy took my hand. I saw no need to pull away. Talking all afternoon, we shared personal stuff: Me, the pain of moving to a strange place; Roy, how his broken home and feelings of worthlessness had made him hate life at times.

"My dad left my mom when I was little," Roy said. "Life was really awful for a long time. But you've changed everything." He turned over to prop his head on his hand and look directly at me. "I've been thinking about you hard ever since last week. I really, really like you, Linda."

My heart swelled, but I didn't know how to respond. His boldness made me hold back from saying I liked him, too. This did not sound like just friendship. My non-response didn't seem to bother him, though.

He sat up and scooted closer to wrap his arm around my shoulders. "You know, I thought I knew myself. But now that I've met you, I'm not sure anymore." He took my hand in his. "I want to take you to Canada. You'd love it up there! I want to love you . . ."

Panic closed my throat. *Love? No, that's way too serious.* "Geez, Roy, I don't know what to say. I mean, I like you, but I've explained to you that I'm not over Ben yet . . ."

"I'm beginning to feel like Ben's brother, because from what you've told me about him, Ben and I are much alike."

You are? I'd have to think about that.

By now the sun hung low on the horizon, and the air took on a chill. We left that lovely spot, and Roy dropped me off at my house.

Later, in bed, I made a twisted mess of the sheet and blanket with all of my tossing and turning. Finally, I lay still, staring into the darkness, unable to sleep.

Roy said he thought he and Ben were much alike. Are they? Does that explain why I like him? Because somehow he reminds me of Ben? Because there is a notch already cut into my heart for Ben—the one he didn't stick around long enough to fill, that Roy can? What is wrong with me? Why can't I relax and see what good might happen with Roy? WHAT am I afraid of?

It made me angry that I thought I still loved Ben. *You don't even know if what you feel for Ben IS love!* Was I falling in love with Roy? For some stupid reason this made me feel I was betraying Ben. Which in turn was ridiculous. I'd not heard from Ben since the day he told me about joining the Navy. Did I believe Ben would reappear, saying he'd made a big mistake? That he still loved me? My mind fluttered from Ben to Roy. Maybe Ben was becoming just an excuse to not get involved with anyone else—to avoid setting myself up for another painful rejection. And geez, who was this Roy guy, who had worked his way into my heart, despite my best efforts not to let him do so?

Sunday evening, Roy called, and we again went cruising, ending up on a dirt road near the geographic feature that defined Prescott: Thumb Butte. This volcanic pillar could be seen from just about every point in town—a great landmark in case one got lost.

Roy parked the truck, and reached under the seat, producing a flat glass bottle of blackberry brandy. He unscrewed the cap, and offered it to me. I'd never had anything other than wine or beer before. I took a tentative sip. A burst of fruit flavor accompanied the pleasant burn as it slid down my throat. I handed the bottle to Roy, and he also took a swig.

"Let's look at the stars," he said.

We climbed into the bed of his truck, and lay side-by-side, staring at the incredibly dense pinpoints of lights filling the indigo sky.

Roy pointed. "That's Venus."

The planet shone brighter than any star in the sky.

"And that dense cluster . . . that's Andromeda. Another solar system. Isn't that amazing? I wonder if there's life there . . ."

He guided my arm to help me find the location. Although I loved to star gaze, I'd never had anyone to star gaze with, or anyone who knew the constellations, planets, and solar systems. I was intrigued by the thought of life elsewhere. A meteor streaked a brilliant white arc, and we gasped.

"Have you ever wondered," Roy asked, "if someone on another planet in another solar system is doing what we are right now, and wondering the exact same thing?" He laughed. "Little green men sitting on the tailgate of their spaceship wondering if there's life out there . . ."

That made me laugh. "Do you think they think we are also green?"

Roy laughed, and we had more fun coming up with images about that far away planet and its inhabitants.

Next, taking the bottle with us, we sat on a log to play our guitars for a while, sipping more brandy between songs. I'd never been able to play in front of anyone besides my family before, but Roy—and maybe this time the brandy—changed all of that. He showed interest in my music, and even though our tastes weren't exactly the same, we both appreciated meaningful lyrics.

Roy set his guitar down. "I've been wanting to say this all evening, Linda."

I held my breath. What would he say now?

"I want you to know that I love you."

I sighed inaudibly. *Oh, Roy. Why did you have to ruin our nice, casual outing? I can't believe you. It isn't possible, for one. And two, there's no reason why you'd feel this way. What was there to love about me?*

"It's true," he said, sliding his hands down my arms, warming my skin. Then he grasped my hands, and squeezed them gently. "I know this is love. I've never felt like this."

Despite my reservations, hearing him say this over and affected me . . . wouldn't it just about anyone? I let him kiss me, our first, one that lasted a minute or so. I reveled in the feel of his mouth on mine tasting of blackberries, the scent of his skin, his hands in my hair . . . his kisses became more intense. Where might this be going? I ended our embrace. "We'd better get back."

He seemed confused, but I needed to be alone. I needed time to think. Time to sort out my emotions. What did I want? (him?), What did I feel? (love?) But I can't love him. I love Ben.

We packed our guitars and got ready to go, but paused a minute when Roy sat on the tailgate. I did too, feeling the cold metal penetrating through my jeans.

After a few moments of silence, Roy lowered his eyes, and said, "Have you ever thought about giving up on life? I mean, are there ever times that you just don't see the point?"

Surprised at the sudden change of topic, but relating to his comment, I had no problem responding.

"There have been times . . ." I said, also lowering my eyes.

Roy nodded. "I've thought about suicide. Put a gun to my head, and be done with it. Sometimes life just plain sucks. People judge me for being poor. Girls ignore me 'cause I'm not a handsome jock."

To hear Roy talk this way made me ache for his troubles. A while ago he'd shared with me a few details of his rough home life and a biological father who was unavailable. His mother, a sweet lady, struck me as a bit meek and submissive. I'd never met a single mom before. Chuck had told me a while back that Roy had dropped out of school in his junior year after the divorce in order to support he and his mom. That explained why I'd never seen him around campus before Chuck introduced us—he'd already quit.

But I didn't care how much money he had, and admired how hard he'd worked to help out his mom. No one could deny that he was a fantastic musician . . . I didn't want to get serious, but something drew me to him . . . what?

"I'm sorry," I said, feeling completely inadequate. I didn't know what else to say.

"Well, let's go," Roy said, hopping off the tailgate.

Parked in front of my house, I opened the truck door. Roy touched my arm. "Linda, I love you."

The honest emotion in his eyes caused deep emotion to rise within me. I kissed him on the cheek, and left him wide-eyed and wondering, which left me wide-eyed and wondering all night. If I admitted to myself that I loved Roy, then it meant that I didn't love Ben, and *that* I couldn't bear to accept. I wasn't ready to give up on Ben. Only one alternative remained with all of this uncertainty. I would have to tell Roy I couldn't do this.

My opportunity came the next morning when Roy called and we talked a few minutes. I told him that things HAD to be different from now on. I explained that I would only be his friend. He said "okay" and he'd call later. I felt much better having been honest with him.

By this time, Kim, who was also two years younger, became a friend of sorts. Not sure how we met, and although we didn't have much in common, she was the only person, aside from Roy and Chuck and a girl I'd worked with at Sandee's, who showed any interest in getting to know me. Sometimes I felt bad for Kim. Like me, she didn't have many friends. But she also lagged behind other sixteen-year-olds both physically and emotionally. How awful to have the bad luck of needing to wear braces. She was also wardrobe challenged. True, her clothes could have been hand-me-downs; but still, I didn't own or want fancy clothes, and managed to avoid looking frumpy.

Kim and I went shopping a few days after Roy's and my conversation. We approached my house just in time to see Roy's truck pulling away from the curb.

"That's Roy," I said to Kim, pulling into our driveway and parking. "Did you know he was coming over?"

I shut off the engine. "No, I didn't. I wonder what he wanted to see me about."

We gathered up our packages, and Kim left.

Shortly thereafter, Roy called. "I just have to know. Was it something I said or did?"

My stomach twisted. *Oh, God.* I'd hurt his feelings. Did he think I was rejecting him? In a way, I guess I was. How could I say this gently? I didn't want to hurt him more. I shouldn't have let him kiss me. Tears spilled down my cheeks. "Roy, it was all my fault for not sticking to friends only. There's nothing in the world I can do or say except that I am sorry I let you think I wanted more."

Dead silence.

A tightness in my throat made it difficult to say, "Look, I'm really sorry. If you can't be my friend, I'll understand completely. If you change your mind, I'll always be here."

More uncomfortable silence.

Roy finally spoke. "I don't know what to say."

"I'm really sorry."

A click and silence.

Based on the disappointment in his voice, I probably wouldn't see him for quite a while. However, I had faith that he'd be fine—probably as soon as tomorrow. Tonight, well, I'd be awfully proud of him if he didn't give me a second thought. I felt badly, but also proud that I'd handled the situation the best I could have.

Late that night, I tried to evaluate my so-called love for Ben and the feelings I had for Roy. Is the way I feel about Ben the same way Roy feels about me? We both love someone who can't reciprocate. If this was true, then it couldn't be real love. Real love was equally shared. Otherwise, it was the typical one-sided love that had little meaning and bordered on self-indulgence. Roy had me analyzing love and its meaning more than I ever had before. For the first time in my life, I felt what it meant to have a heavy heart.

AT THE SWAP meet the next Saturday, Chuck asked me to join him for the Spook Night event in Jerome, a ghost town of sorts. What a perfect place to spend Halloween. He'd call later. Imagine my surprise when it was Roy who did the calling. Seemed he was going too. They picked me up at seven.

Chuck and I talked while Roy sat in the backseat, getting loaded on brandy, staring out the window, and saying nothing.

Chuck carefully maneuvered the treacherous, switchback road up and over Mingus Mountain to reach the former mining community, built precariously on nearly vertical slopes. Most of the structures had met with ill fate, either tumbling down those slopes, or sagging from neglect and rotten timbers. These old buildings fascinated me. What was it like to live here in the late 1800s? I could only imagine how the homes looked before the years had taken their toll.

Arriving in Jerome, I put on my Levi jacket before stepping into the crisp autumn-night air. The three of us meandered through the streets crowded with revelers, some even in costume. I loved Halloween. I always considered it "my" holiday, since it fell three days prior to my birthday. As a kid, I had a blast making spooky decorations, going through boxes of old clothes to assemble a costume, and looking forward to our farm trip to find the perfect pumpkin. At carving time, it took a number of sketches to come up with my pumpkin's perfect expression. Once a teen, though, I skipped decorating and was too self-conscious to dress-up, even though I kind of wanted to. What I loved about Halloween now was that it made me nostalgic for those childhood memories, but also because it fell during my favorite season.

A rock band played in Jerome's small park, and we stopped to listen. Roy discretely reached for my hand. Mildly annoyed, I pulled it away. He put his arm around me. Irritated, I slipped out from under it. I wanted Roy to quit making passes at me, but I also didn't want to make a scene. Why was Roy was being so pushy? Had I given him a reason to think my saying "no" meant "not right now" or "maybe later"? Chuck didn't know what the hell was going on—but now wasn't a good time to fill him in.

When the band took a break, we moved on. Lots of crazy, costumed people milled around, no doubt influenced by a few too many drinks. It was fun at first, but when the event wound down, and we headed home, it suited me fine.

On the road ten minutes, max, Roy leaned over from the back seat. "I don't know where you come up with the ridiculous idea of friends only, Linda. There's no such thing."

My spine stiffened. "Of course there is. Chuck and I are the perfect example."

"*No*, there isn't," he said with conviction. "Somebody always wants more. You can't tell me that sex won't get in the way. It always gets in the way!"

I clenched my jaw and turned around to look at him. "You have no idea what you are talking about, Roy. You're drunk." I shifted back to looking out the windshield.

That didn't end it. All the way back, Roy insisted I was living in a fantasy world, and that I needed a reality check. He accused me of leading him on and getting joy out of it. He swore at me. Called me names. Told me where to go. Nothing I said made any difference. This went on for an hour. Chuck didn't intervene, and although I understood why he might have chosen not to do so, I also wished he'd backed me up. He could have at least told Roy to shut up.

The next morning, I continued to relive the entire argument. Chuck and I managed a friendship, so why couldn't Roy and I have one? Roy was just plain wrong.

Later in the day, I began to calm down. I recalled other things Roy had said that were not antagonistic—that, in fact, touched a part of my soul no one had ever touched before. At one point he said, "You know, I was nothing 'till I met you. You help me live. You make my life worthwhile."

I make his life worthwhile. That left me in awe. Why couldn't I feel that way about him?

Roy called before noon the next day. "I really didn't mean all of that shit I said last night."

My thoughts skipped to something I'd heard a number of times: Drunks tell no lies. "I'll have to think about it, Roy. I'm pretty mad at you right now."

Silence went two beats too long. "Okay."

I gently placed the received in the cradle, felt tears form, and swallowed hard.

After only two days of not hearing from Roy, I prayed the ringing phone was him, and it was. There was no denying that I'd missed him.

"Have you forgiven me yet?" he asked.

"I have . . ." I said, and coerced him to talk to me for forty-five minutes hoping I didn't sound as anxious as I felt. I enjoyed talking to him, something about the way he said my name really got to me, but I wanted our relationship to stay casual—I couldn't handle anything more. At the same time, I thought, *Heaven forbid it ever gets to the point that Roy never calls again.*

THE CLASSIFIED SECTION in the next afternoon's newspaper held promise: A job to answer phones in a busy real estate office, another for a file clerk in an accounting firm. Although neither paid squat, and were not particularly of interest to me, I figured something was better than nothing. I applied for both, and started the waiting game.

Later that week, while out cutting firewood with my mom, I twisted an ankle. Now laid up and unable to walk, I spent the day with it elevated on a pillow, using ice packs to reduce the swelling. When the phone rang, I had to hobble into the kitchen to answer because everyone else was out. I should have let it ring. It was yet another reminder that no one was going to give me a job. Ditto for the second call an hour later.

My ankle felt a little better in the morning, but not well enough to go anywhere. Bored, I forced myself to get out my oil paints, which I'd not used in ages. I wanted to paint a landscape scene for Roy. Engrossed, the afternoon flew by. Once completed, I thought it turned out well, and hoped Roy would like it.

Snow falling the next morning improved my outlook. I loved watching and experiencing snow. Kim called to invite me to a gathering at her house that night. "We're all a very friendly group," she said. "I can't wait for you to meet everyone. You'll have a great time!"

I didn't particularly want to go—Kim was always trying to convert me to her Bahai faith—but I decided it couldn't hurt to meet new people. With my ankle feeling better, and Kim living only a few blocks away, it also gave me a chance for a delightful walk in the fresh layer of white powder coating the sidewalk.

Lights shone from every window; music and voices were loud enough that I had to ring the doorbell twice. Kim answered the door, invited me in, and promptly left me on my own. I stood against a wall, watching people standing in groups, engaged in lively conversations, as though at a cocktail party. Not one single person acknowledged my presence. Too shy to introduce myself, I edged sideways, making my way to the refreshment table. I poured a cup of punch. Feeling out of place and invisible, I finished it, and slipped out the front door. *I'll never do that again*, I thought, scowling as I marched home.

In the morning, surprised by an actual letter from Roy, I went into my room and sat on the bed to read. Not really a letter, Roy had written me a poem. Should I have felt honored? Instead I felt lost—lost between the lines, between words that were said and words that were implied: *"for I was born upon the floor . . . filled with clouds of confusion . . . drowning . . . dying . . ."* And the mention of me—standing at his grave.

The graveside description scared me. What was he trying to say? This dark side was new . . . disturbing . . . yet, I found myself more intrigued and curious about this guy, and the magical effect he had on me. Another effect I couldn't squelch was the chemistry that I'd begun to feel around Roy. I started to fantasize. What would it be like to sleep with him? When he'd first brought up love, it had turned me off . . . I had been in the friends only mode. But now, he had me curious, especially after showing me a different side than the one always talking of love. Roy was so different from quiet and reserved Ben. If I indeed loved Ben, why didn't I fantasize about him much? If I didn't love Roy, but he loved me, would that make sex with him okay? I was torn between what I thought was okay and what society thought was okay.

At six that evening, Roy called. "You want to come over and play guitar?" How perplexing to hear him speak so casually after the serious poem he'd sent.

I joined him at his house. For several hours we recorded our music, critiquing the playback in order to improve. Then we went for a ride.

Roy drove us out the forested and quiet Senator Highway. My hands rested in my lap while I stared out the window. I may have appeared calm to him, but inside every nerve-ending sparked. After the fun we had playing music, and now alone with him in his truck, all I could think about was what it would be like to be with him. Could he tell? I'd even dreamed about making love with him. Wasn't it wrong for me to want Roy in this way?

Roy placed his hand over mine. "I know I've probably said this a million times, but I'm going to say I love you until you believe me."

What *do* you say when someone tells you they love you, and you can't find the words to describe how you feel toward them? The power of his words made me want to believe this was about more than sex, but my gut-instincts just wouldn't let me.

Roy let my hand go and took the steering wheel. "By the way, I'm planning on leaving Prescott the end of the week."

Icy cold tendrils wrapped around the previous warmth. *You're what?*

"I cannot let you go," I said, recognizing that this was just one more weird thing to come out of my mouth lately that probably drove the poor guy crazy. A knee-jerk reaction. I couldn't let him go until I was sure about us. What if he never returned?

Roy swerved onto the first side road and parked. Once he shut off the engine, he leaned toward me. I met him more than halfway and kissed him first, touching his tongue with mine, hungry for more. Caught up in the passionate moment, when we paused to catch our breaths, for some stupid reason I confessed that I'd had quite a dream the other night.

Roy sat up straight and leaned away from me, his eyebrows raised. "Really? What about?"

OH NO! Why in the hell did I say that? I backed up, saying, "Forget it! There's *no* way I can tell you."

Now he was quite animated. "Was it about me?"

Oh, Lord, why did I bring this up? "Umm . . . yes."

"Was it about something I did?"

My shy smile formed. Well, of course it was.

His brow creased. "Did I hurt you?"

Oh my God, no! I made a flash decision to tell him. If I didn't, who knew how much more he would have misinterpreted my reluctance to elaborate. "I dreamed you made love to me."

Roy's eyes widened. "You dreamed I made love to you? Is that what you want? I'd love to."

This was getting way out of hand. "No, I mean, I can't. I just can't," I said, wondering if it was a lie.

He looked puzzled. "Have you ever done it?"

My face burned at this very direct and personal question. "No, I haven't."

"Me either," he said. "Look, I want to give you everything I have. All of me. I love you so much, maybe too much, please love me." Roy squeezed my hands. "I hope you know I don't want just your body. I want *you*, too. I can make your dream come true, or make love to you and still be there to continue to love you. You can have your cake and eat it too," he said, quoting Bob Dylan while giving me a lopsided smile.

I wanted to believe that, oh, how I wanted to believe that. But I didn't. I was not lovable. Getting dumped by both Richard and Ben had proven that. And maybe I questioned what I wanted from Roy. If I was going to get physically involved with someone, shouldn't there be some kind of love between us?

Roy must have picked up on something from me, because his tone changed. "It's pretty clear Ben is still getting between us."

Shocked he'd bring up Ben, I said, "No! I don't want Ben anymore."

Did I say that hoping Roy would believe it? Or to make *myself* believe it by saying it out loud?

Roy threw his hands up in frustration, and then gripped the steering wheel hard, shaking it. "You want Ben SO damn bad, Linda. You really do."

I didn't reply. Could he tell what I was thinking? *No Roy, I don't. You are wrong. I think I want you, but for what? One night? One night that I'd probably regret?*

In the morning, thoughts of Ben and Roy continued to play in my head. Why did I cling to Ben, who didn't want me? That Roy found me irresistible stirred up plenty of desire. I'd always told myself Ben would be the "first." Why did I now want it to be Roy? To prove to Ben that he didn't matter? I rolled my eyes. *As if he would know.*

No one was around to help me sort everything out, to help me understand my inner turmoil. I wanted to confide in Gail, my best friend in the world, but worried that even she would judge me for thinking about having sex with Roy when I didn't love him. It even sounded terrible to me! I had only a couple of girlfriends here, but none of them were close. My friendship with Kim was an odd one. She acted more like a clingy younger sister than a friend. No way could I discuss my physical attraction to Roy. Her religion didn't condone sex before marriage. Thank goodness I had my trusted journal, my only other real friend, who was always there to listen non-judgmentally. In my journal, I poured out my deepest secrets—my scary and puzzling attraction to Roy. My need and longing for real love. My fears of the future. The times I thought life was too hard, and I didn't want to live anymore. Sadly, there were times when writing in my journal wasn't enough, and this was one of them.

Desperate, late that night, I called Chuck, asking if we could meet.

While we sat in Sambo's, I filled Chuck in on Roy's declaration of love. Chuck's face registered surprise, which surprised *me*.

"Roy didn't tell you?" I asked, both stunned and hurt that Roy wouldn't tell his childhood friend about being in love.

Chuck, the good and wise friend that he was, said, "Roy's the type to want to cling to someone and keep it to himself. Don't worry about it."

My concern faded a bit. "I suppose . . ."

He patted my hand. "Look, Roy is very immature in a lot of ways, but mature in a lot of other ways, too."

A ton of anxiety melted off of me like snow in the sun. Knowing that someone else was familiar with Roy's complexity helped. Our conversation drifted to marriage in general, friendships with the opposite sex, and serious relationships. We both agreed that serious relationships at our age were usually nothing but games, and, overall, pretty senseless—it was nice to know that my feelings were not uncommon, and that he and I were on the same page.

After he dropped me off at home a bit before one a.m., I quietly slipped into bed, hoping my parents didn't hear me come in. While they'd never dictated a curfew, I didn't want to take chances that they would think I needed one. Under the covers I thought about Roy, letting all that he'd said to me lately sink in. I had to admit that his fascination with me was quite flattering, and romantic. Maybe this could go somewhere. My heart fluttered when I thought about making love. Sure, sex with Ben had crossed my mind a time or two, but I didn't get the skin tingling with him that I got while thinking about Roy.

THE DAY BEFORE Halloween, I drove down White Spar Road to find a place to walk in the forest. Not ten minutes out, to my horror, there lay a dead German Shepherd in the ditch. My heart broke, not only for the poor dog, but for the owner, who would certainly be devastated.

I drove on, and once I passed the Prescott National Forest boundary, I parked. I slung a canteen over my shoulder, and walked into the tall trees. Pine needles snapped under foot, releasing their heady scent that always calmed my mind and relaxed my body. After walking for an hour, contemplating not only my dilemma with Roy, but the demise of someone's beloved pet, I headed back to the car. At home, I mentioned the dog to my mom.

"Oh my, that's so sad," she said. "You know, there was an ad in yesterday's Lost and Found section about a missing German Shepherd."

I retrieved the newspaper, found the ad, and called the listed number. I'd want to know if it was my dog. A man answered, and asked me to take him to where I saw the animal.

Kneeling next to his pet, tears filling his eyes, he said, "Oh, God, it's him."

The two of us loaded the dog into his truck bed, and drove until we found a secluded spot to bury him. We stood over the dog's grave in silence for a moment. I wiped a tear away with the back of my hand, and left.

At one-ten p.m., Roy called. I appreciated the distraction from feeling sad about that poor dog. After a minute or two of nonsense conversation, he finally asked, "When will I see you again, Linda?"

Not wanting to delve into my rethinking of friends only, I decided to play it cool, and said casually, "I don't know, soon I guess."

"How soon? Today?"

I paused. *What's he getting at? Is he hoping I'll go to bed with him if I say yes?* I wanted to keep the upper hand. "I don't think so."

"Why not?"

"I don't know about you, but I have a lot of thinking to do." *Boy, do I ever.*

From his end, I heard voices in the background, silence from him. He said quietly, "If I was alone at the moment, I'd say what I said last night."

I pretended to not hear Roy hint again that he loved me. A moment later we said goodbye.

Roy called later that afternoon. "Want to go to dinner?"

I accepted because I couldn't bring myself to say no. All day I'd been worried sick about what to do next. Was it selfish to continue to see him? I didn't want to be selfish. But I didn't want to stop seeing him. The question still hung in plain sight: *What do I want?*

We went to a casual place; I didn't even notice the name. Unlike a "real" date, of which I'd not yet had, I wore Levi's, not giving a second thought about wearing anything else. I couldn't talk to him at first— rare for me to be at a loss for words. Could he read my mind that I found him attractive?

After dinner we went to Lynx Lake, talking at the edge of the still water under a dark sky. What could we do about our on again off again relationship? The only solution I could come up with was to wait. Maybe we were too young to feel this way.

"Come back in a year, and then maybe I could love you, if you still love me . . ." I said, hoping this would make sense to him. I didn't know what else to say.

Roy stared into the inky darkness. "What are you inwardly fighting?"

Fighting? "I'm not sure . . ."

"Well I know what I'm fighting at this moment," he said, choking back a sob. "I'm fighting crying."

This confession hurt. I hated tormenting him, but I didn't know how to change what was going on between us.

Later, in bed, where I did most of my deep thinking, I recalled my two last breakups. Both Ben and Richard just stood there when they ended our relationship, acting like it was *nothing*. Couldn't they see my pain? With considerable remorse, I decided that Roy and I would only be okay if we never saw each other again. But could I live without him in my life?

Chapter 4

NOVEMBER 3, 1973. My eighteenth birthday. I guess turning eighteen should have been a big deal, but the whole day was rather low-keyed. The last thing I wanted was for anyone to make a fuss, not that I didn't appreciate the cards and the few dollars tucked into the ones from Gail and my maternal aunt and uncle. Profound melancholy, with no sense of where my life was going, lurked over me all day. Would I ever get a job? Would I ever figure out Roy? Ben? The weather matched my rotten mood. For the first time in three months, it rained most of the day, mirroring my tears, and it turned cold, mirroring my soul.

At five o'clock, to everyone's surprise, my dad insisted on driving all of us the thirty miles to the Realto Pass Steak House for dinner. This place was considered a landmark, but it was way too cowboy for me. All I wanted to do was stay home, shut myself in my room, and drown in sad music. Naturally, what I wanted was not an option.

In the dim interior, we took a booth where a candle burned inside burgundy-colored glass. A band in a corner played irritating, twangy Country music. I frowned. *Great. How long will I have to suffer through that?*

Now that I was of legal age, my dad let me order a glass of wine, not that it mattered. My parents didn't know I'd started drinking at sixteen. I took a sip, and scanned the room. *Oh, God, everyone in the entire restaurant is older than me.* I opened the menu, made a snap choice, and prayed we'd be out of there in less than an hour.

After more than two hours, we finally headed home.

Only two days had passed before Roy stopped by unexpectedly. The visit didn't really surprise me for some reason. Had he resigned himself to a casual relationship? While we listened to records, I found myself on guard, waiting for him to bring up love, the last thing I wanted to hear. But no, we only listened to records and talked about music. *Thank goodness*, I told myself, *he's not hung up on me anymore.*

Friday afternoon, Chuck gave me a call. "Hey, Linda, Roy and I are going to hear a blue-grass band at Prescott College. Want to come?"

What a tough decision. I wanted to go, but worried whether Roy would start pressuring me again like he did in Jerome. *Stop it. Go.* Decision made, I joined them. Roy ignored me all evening—totally opposite of what I'd expected. Ironically, this stung like heck.

That slight, and self-doubts, kept me up all night. How could anyone as ugly as me ever do anything right? Mastering guitar? It was dream that would never come true. Ben coming back to me? Unrealistic. *I wish I'd never moved to Prescott.*

My rotten mood continued all day Saturday. Even though I knew it was a stupid idea, I shut myself in my bedroom, picked up the phone receiver, and punched in Roy's number. As the phone rang on the other end, I scrambled for what to say when he answered. I latched onto something lame: "I'm curious what you thought of the band the other night . . ."

Did he buy that? Who knows, but after talking for a while, he offered to come pick me up so we could practice guitar. When we approached the town plaza, he said, "Hey, let's stop and look around."

The stately courthouse sits proud and historic in dead-center Prescott, surrounded by a plush lawn, and tall, leafy elms. A bronze statue of "Rough Rider" Bucky O'Neill on horseback posed at the main entry. Saturday nights attracted activities of all kinds: musicians, artists, dog walkers, non-dog walkers, people-watchers, pigeon feeders . . . you name it. Roy knew many local musicians, and talked with a few who were set up on the grass, entertaining crowds on this busy night. We sat on the lawn and listened to them play some great music for over an hour. Finally, we climbed back into Roy's truck.

"Where to?" he asked, glancing over at me.

I'd lost interest in practicing guitar by then, realizing I'd never be as good as the musicians we'd just heard. I shrugged. "Doesn't matter."

He turned over the engine, and drove.

We ended up cruising Prescott's meandering streets for hours, talking while the tape deck softly played Bob Dylan. My body relaxed into the seat, enjoying the music, the darkness, the soothing twists and turns of the road, our casual conversation . . . casual, that is, until Roy turned to look at me, and said, "I really do love you, you know."

I sighed audibly. "Roy, please stop staying that."

"Why?"

"Just stop it, please." I hated being reminded how he felt about me, especially when I didn't know how I felt about him.

We rode in silence until he found a place to park. Roy leaned over and tried to kiss me. I tipped my head away, and said, "No, please don't."

About ten minutes passed before he tried again. Annoyed, I pushed him away. "I said no! Please take me home."

He sighed, and obliged. A block from my house, he turned to me and said, "I would rather kill myself than not have you."

Whoa, what? Panic closed my throat.

Roy's tone switched abruptly to anger. "You're getting some kind of perverse pleasure out of hurting me, aren't you?"

My head snapped to look at him. "What the hell are you talking about? I most certainly am not!"

"Then why do you keep insisting we be just friends, and then turn around and kiss me? I just don't get you."

"I . . . it's not that . . ."

I didn't get me either. I didn't know how to make the decision that must be made—stop making excuses and either go for it with Roy or not. An exhausting, emotionally draining conversation that went around in infuriating circles made my head want to explode.

When he dropped me off, I leapt out of his truck, turned, and screamed at him, "I don't ever want to see or hear from you again!" I slammed the door, and ran into my house.

Wound up from the argument, I pulled out my journal to vent:

> *God how much I wish I'd never SEEN Prescott. Tonight Roy started saying how he would kill himself over me, etc. I'm so afraid he's serious. Really. I could never die for him, but over him? I know how bad I've hurt him, I know how it feels. But god he seems to think that he's the only one that's got any feelings. I'm so tired of all this.*

WHEN THE PHONE rang in the morning, I grabbed it on the second ring.

"How are you?" Roy asked.

Annoyed that he had the nerve to call, I rolled my eyes. "Fine. I thought I told you I never wanted to hear from you again."

"Oh yeah, you did. Are you sure you don't want to go out today?"

My jaw set. "Yeah, I'm sure."

"Really positive?" His tone was almost . . . teasing?

Exasperated, I let out a sharp: "YES."

"Oh. You don't want to go?"

By now, I'd stood up, and paced my bedroom, ready for this conversation to end.

"You've got it."

"Oh."

The resignation in his voice made me soften my tone. I never could be mean to someone, even if they deserved it. "Well . . . I guess it's goodbye."

"Yeah, maybe I'll be seeing you around?"

"Maybe. Goodbye."

I slammed the phone down and screamed in frustration.

TWO DAYS LATER, I found a letter from Roy in our mailbox, full of apologies, swearing he wanted to be just friends. What else could I do but call him? In the back of my mind I questioned what we were doing. How long could we keep hurting each other? Who would finally say, "I've had enough?"

Chapter 5

IN MID-NOVEMBER, a bicycle swept into our carport and the paperboy tossed the skimpy Prescott Courier onto the concrete. As I did every afternoon, I collected the newspaper, and checked the want ads. *Nothing.* I folded the page and flung it on the couch. I still didn't want to work in grease pits or retail, not that those jobs were plentiful. Kids looking for after-school jobs got those anyway. What could I do? The realist in me knew my interests didn't prove promising in the real world. I dearly loved music, but making a living playing guitar was next to impossible. Besides, half the time I thought I was good, the other half I cried myself to sleep knowing I wasn't. I enjoyed drawing and painting, but a career in art was also unrealistic. What was I going to do with my life? The indecision over what to do with my life, as well as with Roy, Ben, and just about everything else, sunk me lower than low.

How could I say "no" when Roy called wanting to go hiking a few days before Thanksgiving? I loved to hike, and, well, I'd missed him. In truth, I couldn't remember why I was supposed to be mad at him.

At Watson Lake, another of Prescott's lakes nestled in the Granite Dells, we tossed a stick for Roy's new black lab puppy, Yankee, to find and fetch. Gangly and clumsy, the puppy had huge feet, which I'd heard meant he would grow into a "really big dog." Yankee loped into the lake, snatched up the wet branch, and brought it to Roy. I smiled at the scene of guy and dog, both of them full of love and camaraderie.

"Good boy," Roy said, rubbing the dog's shiny black head. Yankee took that moment to shake dry, showering the surprised two of us with cold, odorous, lake water. Roy pitched the stick even farther away for Yankee to take longer to fetch.

"He's a great dog," Roy said, watching Yankee lope off in his quest.

I agreed, also watching the dog until I realized Roy had turned to me.

"He really likes you." Roy's smile reached his eyes, and my heart. He briefly touched my hand with his fingers. "I can see why."

A deep longing welled up inside me. I wanted him to touch me the way he used to. *Ridiculous! Start that emotional ride again?* A line from the movie *Sunshine* came to mind. "Never go to bed with a man you don't love. Love is so beautiful, that if you do, you'll always regret it." I should keep us just friends.

SNOW FLURRIES FELL hard the day before Thanksgiving, swirling and dancing, secretly turning the mountains white while they were hidden from view by low-lying, gossamer clouds. Roy called and invited me to experience the storm with him and his friend Nick. Why not?

When Roy pulled into our driveway, Nick jumped out so I could sit between them. Roy's crooked smile made me melt, and I couldn't help but notice how damned good he looked in his Levi jacket with a fleece-lined suede vest underneath. He hadn't shaved that morning, the bit of stubble looking sexy. *Damn. Sometimes I really do love this guy . . .* but other times were more critical; times when he acted childish and I just wanted to slap him. But, like now, I just wanted to go to bed with him. What was it about him that made me feel this way? He wasn't that great looking, and he didn't have a great body. These seemingly new feelings (of love?) for Roy . . . where had they come from?

"I thought we'd go sledding," Roy said, grinning at me.

Finding a suitable hill in a forest clearing, Roy tugged his sled up to the top with Nick and me at his heels. On the sled, I wrapped my arms around Roy's waist, settling in against him for a wild ride. Nick gave us a shove, and off we sailed down the slope, snow stinging our cheeks, our laughter echoing in the canyon as we whooshed through the powder. Dragging the sled back up, we let Nick give it a go, smiling at Nick hollering, as he too slid through the snow.

Hours later, exhilarated beyond noticing my wet feet and icy hands, and glowing from the silly and laughter-filled day, I waved goodbye when Roy dropped me off at home. After changing into dry clothes, I reflected on the fun Roy and I had together. Laughing with him made me dizzy and high as though I'd been drinking wine—what a great feeling. I decided to not let doubt and worries about him get in the way—no overthinking allowed.

AT LONG LAST, that Friday I got a non-typical job offer. Lucky me would enter the world of jewelry making. With silver and turquoise jewelry the current rage, I would cab turquoise, the process in which raw stones are turned into polished gems, ready for setting. Perfect! No milkshakes, typing, or phone answering involved. I would start on Monday.

Saturday, I called Roy to deliver the good news.

"I'm glad you got the job," he said.

He sounded really down, but nothing I said cheered him up. After a minute or two, we hung up. It made me sad to think of him as sad.

The next day I called Roy to see how he was doing. Maybe he was just having a bad day yesterday. Besides, after our fun-filled day of sledding, I decided to share those euphoric feelings with him. I took a deep breath. How would he react? Both excitement and anxiousness competed for space in my chest.

"I think you've matured a great deal since we first met," I said. "You've become a part of me . . . a part I want to keep in my life."

I waited for his reply. Would it be what I wanted to hear?

After a pause, he said, "I'm so happy our feelings are now mutual. Let's go somewhere after Christmas."

This wasn't the first time he'd mentioned taking off with him.

"I wish I could! But my new job starts tomorrow. Maybe someday?"

Afterward, I mulled over his offer. The unspoken rule at home was that no daughter was going alone on a trip with a boy. If we went, I'd have to figure out how to pull it off without my parents finding out.

Chapter 6

MONDAY MORNING, MY mom let me use her car, and I arrived at my new job with the jewelry manufacturer. I met my coworkers: Tom, Cathy, and Tony, all of whom also started today, and our supervisor, Lynell.

Lynell immediately took us to our work stations for a two hour training session. Afterwards, we sat at grinding wheels, holding slabs of raw turquoise attached to a wooden dowel, to shape and polish each stone under a stream of cold running water.

Lunchtime rolled around, and my coworkers and I gathered at a table in the makeshift kitchen. Rather blurry-eyed from the deep concentration of learning something new, I boiled some water in a teakettle on a hotplate for my instant soup, and sat next to Cathy, who was tenderly inspecting her lower arm.

"Man 'o man!" she said. "My arms are chapped and sore. Are yours?"

I'd been so preoccupied, I hadn't noticed, but now that she mentioned it, my arms *were* blotchy-red and painfully raw. We surmised it came from the cold water running down them all morning.

A little past five, I drove home in winter twilight, pleased with my job despite the rash, and looked forward to tomorrow.

Around eight that night, Roy called. I expected we'd talk about getting together soon, but instead, our conversation went south in seconds flat.

"I don't know about us anymore," he said. "You don't believe me when I tell you that I don't just want sex from you, and that's a problem."

Why was he bringing this up again? I thought things were good between us.

"I've lost the battle, and have no desire to fight anymore," he said, his voice lifeless.

Where was this coming from? "Fight what?"

"I don't want to talk about it."

"Tell me, please."

"No."

End of conversation. We hung up.

I crawled under the covers and let my mind search in between his words in order to decipher what he meant. I decided it was possible that he didn't know. Or, that like all of the other guys I'd fallen for, he'd changed his mind, and didn't want anything to do with me. That's what happened with Richard and Ben, so why not him? I tried to sleep, but instead I stared into the dark void of my room for most of the night.

Daybreak was welcome because it saved me from not sleeping. I went to work. My coworkers and I convinced Lynell to buy rubber gloves to protect our skin. Later, we had the gloves. But here, on only day two, I discovered this new job was beyond boring. For hours on end I did the same thing, over and over. The fact that I'd probably slept a total of three hours last night didn't help the tedium. My eyelids kept trying to shut, so I had to force them to stay open. Cathy and I were able to talk to pass time, but Tom and Tony were at the saws cutting the turquoise into smaller, manageable pieces. The noise prevented conversation with them except at break time.

Workday three, Tony asked me out to lunch. No big surprise. He'd flirted with me on day one. I accepted. Tony was attractive, with smooth olive skin and shoulder-length black hair. My inner voice warned me to be wary. Guys who came on strong this early usually only wanted one thing: sex. But, I didn't want to jump to conclusions. *Maybe I'm wrong . . .*

My original instincts were right. Once we were away from work, his flirting went over the top, with him commenting on my clothes, hair, body shape. All of which screamed, "This guy is a player!" When we returned, my other coworkers eyed me with interest. Did they think something romantic was brewing between me and Tony? They were wrong, wrong, wrong. Now to end whatever *he* thought we had going on.

MY MOM AND I had just finished watching our favorite evening TV show, *Perry Mason*, when I took a call from Roy in my bedroom. With pillows propped on the headboard, I asked him how he was doing. Maybe he was ready to explain now.

"I want to tell you something," he said. "You know, for a while, I thought I wanted to marry you."

Okay, I'd sensed that, but with every fiber of my being I knew I was way too young to get married. *We* were too young to get married. After all, he had just turned seventeen! Where was he going with this?

"It's just that . . . it's just that I love you so much, it can't possibly be real. This won't work. I now feel that there will be less hurt if we end our relationship right now than if it's dragged on and on," he said. "I'm sorry if I've hurt you."

He was telling *me* goodbye. *Now?* After I'd finally admitted to myself, and to him, how much I cared for and needed him in my life? I started to cry.

"Is there anything I can do to make it up to you?" he asked.

Barely able to speak, I said, "No, Roy, there is nothing you can do to fix how much you've just hurt me. I can't talk to you. Goodbye."

After a crying jag that left my eyes red and puffy, I wondered if maybe I deserved this. Considering all that I'd put him through, it didn't surprise me that he would turn the tables. I hated myself for screwing everything up by not knowing what I wanted.

What a struggle to get up and go to work in the morning. When I stumbled in, I was met with more bad news: another turquoise screw-up added more worries that either I, or everyone, would get fired. I couldn't stop myself from clock-watching, which of course made the long day longer.

I was in the living room that evening when the phone rang. My dad answered, and handed the receiver to me. "It's Roy."

Now what? I took the call in my room.

"I've only got a minute, but I want you to forget everything I said last night," he said.

I tried to produce some sort of answer, and muttered a few incomprehensible sounds, but he only said, "We'll talk later."

The phone clicked into silence. I wanted to scream. *What he says, does, and thinks never EVER match. NEVER.*

After I got home from work the next day, I made the mad dash across our busy street to check the mailbox. A letter from Gail would be perfect. It had been ages since I'd heard from her. Sometimes I felt guilty for the weekly long letters I sent, detailing all that was going on with my life, especially Roy. In past letters she'd expressed worry about my relationship with him. I knew she had my best interests at heart, and didn't want me to get hurt. Her concern was appreciated, but I just couldn't follow her advice and cut him out of my life. *I sure could use some support from her right now*, I thought, sorting through the various envelopes. I blinked hard at the familiar handwriting before it registered who it was from. Neon lights exploded in my head; those silly stars you see in cartoons floated in front of my eyes.

I tore open Ben's letter.

Written in his loopy cursive, Ben explained why he had been so aloof to me that day when I came to his job last summer:

> *When you came to see me, I was in a bad mood, freaking about my decision to join the Navy, wondering if I'd done the right thing. I was so bull-headed about not telling you what was going on. I felt awful the next day for behaving as I did towards you, and even worse for not calling you to apologize. I am now apologizing,"* he wrote. *"I will be in California soon. Is it okay to come see you?"*

Strangely calm, I stared at the news that should have sent me over-the-top with joy. But it didn't. I took a deep breath. *Just take this as it comes*. If he got here, great. If not, I would try my best to accept it. I still cared a great deal about him, but I was afraid of the changes that may have taken place—in both of us. The thrill that he wanted to reconnect, though, tugged at me—hard. I wanted to see him again.

I sat down at my desk to compose a response, choosing ordinary notebook paper over formal stationary.

> *Dear Ben,*
>
> *It was nice to hear from you! I have missed you and wondered if you were okay. I accept your apology, and would like to see you . . .*

This wasn't a lie or a ploy . . . I simply could not think of any other way to find out if we still had a chance. I wrote about what I'd been up to, leaving Roy out, seeing no point in bringing up a relationship that I didn't know how to explain . . . to him, or to me.

Letter mailed, I settled in to finish some of my sewing projects. The doorbell rang. With no one home but me, I got up to answer, and had to hold the collar of frantically-barking Peanuts so she wouldn't kill whoever was at the door. Upon opening, I stood, stunned, to see Roy on the stoop. With his felt brimmed hat in hand and sorrow in his eyes, he smiled, squatted, and stroked Peanuts on the head to quiet her tirade. "I thought to see if you'd like to go hiking."

I almost said, "Sure." He'd hit a tender spot with the remorseful look on his face, and, as usual whenever we'd been apart, it felt good to see him again. But that didn't last long. I squared my shoulders and clenched my jaw. True, he'd told me to forget what he'd said, but did he really think it was that easy?

"I've got things to do," I said, frowning. "Plus, I'll have you know, I heard from Ben."

Was this mean? Maybe. But I wanted a reaction from him. Something to show that this mattered.

Roy's face betrayed nothing at the news. "Okay, catch ya later."

I closed the door, and stood there for a moment. *Well, that is that. Now that he knows I heard from Ben, I'll never hear from him again.* Did I feel sad? Resigned? Yes, resigned.

FOR OUR SUNDAY family outing, we chose hiking at Copper Creek, a glorious area with clear creeks and tall trees forming lush green canopies. Scents tickled at my memories of hometown Syracuse. History fascinated my folks, and I had to admit, exploring old copper and gold mines had its perks. My mom and I never could resist collecting pretty rocks, and there were plenty here to choose from.

"Oh, Mom, look at the blue streaks!" I said, inspecting a large stone with a matrix of Chrysocolla.

"Lovely! I found this one with flecks of pyrite," she said, holding her big rock that glittered like gold. "Too bad we can't take it home, though."

I agreed. Carrying heavy ones for long distances would not work, so we stuck with pocket sizes.

That night after dinner, Roy's phone call surprised me yet again.

"I've been thinking," he said. "I've decided that you are the only girl I'll ever love. I've thought about this a lot. I can't imagine wanting anyone else to have my baby. I've never met anyone who cares about me like you do, and I don't think I ever will."

The cynic in me screamed: *This is crazy! Just crazy!* I wished some real nice girl—*Other than me*, I thought with a laugh—could prove to him that there are other girls out there who want to marry and have kids. I didn't want to get married . . . to him, or to anyone, at least not now. Even crazier, though, I still had feelings for him. Should I believe him? Or wait for him to pull another one-eighty?

Not much more was said, and I hung up the phone, more confused than ever.

ONLY A WEEK into my new job, Lynell called a Monday morning meeting in the break room. Unconcerned, I sat at the table with my coworkers.

"The owner isn't happy with you guys," he said.

My eyes flew wide open. *What?*

"That last batch of turquoise cabs is totally screwed up. I'll take the blame; I wasn't paying attention and should have been. I explained that to him, but it didn't seem to matter. He is considering making me let you all go. But I refuse to do that. There's no good reason. I'll quit first."

Not one word was spoken between us other than what was necessary to complete our tasks. *What did I do wrong?* I dreaded starting yet another job search.

The next morning, I got up and went to work as usual, wondering if I'd been fired. But no, I still had my job. Amazing, considering that Lynell relayed more complaints from the owner about our lack of skills.

Cathy whispered in my ear, "Well isn't that just peachy? We've been here a whole week, and the guy expects perfection."

With a deep sigh, I shrugged, and headed for my work station.

"Linda looks good today," Tony said to no one in particular, delivering yet another compliment, which I ignored.

"Linda always looks good," Tom said.

Embarrassed, I turned to see Tom grinning at me. Did he mean it? I mumbled "Thanks," and sat down, smiling at the thought that maybe he did.

On the way home, though, I felt like a complete failure. I couldn't seem to please the owner, and worried that I could still get fired. Add to that all of the contradictory messages from Roy—what more could go wrong? I didn't even stop to check the mail after I parked the car in the driveway. Instead, I went inside and flopped onto my bed staring at the ceiling.

After giving it much thought, I decided there was only one way to stop the roller-coaster ride with Roy. We had to stop seeing and talking to each other. I would have to initiate the end. But could I? I wrote him a letter. I knew what I wrote would hurt him, and I hated inflicting pain. But in reality, I think it hurt *me* more to end our relationship for good.

Chapter 6

"I'LL DRIVE," TOM said, after we all decided to go out to lunch. "Where to?"

On the way to McDonald's, my coworkers and I vented about work hassles, and speculated about the mysterious shop owner, whom no one had met, or even seen. I'd never had a job where fellow workers went to lunch—it felt like a school field trip.

Back at work, still a rambunctious group, I cracked a silly joke when we left Tom's car.

"That's a good one," Tom said, laughing as he put his arm around me for a friendly squeeze.

Once inside the shop, I noticed a Christmas gift-wrapped package near the door. Curious, I read the tag. "To Linda from Roy." My face blanched. *Oh, Roy*. Obviously, he'd not yet received my letter. I felt like the most horrible person on the planet. No way would I open it here—I set it aside to take home.

After dinner that evening, I took the gift into my bedroom. First, I lit my candle, which filled the room with the scent of melting wax, and flickering light. Sitting on the bed, I removed the wrapping from the square box. Inside was not just one gift, but several. Knowing that I kept a journal, Roy had selected an ornate fountain pen and a bottle of dark blue ink. He remembered that I love seashells and candles, so purchased a porcelain, scallop-shaped soap dish, and a pillar candle with shells embedded in the wax. Also tucked in the box was the Irish Blessing, framed in a tiny gold-toned easel. I read the sentiment:

> *May the road rise up to meet you.*
> *May the wind be always at your back.*
> *May the sun shine warm upon your face;*
> *the rains fall soft upon your fields*
> *and until we meet again,*
> *may God hold you in the palm of His hand.*

I swallowed hard. What in the hell should I do now? This was not only incredibly sweet, but romantic as heck. When he read my letter, would he call? Or would it break his heart? I guessed it would break his heart. I hated myself at that moment.

The phone rang. I answered, and heard Roy's voice.

"Did you find the package I left?"

"Yes, I did, and thank you. They are all lovely."

Because he didn't mention the letter, I didn't either. How could I? I was too ashamed. We talked a bit longer, and hung up.

My heart didn't just hurt, it felt like it burst. *What have I done?*

Shortly thereafter, Chuck called. Just what I needed.

"What's new?" he asked.

"I heard from Ben!"

"I'm happy for you. I know this is a big deal."

How wonderful to be able to share this news with someone who understood and cared. We chatted for over an hour. After I explained my letter to Roy, he said, "You did the best you could by letting Roy go."

What a relief to hear this. I had to let go of the guilt.

LYNELL CALLED IN the morning. " You don't have to come to work today. The turquoise shipment didn't come in," he said. "I'll let you know when it does."

With an unexpected day off, I called Kim to see if she wanted to go for a walk. We picked quiet side streets for our route. Kim often turned to me for advice about boys, and today was no different. The guy she had a crush on didn't know she existed, and she wondered what to do.

I almost said, "Don't look at me; I've got my own problems." But then I thought better. "Well, make an effort to start up a conversation with him. Find something he likes, and ask him about it."

"Good idea. Okay, I'll try," she said.

Our walk and talk did us both good. Exercise always made me feel better, and Kim made a plan to talk to the boy she liked.

A few days later, Tom asked me out to a movie. A movie sounded like fun. Wary of getting involved with someone again, though, I hesitated. "Thanks, Tom, that would be nice," I said. "But I feel I must tell you I'd like to keep this as friends only, okay?"

"Sure," he said lightheartedly. "Not a problem."

Later that night, before falling asleep, I reflected on how quickly I'd accepted Roy's sudden disappearance from my life. He'd never contacted me about the letter I'd sent, which I figured would happen. That didn't mean I didn't still feel awful, nor did it mean that I didn't miss him. Despite the emptiness in my heart, I would have to try to move on.

Date one went well; Tom was fun to be around and we enjoyed the movie. On our second date a week later, we went parking in the forest after dinner. Chemistry had kicked in, so I knew we would be making out. Kissing him made not only my request to stay friends vanish, but the entire world outside the car. Our passion grew, and he started to unbutton my shirt. I placed my hand on his. "No, Tom, this is moving too fast. Could you please slow down?"

He sat up straight. "Oh, okay . . . sorry . . . it's so easy to get carried away with you. And hey, no need to worry. I believe in waiting until marriage to have sex."

I almost laughed, thinking he must be kidding. The expression on his face told me he meant it. Although I was in no hurry to have sex, I sure didn't plan on marriage first. I suggested gently that we should probably get going . . . which he agreed to. Easier said than done, because we made out for two more hours before we finally hit the road.

Parking at the curb in front of my house, he shut off the engine. "I want to tell you something, but I'm afraid you'll think it's too early."

I immediately worried where this was going.

"I think I love you," he said.

No, you don't. But that's okay. I smiled, but didn't reply other than to say, "Goodnight, Tom, thanks for a great evening."

Once in bed, I thought about the nice evening and the fun we had at work. I enjoyed Tom's company—and the lack of exhausting drama I'd had with Roy. Two weeks had passed since I'd written Ben, and no response yet. I found it easy to push aside a relationship that didn't have much chance of surviving. My current reality with Tom had more significance. Clearly, I had a strong attraction to him, and I wanted to see where it would lead.

I didn't see Tom for a couple of days. Then we did what most teens did here—cruise Prescott's quiet mountain streets. We chatted of nothing and listened to a John Denver cassette. Tom's favorite musician was quickly becoming one of mine. Finally, we parked in a wooded area, kissed, and hugged until Tom held me in his arms, resting his head against mine.

"I want you to travel with me someday. To Canada, Northern California. It's so beautiful up there. Forests unlike anything you've ever seen. The ocean. The lakes. I'll take you out in my canoe. I'll teach you how to fish. There's so much I want to share with you if you will let me," he said. "We'll have fun. I know we will. I think you must know . . ." He paused. "I've decided that I don't just think I love you, I know I do."

"Tom," I said, when my voice started working again, "I'm not sure I can say the same thing. I mean, I love our times together, and I am attracted to you . . ."

"It's okay, Linda. You just take your time."

The breath I'd been holding let loose. He'd said the right thing by telling me to take my time. As far as I was concerned, there was lots of time to see how, or if, my feelings would grow.

FOR AS LONG as I could remember, Christmas Day had always delivered a plethora of gifts to the point that stacks of presents surrounded the tree and spilled into the entire living room, taking ages for my family to unwrap. Of course, as a child the excitement of what lie underneath the wrapping was all the fun, but as a young adult, I stopped thinking about what I was going to get, and now found accepting gifts uncomfortable. I didn't feel worthy. Instead, I preferred the joy of watching everyone open the gifts I'd picked out, or handmade. This was what made Christmas Christmas.

Tom came over after the family wrapping-paper-frenzy had ended.

"Hello, Mrs. Strader," Tom said to my mom when he came in the door.

My mom smiled at him. "Hi, Tom. Merry Christmas!"

"And a Merry Christmas to you, too," he said, giving her a one-arm hug. "You are looking particularly lovely today, may I add. Just like your lovely daughter." He smiled at my mom, who laughed lightly. I'd never seen my mom embarrassed, but for a moment there, I thought she blushed. I'd never had a boyfriend who flirted with my mom. I wasn't sure I approved.

With my parents busy in the kitchen fixing our big Christmas dinner, my sister in her room on the phone, Tom and I sat alone side-by-side on the couch in the living room. Smiling, he pulled a small jewelry box adorned with a tiny gold bow out of his shirt pocket. Apprehensive and nervous (is this an engagement ring?), I didn't open it right away.

"Go on, open it," he said, grinning widely.

My hands trembled a bit when I unwrapped the box. Inside, I found the very turquoise and silver bracelet I'd admired in the display case at work, though different in a significant way. He had exchanged the blue stone for one in my preferred color, more on the green side, with swirls of matrix that added texture and interest. He quietly said, "I inscribed, 'I love you' on the silver underneath the stone."

Relieved it was just a bracelet, but also touched that he'd gone to all of that trouble, I slipped it onto my wrist. "Thank you, Tom, that was very nice of you."

I rose from the couch and retrieved his present from under the tree. "It's nothing fancy," I said. "I hope you like it."

Tom unwrapped the special pen. "Hey, thanks. This is perfect for writing in my journal."

What a relief he liked it. It had taken me days to figure out what to buy him.

After Christmas, Lynell took Tom and me aside.

"I'm planning on opening my own store soon, and would like you two to make jewelry for me. I'll teach you silversmithing after work, in my garage, where I have everything you'll need. Once you get the hang of it, you'll have to buy your own equipment, but I have extras I can sell you at a discount."

Why not? This sounded like a great opportunity. Plus, the thought of learning silversmithing lit a creative spark in me. I didn't hesitate for a second to accept, and neither did Tom.

TOM AND I hiked several times a week. We shared the love of the outdoors, with the fragrances that overwhelmed the senses, the beautiful pines with mountains rising in the distance, and the gurgling clear, cold creeks. What fun to learn his wilderness survival skills: how to start a fire with a magnifying glass, how to walk in the forest without leaving a trace or making a sound, and how to use a mirror as a signaling device. All the while he showed me these things, he made me feel special and important, which was exactly how I wanted to be treated by a boyfriend.

Despite the cold, late December weather, Tom drove the two of us out the scenic Senator Highway at sunset to find a secluded spot. The road wound through the dense ponderosa forest as the late afternoon sky took on a tinge of lavender and orange. He edged his car down a dirt side-road until he worried about undercarriage clearance.

"We'd better walk from here," he said, shifting into park. From the trunk he collected two blankets, and a brown paper bag containing a bottle of wine, corkscrew, and two plastic cups. He pocketed a flashlight. Hand in hand, we made our way through the forest as daylight waned.

After we'd walked awhile, Tom picked a wide clearing among the trees. "This is a good spot. Let's collect some wood."

Before long, tall, orange flames offered welcome heat. Within minutes after sunset, temperatures had fallen dramatically. Tom had dragged over a log to sit on, and I perched there, holding my palms close to the fire. After covering our legs with the blanket, Tom uncorked the wine, filled our glasses, and made a toast.

"To you and me, and a lifetime of love."

I smiled shyly, and we touched cups. We sipped, snuggled, kissed, talked, and watched the crackling fire. After we finished our wine, Tom spread one of the blankets on the ground. We lay side by side, our kisses turning more passionate, while Tom's hands moved through my hair, pulling me tight to his mouth. He unbuttoned my shirt, and with my help, removed both it and my bra. Then he tugged the other blanket to cover us against the brisk night air.

Tom searched deep into my eyes. "Oh, Linda—I know I said it before. That we should wait until we marry. But I don't want to wait. I want to make love to you."

Intense desire stirred in me, generating plenty of heat to keep us both warm. I wanted him, completely, totally . . .

Breathless, I said, "Oh, yes, yes, I want you too, Tom."

As he unbuttoned my jeans, Tom told me that he loved me, more than anything. Then he said, "I'll try to be gentle, but this will probably hurt you, and I'm sorry."

I whispered, "I know, but that's okay."

Bravely, I held in a painful scream by taking in a quick, deep, and uneasy breath.

Tom paused. "I'm sorry, Linda, I'm so sorry."

I met his eyes with mine. "It's okay, really."

"Are you sure? I mean, will you be okay?"

I nodded. Even though the pain had briefly ruined the romantic moment, I felt like the sexiest girl in the world.

We snuggled and kissed more. The fire had died down, leaving only red embers. Tom touched my shoulder. "You're freezing."

Tom dressed, and got up to add more wood to our fire. I wished we were someplace where I could revel in how womanly I felt. I'd always hated my body, but at that moment, I almost wanted to parade around naked in front of Tom, making him lust for me again. Instead, shivering, I pulled on my jeans and my flannel shirt. Tom returned, and again covered us with the blanket. He hugged me close, and kissed the top of my head.

"Linda, will you marry me?"

Marry? Us? Now? If he could have seen my face, he would have witnessed my shock.

"Not right away," he said in a rush. "I mean two years from now, if we are still together."

Why did I say yes? Because no one else had ever asked me? Because I couldn't figure out how to say no? Maybe getting caught up in the romantic night, and feeling that maybe I loved him, too, saying yes felt right. But the fact that he'd added two years to this marriage "proposal" offered me some safety. He was talking two whole years. That would give me plenty of time to know if this was right.

Tom grabbed the wine bottle and refilled our glasses. Now chatty, he expounded on our future. "When we marry, you can stay home and raise our kids," he said, smiling at me.

Kids? I didn't want to stay home and raise kids. Before I could gather my thoughts to protest, he jumped up to gather more wood. We stayed there a bit longer, until wood ran low and we got cold.

All in all, it was a beautiful evening, despite the flat tire and the long walk home at four a.m.

MY EYES POPPED open at nine a.m. to blinding sunshine and memories of last night. Before rising, I tried to put words to my feelings for Tom, but couldn't. I recognized that I'd been lost for words lately. For one, I didn't know *how* to love Tom. Not "in which way"; I just didn't know *how* to go about it. Could feelings of love be manufactured like the jewelry we made? *Of course not.*

What he said, though, about us having children echoed in my ears. Raising a family had never, ever been my life's plan. That I didn't say what was on my mind was not unusual for me. I had a rough time standing my ground. Most likely based on my experiences with my dad. Voicing my opinion always resulted in him yelling at me that I was wrong or had no right to have an opinion that didn't match his. In other words, an argument that I couldn't possibly win. Avoiding uncomfortable conversations made my life easier.

Half an hour later, I figured I'd better get up. I studied my face in the bathroom mirror. There was definitely something different. Something different on the inside, too. Would anyone be able to see that I was no longer a virgin? I panicked. Would my parents notice?

Chapter 7

AT THE SMALL Prescott airport, I watched the commuter plane land, hardly able to contain myself from rushing to open the door myself to welcome my best friend, Gail, who flew out from Syracuse to visit me. I waved wildly when she stepped off the plane. Her silky blond hair shimmered in the sun, and a broad smile lit up her face. She trotted over and greeted me with a hug. Gail stepped back and grasped my hands. "Oh, Linda, it's so good to see you."

I squeezed her hands in return and grinned until it hurt, my heart filling with love and friendship, my eyes blinking back happy tears.

Prescott must have wanted Gail to feel at home because it snowed like crazy the next day. Excited to show her around the town plaza, despite the serious flurries we strolled and wandered into a few of the fun gift shops in which we were the sole customers. It didn't matter that we were freezing to death, or if we found anything to buy—we simply wanted to have time to talk alone, which we did—nonstop.

After dinner, Chuck picked us up for a snowy drive in the Thumb Butte area. Huge white flakes drifted from an indigo sky, his jeep navigating six inches of snow on the road with ease. The whole adventure was filled with lively conversation. My heart swelled knowing that my two best friends in the world had no problem finding things to talk about, and, based on all of the laughter and genuine smiles, that they enjoyed each other. Nothing could've made me happier.

Gail and I walked into the house a few hours later, both of us exuberant over the fun we'd had. I'd just hung up my coat when Tom called.

"How's it going?" he asked.

"Just got in from going to Thumb Butte with Chuck," I said. "We had a great time."

The silence on the other end had me thinking we'd been disconnected. "Tom? Are you there?"

More silence. "Yeah, I'm here," he said flatly. "So . . . you and Chuck went out?"

My mouth opened but no words came out. I'd told Tom when we first started seeing each other about the friendship I had with Chuck. I thought he understood. Was he jealous? I couldn't hide my annoyance. "We weren't alone. Gail came. You remember Chuck and I are just friends, right?"

Tom didn't respond right away. When he did, he said, "Oh. I see."

At the end of our call, I hung up and frowned. *What is his problem?*

Late that night, Gail and I sat on my bed, talking, keeping our voices low so as to not wake my parents. I always trusted her to give me an honest assessment in the boyfriend department. No one knew me like Gail. Not even me. What she brought up was Ben's excuse for brushing me off after he'd dropped the Navy bomb.

"Don't you think he's leaving something out?" she asked in a whisper. "Maybe there was more to it than him being preoccupied. My guess is he was a bit afraid of you, maybe even afraid of what he could feel for you. Long distance relationships are easy. You don't have to actually deal with a real human being."

Deep inside I knew that was a possibility. Maybe we'd built each other up to be someone we were not. Despite that, I believed I did still love Ben. But did I really love Tom? I feared Tom was just a fill-in for Ben. What in the world was I going to do if Ben ever really *did* come to see me?

The weather didn't improve the following day. Tired of the wet and cold, we opted for a movie with my older sister and her boyfriend. The day after was also overcast, but at least it had stopped snowing. My parents, Cindy, Gail, and I headed out to Rich Hill, famous for its abandoned gold mines. We had a blast exploring and searching for gold nuggets, joking about how if we found some, they'd make us rich.

That night, Gail and I again stayed up late. She was leaving the next day and I didn't know when I'd see her again. I wished I could foresee every future important event so we could talk about it right then. Once worn out, we went to bed, but I stayed awake most of the night, dwelling on the sad reality that my best friend had to leave. Her absence would leave a substantial vacancy in my life.

In the morning, Tom and I drove Gail to Sky Harbor airport in Phoenix. Her four-day visit had zipped by like a passenger train at top speed. Gail and I hugged goodbye with my eyes brimming tears. I hated that we lived so far apart.

STUPID WEATHER. THE warm and sunny days that I'd hoped for during Gail's visit showed up a week later. Work was still a grind, except for when Tom and I stayed late, learning the ropes of silversmithing from Lynell. My first ring made me proud, and I already had design ideas for the bracelets and earrings I wanted to make. I also spent a few apprenticeship hours at Lynell's home on the weekends. Tom rented a room from Lynell, so he attended as well.

That Saturday, after several hours of instruction, Lynell's wife brought us snacks. She'd barely cleared the door on her way out, when Tom whispered, too loud in my estimation, "Man, she needs to lose weight."

"Tom!" I said. "Shhh . . . she could've heard you."

"So what," he said, snickering. "She's fat."

Shocked into silence, I didn't defend her. Later I thought I should have. He was mean.

Home from work on Wednesday at four o'clock, I looked forward to sitting outside and enjoy what little warmth was left in the day. A letter from Ben sat on the kitchen table. I held it in trembling hands, thrilled, but nervous. What did he have to say?

Sitting on the floor of my room, leaning against the bed, I pored through his letter. Tears fell freely by the time I'd finished. I fished a tissue out of the box, and blew my nose. It was a casual letter, saying he missed me and hoped all was well—but that wasn't what upset me. He'd contacted me again, and there was no denying that Ben still mattered to me. I wiped tears from my face, and did my best to smile when I told my mom I was going out. There was no way I could hide these emotions. I had to be honest and tell Tom what was going on.

As soon as I found Tom, I grabbed him by the hand. "I heard from Ben," I said, my voice catching. There wasn't much more he needed to hear. Without speaking, we drove a spot in the forest to talk.

"I'm going to lose you to Ben, aren't I?" he said, choking on the words, his head hanging down.

I lowered my eyes to avoid the pain in his. "I don't know, Tom."

Would he? I didn't want to end our relationship over one letter, but I couldn't deny that letter from Ben stirred up plenty of intense emotions and plenty of questions. My heart told me I still loved Ben.

But my brain wondered if this made sense. How could we possibly have a relationship with him in the Navy?

That night, I wrote Ben a long letter. I asked questions about where we were going, or not going. I told him how much he'd hurt me, and how I didn't know if I could get past that hurt. I told him I was dating Tom. I'd already sealed the envelope when I had a second thought. I carefully peeled the seal apart. Below my signature, I added that I still wanted to see him, if he still wanted to see me after reading all that I'd written. Envelope re-sealed, I walked it to a blue postal mailbox instead of placing it in ours with the flag raised. I didn't want to chicken out and retrieve it later. With the letter mailed, I tried to put Ben out of my mind. I'd asked some pretty blunt questions, uncharacteristic of me, and I figured he'd take offense, or not like me anymore. *If that's the case, then so be it.*

Except the next day I reread Ben's letter, horrified that I'd jumped on his case. Now I saw so much innocence. All he did was write a "hi, how are you doing" letter. What had I done? Why did I bring up Tom, when I wasn't even sure where *we* were going? *I should never have mailed that letter.*

AFTER THE INITIAL shock, Tom had taken the news about Ben in stride, and behaved as though I'd never heard from him.

The morning of New Year's Eve, Tom asked me out. "Let's go to dinner and a movie." He'd picked one of the nicer restaurants, and I dressed up for the occasion. At the theater, we walked toward the ticket window, with Tom on my right. When I turned to say something to him, he wasn't there. He reappeared on my left. "Oh! Why did you . . . ?"

"I just realized I was on the wrong side," he said.

"Wrong side?"

"A gentleman should always walk on the street side, to protect his lady from a wayward car."

The expression on his face was so darned serious, I had to stifle my laugh. *He's living in the dark ages.* "I don't think you need to worry about that, Tom."

We'd barely settled into our seats, when a black man took the seat next to me. Tom rose up, eyes wide, and said, "We need to move."

At a loss as to why, I checked immediately in front of us. Had someone blocked his view? But no, not a soul sat in that row.

Tom nudged my arm and leaned toward my ear. "I will *not* let a nigger sit next to you."

I turned to him in disbelief. Did he really just say that? My face burned with embarrassment. Ashamed to be associated with him, I considered leaving. But, instead of making a scene, I decided it was better to stand my ground. "We are *not* moving."

Tom didn't argue with me, or force me to move, but throughout the entire movie I wondered how in the hell I ended up with a racist. My parents didn't raise me that way. What should I do with yet another side of Tom I didn't at all like? But then again, what relationship didn't have conflicts? Didn't most girls stick with their boyfriends for the long run? After all, he could change.

Only two weeks into the New Year, there went my job. Or rather, everyone's job. The owner ran into trouble with the IRS, and he closed the shop. Good thing Lynell had been teaching us silversmithing the past two months. Lynell now wanted Tom and me to consign our creations to him. He would sell our work at trade shows until he opened his own store. With no other option at that point, both Tom and I accepted, hoping it would pan out, and we could make decent money.

On a rainy Sunday afternoon, Tom and I went for a drive along the scenic White Spar Road. We found a place to park. As we talked, I couldn't help but notice that the topic of Ben did not come up, but to be honest, I was glad it had not. I didn't want to be grilled about making a decision. Instead, we talked about music, silversmithing, and the potential to sell our jewelry. Hours passed, the sun set, the rain continued to fall, and it grew too cold to sit there any longer. Back at my house, with everyone else asleep, I quietly made tea. The kettle whistled, and I poured two mugs. Tom lit a candle for light, and set it on the kitchen table. I wrapped my hands around the mug to warm my cold fingers. From across the table, Tom wrapped his hands around mine, and leaned towards me, focused on the rising steam.

After a few moments, he gazed into my eyes and said, "We'll go camping under the stars sometime in California at this lake I know, and I will make love to you in the beautiful darkness and keep on loving you the way I do."

My heart warmed at his incredibly romantic words. Did we have a future? At this moment, I didn't want to know. As the pleasurable minutes passed, I told myself to always remember this moment, to always cherish the silence and peace between us, with the candle gently burning, and the rain drizzling silently down the windows.

THE NEXT DAY, Tom and I drove the long two-hour haul to Phoenix to see my favorite musicians, Jackson Browne and Linda Ronstadt. What a great concert! Linda and Jackson were both amazing. We had good seats and the acoustics were excellent. But during the long the drive back, my good mood slipped. The excitement, the crowds, the people watching . . . you'd think that would have been fun. Instead, I wondered if everyone had a more interesting life than I did. Where was my life headed? It sure didn't look promising. Tom's talk of marriage scared me. *No way* will I marry for the sole reason of "what else is there to do?"—which I'd actually heard spill from the mouths of girls around here. Not that I was opposed to marriage, it's just that marrying too young could be a problem. What if I hadn't met the right person yet? I'd never know. Being in a loving relationship with someone without getting married was an okay option. I wanted my freedom—to live how I wanted, not be forced into the role of wife and mother. I had to tell Tom that I wasn't ready to be tied down. Because I doubted he would want to be just friends, we would have to break up.

STILL FEELING AS though I was not quite rooted in reality, I let life float me along for the ride . . . waiting . . . waiting for what? For me to make a decision? Or for life to lead me in the right direction? Maybe, but I didn't feel pressure from anyone at the moment to do anything. So I didn't.

Tom and I lounged on the couch one afternoon, watching a movie on TV. Kitty Tabitha jumped up onto the back cushion, tucked her paws neatly, and purred. I stroked her fur, speaking softly about her being such a sweet girl. Tom reached up and tugged Tabitha's tail, hard. She flattened her ears and glared at him.

"Geez, Tom, don't do that," I said. "Cats don't like their tails pulled."

"Aw, she loves it," he said, laughing.

Tom tugged her tail again. Tabitha hissed, and leapt off the couch. Tom's laugh was almost sadistic. Now *I* glared at him.

"That was mean!"

He shrugged. "I was just teasing."

Certainly he would not do this again. People change, right?

ONE OF MY favorite pastimes was to pore through sheet music at the music store for a gem-of-a-price I could afford—which was technically free—but I saved up for an occasional two-dollar splurge. Tom shared my love of music, and one afternoon we visited the Prescott Music Center together.

"I'm gonna go look around," Tom said.

I nodded, and continued browsing the sheet music until I heard a familiar voice from behind me.

"Hey, look who's here. Someone I know."

I turned around to see Roy grinning at me. My heart somersaulted from the undeniable thrill of seeing him. I flashed a big smile. "Oh. Hi." Automatically, my eyes darted around the store to locate Tom. A wave of relief swept over me when I saw Tom engrossed in the guitar section. He would lose his mind if he saw me talking to another guy.

"What's new with you? I'm headed to Florida tomorrow," Roy said.

I nodded and smiled.

A pained look in his eyes flashed and died when he turned away to flip through a rack of albums. "Uh . . . I heard you're getting married."

I'd told Chuck about Tom's two-year conditional proposal.

"Marriage is uncertain as of now," I said, noticing how awkward and unfitting the word marriage felt like coming out of my mouth. Until that moment, it had never crossed my mind that I was sort of engaged to be married.

"Is he here?" Roy asked, scanning the shop.

After I pointed out Tom, Roy's eyes followed him as he continued to wander through the guitar section. I could see the ache in Roy's eyes—and, as if commiserating without my permission, my heart ached too. Roy's rapt attention on Tom made my insides squirm more by the second with the fear that Tom would see us talking and make a scene.

To rush things along, I said, "Hey, I'd love to have you write me now and then . . . tell me how you're doing?"

I scrounged in my purse for a scrap of paper, found one, and wrote down my address.

"Here," I said, handing it to him. Then it dawned on me he might need more information. "Oh, wait. I'd better put down my name in case you forget whose address this is."

As I began to write, Roy stared at the paper and said, "Linda, there's no way I'd forget."

I didn't raise my head to look at him because I couldn't. Could he see me tremble? Good Lord, after all this time, he still got to me. With my note in hand, he left the store, but he did not leave my thoughts.

MY MOM CALLED me at work right before lunch the next day. She'd never, ever, called me at work before. Was something wrong?

"A small package came for you in the mail today—it's from Ben."

My breath caught. *A package?*

I had to know what Ben had sent.

"I'm going home for lunch," I told Lynell, and, having borrowed my mom's car that day, drove there in a trance.

My mom looked up when I stepped in the carport door. "Oh! I wasn't expecting you . . ."

"Where is it?"

"On the table . . ."

I took the tiny rectangular package into my bedroom, where I tore off the plain brown wrapping and revealed a cassette tape. Sitting on the floor and leaning against my bed frame, I plugged it into my tape player with a click. Static crackled as the leader passed through the wheels. Glued to the machine, I sat perfectly still to avoid missing a single word. Ben's gentle voice filled my room.

> *. . . I've been thinking about all the times before you split, when we were in the halls, sitting there in ol' Nottingham during lunch, there were so many times I just wanted to take you into my arms and tell you how I felt. But I couldn't. Something stopped me. I don't know what . . .*

What came next made me melt. He apologized for hurting me. He knew he screwed up by letting me go. He regretted losing the best thing he'd ever had. He had never been in love with anyone before me.

"*I want to be with you again,*" he said. "*I miss you. I still love you. But I don't want to get between you and Tom.*"

With the sound of ocean waves in the background, he said:

> *It seems like I'm just sitting here talking to you. Like you're right here beside me, and I'm telling you this. It's beautiful, it really is. The sun's setting right now and the sky's all orange and pink and light blue . . . I wish you were here to see it . . . 'cause you're beautiful, you really are. Physically and mentally. I think that's why I love you . . .*

Tears flowed freely while I held my head in my hands for fifteen minutes after the tape ended. Tears of joy that Ben really wanted me back. Just like I'd hoped and prayed for a whole year. Tears of grief that to be with Ben, I'd need to break up with Tom. I blew my raw nose for the umpteenth time, took a deep breath, and walked into the kitchen. My mom stood at the sink washing dishes. I'd never shared boyfriend troubles with her before.

She turned, and one look at my face and red, swollen eyes, she asked, "Oh, honey, what's wrong?"

The sobs began again.

"Mom . . . oh, Mom . . . Ben says he still loves me. He wants to know if I still love him. I do. What am I going to do?"

She wrapped her arms around me and gave me a strong hug. "If you do love him, then you'll have to make a decision about Tom," she said, stroking my hair.

My head pounded and my eyes ached. I did love Ben. But I loved Tom, too, didn't I? Wasn't Tom, the one present in my life right here right now, the better choice? And yet, my love for Ben was so powerful, I couldn't bear to think of Ben as *not* the right one.

When I awoke the next morning, I had to remind myself that Ben really did say all of those wonderful things to me. And although both Roy and Tom had told me I was beautiful, hearing Ben say so, a man two years older than me, incredibly handsome, and out of reach for so long . . . I could not tone down the thrill that *he* thought I was beautiful, and that he wanted *me*.

Ah, but then, then came the snippets of doubt invading my pleasurable thoughts like tendrils of poison ivy. Ben might dump me again. I might have made him into someone he is not. He might have made me into someone *I'm* not.

It sounds so beautiful for you to say
"I've loved you more when you went away"
and although I know you'll do me wrong
I'll never love anyone this strong.
LMS *1973*

OVER THE NEXT two days, Tom called and left several messages. No doubt he wondered what the hell was going on, but I still couldn't bring myself to talk to him. I needed more time. During this alone time, I picked apart our relationship, realizing there were too many things about him that didn't work for me. Being a racist was huge. So was his cruelty to people and animals. I hated his jealousy. And his values were from my parents' generation. Plain as day: even if Ben and I didn't work out, Tom and I weren't going to work out either.

First things first. As Ben had requested of me, I tape-recorded a short response, assuring him that I felt the same way, and mailed it off.

With perfect timing, Sunday, Chuck and I went hiking. I poured out my troubles in one continuous monologue. He listened without speaking a solitary word. Once I exhausted what I wanted to say, silence on his part followed. To fill the void, birds twittered, flies buzzed, and pine needles snapped under our feet.

"Well," he finally said, "it seems to me that all of your indecision must be coming from the fact that you are not ready to be tied down—to Ben, to Tom, or to anyone."

This struck home. It had never dawned on me that I did not have to "be with someone," for the sake of being with someone. I dreaded telling Tom that we weren't going to work out, but I would have to find a way.

LYNELL DID NOT provide enough jewelry orders to make our venture work. I resorted to applying as a waitress at The Third Base luncheonette. My gut didn't think too much of this—it churned all day and all night after I'd accepted the position.

Late Saturday morning, wearing the hideous white-polyester uniform dress with a zipper up the front from my fast-food stint at Sandee's, I stood listening as the seasoned waitress ran me through the drill.

"Make sure you write down the orders in shorthand—you'll never have time to spell it all out. I'll give you a list of common ones you'll need to learn. Memorize the daily specials the night before, they aren't on the menu. I'll make sure you have them before you leave. Refill coffee and water on a regular basis—customers get really cranky when you aren't on top of things . . . oh, and make sure you smile no matter what, or you won't get any tips . . ."

Each of those instructions made me cringe more. I did not want to do this. However, I toughed it out—for two long days. Throughout my shifts, I felt like a complete idiot. I mixed up customers and orders more than once. A man yelled at me when I took too long to bring more coffee. I spent every "serving" minute terrified I'd spill something on a customer. On the third morning, the boss told me my hours would be cut down to two per day. My way out! Those were not enough hours to make this worthwhile. I quit. It was time to do something besides apply for low-level jobs that sucked the life out of me like a super-duper vacuum cleaner. I headed to Yavapai College to explore education and career options. My parents couldn't afford tuition, but maybe I could get a scholarship or financial aid.

Compared to Prescott High School, and even Nottingham High in Syracuse, the college complex was huge and intimidating. I managed to find my way to the administration office, and spoke with a guidance counselor.

"Here's an application for financial aid," the pleasant woman said. "Fill out all sections, and have one of your parents sign here." She turned a page over and pointed to the signature line. "Bring it back, and I'll see what we can do to help you."

Nervous at the prospect of going to college, but also excited at the thought I *could* go to college, I began daydreaming about what I might study.

"Dad," I said after dinner, "I have some forms here for financial aid so I can attend Yavapai, and I need you to fill out the back of page three and sign."

"Hm? Okay." He set the papers on the table next to his recliner.

At breakfast, I picked up the papers from the table and asked, "Dad, did you have a chance to finish the application?"

He slammed his fork down. "No. And I won't. It's none of their damn business how much money we make."

"But that means I won't be able to go," I said, my eyes watering.

He picked up his fork and attacked the eggs on his plate. End of discussion.

My face burned with shame, as though I'd asked for something ridiculously unreasonable. A tense lump formed in my throat. I stared at the forms clutched in my hand for a moment, wiped tears from my face, walked to the kitchen trash can, and tossed them in.

LATER THAT WEEK, while grabbing a snack, the telephone rang at seven-thirty p.m. I snatched the receiver from the kitchen phone. "Hello?"

"Hi, babe, it's me."

I couldn't place the familiar voice for a second. Then I did.

I sputtered and choked. "Ben. Hi."

Always soft-spoken, Ben didn't have much to say, but we managed to stumble over a few lines: "Good to hear your voice." "How are you?" "I've missed you."

Then he described a dream he'd had. "I came to Arizona, and I saw you, and then I split. But I wasn't alone."

Smiling, I said, "Oh really?"

"Yeah, I found this cat . . ."

We both laughed.

His voice softened. "No, I left with you."

I fell silent for a few moments, envisioning what that would be like.

After hanging up, I lay awake for hours. Ben's voice filled my head. But then Tom stepped in. I hated confrontations, and the one with Tom would be huge. Tom continued to call, and I continued to dodge his calls. To postpone it any longer would be wrong, if not cruel, and yet, how could I find it in me to tell him? *Maybe I'll wait a few more days . . . maybe less.* That thought made me pause. *I can't believe I am thinking of holding back from telling him we are over.* Despite chastising myself, I decided to wait anyway.

AN ACQUAINTANCE OF mine said he would be moving into a new house, and I volunteered to help. While waiting in front of Marty's place for him to arrive with a trailer-load of boxes, I could've sworn I saw Roy drive by. When the vehicle did a U-turn, I knew it was him.

Roy pulled up to the curb, and hopped out. I jumped up from the front steps, delighted to see him.

"I hitchhiked as far as Texas," he said, about his Florida attempt, "but I got tired of no one giving me a ride. I spent many nights sleeping by the side of the road."

That didn't sound at all like fun. Both Roy and Chuck were enamored with hitchhiking. Episodes like that made me wonder why. Our conversation continued, and somehow I found myself telling him details about Tom and Ben. "Tom and I are too different from each other, and not in a good way."

"Yeah," Roy said, giving me a long, steady look. "That's what happened between us."

Words stuck in my throat. *It was?* I'd never thought of us as being too different from each other. What was *the* reason we hadn't worked out? Figuring out the real reason would take more than a few minutes of contemplation. I did notice how, unlike the last time we'd met, he made efforts to keep our conversation going. When Marty arrived and I had to unload boxes, I regretted that Roy left.

After helping Marty all afternoon, I went home and plopped onto the couch, exhausted. The doorbell rang. Because no one else was home, I pushed myself to get up. A young delivery man stood before me with an armful of fresh flowers in a large glass vase. *From Ben?* I set the sunny, colorful bouquet on the kitchen table, and plucked the tiny card from the holder. *From Tom.* Guilt smothered me like a blanket tossed over flames. I could not put this off any longer.

Tom called to check on the delivery, and of course I thanked him for his thoughtfulness.

"You've not returned my calls," he said. "We need to talk."

My body slumped, inside and out. *This is it.*

Tom insisted on picking me up. At his place, we sat side-by-side on the couch in the living room. My hands shook with the combination of nervousness and dread. It felt like forever before one of us spoke; the silence emotionally charged, tense, much like a ticking bomb. When he leaned in to kiss me, I averted my head.

Tom sat back. "Tell me the truth. You love Ben *and* me, don't you?"

The pain in his eyes and the pain in the back of my throat rendered me unable to speak, nor able to face him. I stood up and walked outside. He followed, and stood beside me on the front porch. I hugged myself not only because it was cold, but because I also needed the comfort. Overwhelming guilt was ripping me apart.

"I understand this is hard," Tom said, "but don't worry. I figured you felt that way. Take your time in deciding between the two of us."

What the heck? This was not at all what I'd expected. I'd no idea what to do with this offer. Stay? Go?

After talking some more, Tom wanted to go for a drive. We parked in the forest, where, somehow, he convinced me to make love with him in the back seat. I liked sex with Tom, but I didn't like that we had sex to avoid dealing with our problems. Shouldn't there be more to a relationship?

The next day, I knew there should be more. An all-nighter of thinking, ruminating, sorting, and analyzing of all of the signs made it clear. Tom was not right for me. In the morning, I wrote Ben a letter to say that Tom and I were done, and if he (Ben) and I didn't work out, then we weren't meant to be together, either.

Valentine's Day was coming up. Certainly, I couldn't break up with Tom just before Valentine's Day. I gave myself permission to wait, which took off a ton of pressure. I focused on normal, everyday stuff. On Sunday, I baked heart-shaped sugar cookies, delighting in applying red frosting. After that, I gave the car a thorough cleaning and waxing, pleased with the brilliant shine. Kim came over, and we went hiking up into the big boulders off Willow Creek Road. What a beautiful day to be outdoors, with the sun warm and the sky a perfect blue.

A mention of Tom and Ben brought a shrug to her shoulders. "I've never had a boyfriend, so what do I know?"

Monday and Tuesday I finished making two women's rings, a delicate bracelet with fussy silverwork, and my first turquoise-inlaid pendant. How I loved to see the shine after the final buffing.

Come Valentine's Day, not one single word from Tom. No card, no flowers, nothing. His ignoring me stung. What happened to him wanting me to stay? It also gave me time to think. Maybe I did love Tom in a way, but I loved Ben more. It was time to let Tom go.

The next night Tom appeared at the door unannounced a little past eight. We sat on the back porch steps. Finally, I'd gathered up the strength I needed. There, I made an instant decision *not* to bring Ben into the picture. What was the point? This wasn't about Ben stealing me from Tom, this was about Tom not being right for me.

As gently as I could, I explained why we'd have to break up. "I think you are too serious for me, Tom. I'm not ready to get married, or be tied down. I need my freedom."

To see Tom reduced to heaving sobs almost made me retract what I'd said. But I didn't. I couldn't. No more denying or deceiving. After Tom regrouped, he asked me a very painful question. "So did making love with me mean anything to you, or would you have done it with anyone who came along?"

What the . . . "No, of course not!"

Based on his facial expression, I doubted he believed me. With not much more to say, he left.

If I was destined to be an old maid, well, so be it.

As I'd anticipated, breaking up with Tom left me feeling raw for a few days. It took a letter from Ben to cheer me up. He wrote that he would come visit me on Saturday the 24th. *This Saturday?* I double-checked the calendar. *Four days!* I floated around the house all afternoon.

The phone rang that night. I answered, pleased to hear Ben's voice. But something about his tone sounded off. Then it hit me: *He's not coming.*

"Well, Linda, I hate to tell you this, but I got busted, and won't be able to go anywhere for at least a month."

No! Dammit. This wasn't the first time he'd gotten into trouble. My irritation flared. Why couldn't he follow Navy rules? His behavior denied me the right to be with him. Could this all be happening to prove we weren't meant for each other? Unwelcome doubts marched through my head, each one competing for priority. *Ben is not the one. He won't love me, or I will end up not loving him. Where is my life going? Do I need Ben because I love him? Or do I love him because I need him?* Ben wasn't perfect. He smoked cigarettes and pot too much, and he had a temper, which I guessed was probably why he'd spent time in the brig more than once. How does Ben stand on sex before marriage? Would he be mad if he knew I'd had sex with Tom? Right then, I had no interest in going to bed with Ben. Although Ben and I weren't really strangers, we didn't know each other well, either. When I wrote to him, I always asked questions in an attempt to get to know him better, but he never answered them. Frustrated the heck out of me. Right now, how I would love to hear his voice, to watch him talk . . . but the latter hadn't happened for nine, tortuous months.

The complexity of time confused me. When we moved to Prescott, the first eight months were brutal. I could have sworn each day contained forty-eight miserable hours. But the summer in Syracuse after graduation felt like last week. Now that I'd engaged the memory train, I couldn't stop it. The day after Ben and my friends picked me up at the airport, just having Ben hold me fulfilled all of my hopes and wishes of connecting with him. When Ben and I strolled through the LeMoyne College campus and he stopped to kiss me, I didn't want to wake from what felt like a dream. Despite what happened with Ben, I realized that if he hadn't ditched me, I wouldn't have experienced half of what I did that summer . . . including maturing, I thought, by several leaps. Sure, the summer had turned miserable when I realized I had to go home, but that in itself was a lesson I needed to learn.

WHAT A SURPRISE to hear from Tom. A shocked me let him talk—for two whole hours.

"Please, please, Linda, give me another chance. I know it will work this time. I will do things differently, I promise. Think of all the things we have in common! We love the outdoors, we are both creative, and enjoy listening to the same style of music and playing guitar. Give me two weeks. If you still feel the same way, I'll let you go."

My resolve wavered. Now what? The week had been empty and lonely, especially with Ben blowing up my hopes by getting busted. Should I give Tom another chance? I wasn't sure anymore that breaking up with Tom had been the right thing to do . . . at least, not as sure as I was before . . .

I caved.

Although Tom and I got back together, it didn't take me long to realize we had changed. No—*I* had changed. *Can I put up with Tom's faults long term? Do I want to?*

When Tom called and insisted that because we went all the way, we were supposed to get married—that did it. It didn't register until that moment that I did not share in his old-fashioned beliefs. This time, I stood fast. "No. It's over, Tom."

Tom sighed deeply. "I told you I'd let you go . . . as much as it pains me, I guess this is it."

We said goodbye.

Tom did call me one last time to say he was moving to California. I wished him well.

ALWAYS KEEN TO make a few bucks, I headed down to the swap meet on Saturday to see if I could sell some of the jewelry I'd made.

After an hour, a woman strolled up to my tailgate display, and asked to see the silver watchband adorned with four lovely pieces of turquoise that I'd slaved over for hours. I removed it from my display case.

"This is beautiful!" she said, putting it on her wrist to admire. "How much?"

The ten went into my wallet, my mind reeling over what I could buy with that much money.

Encouraged, I set up at the swap meet every weekend. In mid-March, I bumped into Roy and a friend of his. I played it cool, checked my emotions to hide the fact that seeing him brought on a thrill, and did the non-committal shrug when he asked me what was new. That all changed when his friend asked Roy if I was his girlfriend, and Roy replied, "Naw, she's an ex."

I did a double-take. *An ex? I'm an ex?* No one had ever referred to me as an "ex" before—at least not in front of me. This felt like an insult. How could I be an "ex" when we never were a couple? I couldn't help but notice that he found it hard to say goodbye, repeatedly starting up new topics to keep us talking. If I was nothing but an "ex," then what was that all about?

ALWAYS VIGILANT ON the job search front, I applied for a secretarial position, even though the ad said "minimum three years' experience." That done, I tackled some sewing projects I'd neglected for ages, pleased with the results. I even made time to relax. I listened to records, practiced guitar, and treated myself to an ice cream cone after lunch.

Three days later, a letter arrived from Ben. With trembling hands, I tore open the envelope and read the pages in his loopy handwriting. In those pages he said how much he loved me, missed me, and wanted to be with me—which was exactly what I wanted him to say. But what struck me as strange—no—not strange—*ironic*—was how long I had prayed for Ben to feel this way— and now that he did, you'd think I'd be deliriously happy. But no, I did not feel happy. Maybe because I had a hard time believing him. How could he love me that much? How could he justify it all? We'd spent so little time together. To add to my doubts, I couldn't help but be annoyed that, once again, he'd not answered the questions I'd asked in my last letter. Time to think this through.

Ben had been a significant part of my whole existence for two years now. What was it about him that kept me hanging on? While it was amazing that a man as handsome as Ben said he loved me, of course there was more. I reminisced about the innocent and sweet way he straightened my necklace when we sat waiting for Sheri on the Nottingham campus. How he made me feel like a sexy young woman when he called me "babe." Most definitely I could never forget the pleasant dream he'd had about us leaving Arizona together. Not much to hold onto, but I did anyway.

That night, I dreamed of Ben being here, holding me, saying he loved me. I dreamed I was in Syracuse with him. So many dreams—all beautiful—all untrue. Somehow, someday, maybe those dreams would come true. I would have to wait.

CHUCK AND I drove out to the forest one cool evening to talk. We parked, and he killed the headlights. Dark, mysterious shadows hid secrets only the trees knew.

"I'm going to Colorado next week. Would you like to come with me?" he asked.

I did. More than anything. But would my parents let me? Never. They were old school. Girls did not travel with boys unless they were married. Would my mom trust me? Maybe she would say yes. It wouldn't be easy, but if I wanted to go, I'd have to find the courage to ask.

The next morning, I strolled into the kitchen where my mom was fixing breakfast.

I took a deep breath. "Mom, Chuck has asked me to go to Colorado with him next week . . ."

She plucked a slice of bread from the toaster, and turned to me. "No, I don't think so. That wouldn't look proper."

That's what I feared she'd say. How infuriating that society frowned upon what a "proper" girl could and could not do! Chuck and I had a platonic relationship. Period. Why did I have to be married before I could take a trip with a guy? This lit a fire under my job search. I had to get out of here and live under my own rules. Instead of relying on the classifieds, I started cold-calling. No luck with that, either.

On our usual Sunday family outing, my dad steered us onto Walker Road in the Bradshaw Mountains, which took us deep into the Prescott National Forest. Ponderosa groves stood with nary a sign of civilization. Staring out the window, I let my thoughts wander. Chuck and I had been close friends for almost two years now. I felt special, if not honored, that we were friends. After all, his friend list was quite long. Why did he include boring me on that list? You'd think because my parents weren't about to let me go gallivanting around with him unless we got married, there'd be no good reason for him to keep me around. These feelings of friendship I had for Chuck . . . were they more in disguise? For sure referring to us as good friends didn't begin to touch on the depth of what I felt for him. What did he think of me? Was I also just a friend? Lately, I saw hints that he felt more. He'd always been nice to me, but lately he'd been . . . well . . . extra nice. Heaven forbid should I read into what wasn't there. That would not only be embarrassing, but potentially painful. I already knew first hand that there is nothing worse than having deep feelings for someone that are not reciprocated.

WHILE SEARCHING THE Prescott Courier's classifieds yet again for work, my eyes landed on the "musical instruments for sale" section, and widened when I read about the Martin guitar for sale . . . *a Martin.* Roy played a Martin. My heartthrob, famous singer-songwriter Neil Young, played a Martin. The desire to own a Martin guitar swept in and overtook my everything. Could I afford a new Martin? Never. Could I afford a used Martin? The ad said $425. Did I have that kind of money? No. Besides, I didn't really need a better guitar. My Guild had a beautiful sound, confirmed by several decent musicians who'd heard me play. But none of that mattered. I wanted to see, touch, and maybe play a guitar that could only be mine in my dreams. I called the listed number, and made an appointment.

Late the next day, the seller lifted his Martin from its case, and handed it to me. The guitar's shape fit perfectly against my body, the smooth wood of the neck fit perfectly in my hand. I positioned my fingers on the frets, and strummed a chord, the rich sound filling the room, and my every living cell. After ten minutes of playing, I handed the guitar back to the owner, thanked him, and drove home. There, I sat on the floor in my room, leaned against the bed with knees pulled to my chest. *Martins are too beautiful and too expensive for me to ever own.*

After a half hour of feeling badly, I removed my Guild Madeira guitar from its case, and sat cross-legged to play. *Hello, old friend. I'm sorry I thought about replacing you. Don't worry . . . I love you just the way you are.*

Chapter 8

MY OLDER SISTER, Cindy, had accepted a nursing job in Tucson. First, she stopped in Prescott. That way, our mom could join her to look at apartments. I tagged along, albeit reluctantly, to look for work. I didn't want to live in Tucson, but I knew something had to give.

Tucson's big city traffic freaked me out. How did people deal with this on a daily basis? Cindy pulled into a Circle K and bought a newspaper to scan the classifieds. Within an hour, we were scaling two flights of stairs, and walking with the landlady through Cindy's first option.

"It's a one bedroom with a full kitchen," the landlady said. "We need first and last month's rent, plus a deposit . . ."

Her voice faded as I veered off to explore the place on my own. For sure, it desperately needed a good airing. There were not anywhere near enough windows, and the bathroom didn't even have a tub. Those faults didn't faze me. The desire to be financially able to rent this place made my hands twitch. We barely had time for me to apply for one sales job at a large department store before it was time to return to Prescott. On the ride home, I decided that in order for me to ever be on my own, I would need to save, save, save, every dime I could to make it happen.

THE NEXT SUNDAY morning, our green Chevy suburban, purchased for excursions such as this, bumped over the washboard Walker Road, doors rattling, the air scented with pine and the dust our tires stirred up. We stopped to take a look at the narrow and quiet Lynx Lake, which shimmered blue under a cloudless sky. After strolling a bit there, we drove further, winding through the forest and passing a small community of tucked away cabins.

While staring out the window, I thought about the deeper feelings I'd been experiencing lately for Chuck. Was this infatuation? If it was, I'd get over it. It made no sense to say anything to him. That would ensure our friendship would remain intact.

Evergreens soon gave way to a massive wildfire scar. Blackened trees stood like sentinels from the blaze that had raged through here a couple years ago. Twisted and charred downed trees lay like a game of Pick-Up-Sticks. *Wow, this is awful. Were any animals killed?* A sign of regeneration—a baby ponderosa peeked above healthy green grass—but it would be a long time before those trees once again whispered in a breeze.

After more miles on the dirt road, we reached Hassayampa Lake. There, my dad parked and we ate the tailgate picnic lunch my mom had prepared. We packed everything up, continued to where Walker Road connects to Senator Highway, and headed home.

After dinner, I took a call from Chuck. "Do you want to go to an art show in Sedona next weekend? I really hope you can come! I'm planning on taking my motorcycle, if that's okay."

His enthusiasm about me going with him on this trip topped anything I'd heard from him before. But now I needed parental permission. My dad, a paramedic, considered motorcycles death-on-wheels.

"Chuck has invited me for a motorcycle ride to Sedona," I said at the dinner table that night. "I really want to go. Can I?"

My mom looked to my dad. The silence from my dad, who had the final say, lasted way too long. *He's going to say no.*

"Okay," he said. "You can go, provided you wear a helmet."

I couldn't get to the phone fast enough to deliver Chuck the good news.

"They said yes!"

I could almost see him smile.

"Great, I'll pick you up Saturday morning."

At about eleven, Chuck and I headed to Sedona. In no time, he confirmed that my intuition had been exactly right. Today with Chuck was unlike any other day we'd ever shared. On his motorcycle, I wrapped my arms around him, and rested my cheek on his shoulder, enjoying a closeness we'd never shared before. He responded by placing his hand over mine, his touch warm and comforting, or resting it on my thigh, which sent tingles up my leg and into my spine. We stopped in Jerome, and parked at a café for something to drink. The waitress led us to a red vinyl booth, where we sat opposite each other.

After ordering, I twirled the paper coaster in circles, and said wistfully, "I'd love to go to Canada someday . . ."

Chuck used a tone of voice I'd not heard before when he said, "If you could just take off, I sure would love to take you up there."

Pleasant warmth widened in my chest. In the past, I'd heard comments more in the line of: "Sure you can come if you like," but this time I heard, "I'd really like to take you there because you're *you*." Would he say that to any other of his female friends?

When we straddled his motorcycle to leave, I again wrapped my arms around him, pressing close, enjoying his warmth, feeling more connected to him than ever. Soon we meandered through the red sandstone cliffs of Sedona, and the lush riparian vegetation of Oak Creek Canyon. Oak Creek, as usual, had attracted crowds wanting to experience the renowned Slide Rock State Park. Kids and adults alike screamed and laughed as they rode down the natural water slide. It looked like fun, but not with that many people in one place at one time. Plus, I assumed the water had to be about 40 degrees—brrrr.

Chuck parked in downtown Sedona, where we explored art galleries, gift and jewelry shops. The entire time, he took every opportunity to touch me—on my arm to get my attention, on my lower back when I entered a shop first, or a fleeting feather touch on my hand while viewing a painting we both liked. After walking through the art show we'd come to see, we entered a jewelry store.

An intricate silver and turquoise brooch with amazing detail caught my eye. "Oh, Chuck, look at this!"

He came to my side and put his arm around my shoulder. "That's really nice. I bet you could make one even nicer."

Nothing short of spectacular that Chuck thought my jewelry skills were at that level.

On the ride back, the breeze warm and fragrant with pines and mountain-high air, I rested my cheek on his shoulder, thoughtful. What a beautiful day, both weather wise and beyond. What a wondrous experience riding on his motorcycle. No wonder people liked them—you could see more around you and appreciate it more, too. Just to breathe in the fresh air, and smell the beautiful trees and water—there was so much to take in that you couldn't experience sitting inside a car.

Our new connection confused me, though. Startled by all the emotion that swept over me today, I had a hard time believing this was really "us."

Chuck parked in front of my house, and shut off the engine. Removing his helmet, he finger-combed his mussed-up hair, and smiled at me. "Did you have fun today?"

I smiled back. "I think it was one of the best times we've ever had."

As I knew he would, and as I wanted him to, he planted a friendly kiss on my lips.

"In two weeks, I'll be hitting the road," he said. "But I will be sure to call you so we can spend more time together until then."

That night I lay awake. What did Chuck think of us? Was he planning a fling before he left? Why had he changed his mind about our friendship? Boy, figuring this out was going to be rough. We'd *never* discussed our feelings for each other. Would we be able to? But after all the heavy-duty crap I'd been through lately with Roy and with Tom, our deep friendship connection was a pleasant relief.

In the morning I realized that I was content to be Chuck's good, close friend. What we had was a unique, special—but not romantic—relationship. No way would I ruin everything by letting more happen between us.

Chuck came over after dinner the next day, and we sat in my bedroom and talked. The whole time, the urge to dive into a discussion about the change in our relationship nipped at the edge of my responses. When he was about to leave, I couldn't resist. "Can I ask you something?"

His eyebrows raised for a split second, then relaxed. "Sure."

"What happened yesterday? I mean, you've changed."

Chuck lowered his eyes, blushing a bit. "No I haven't; I'm still the same ol' me."

Smiling, I shook my head. "No, you've changed."

Now he lowered his head. "Yes, I guess I have, in one way."

I hazarded a guess. "How long has it been since your feelings for me changed?"

He paused in thought. "Oh . . . I don't know . . . a month?"

A month! A whole month! My mind scrambled to recall how long it'd been since I noticed that he'd been treating me differently. Indeed, it had been about a month. What I couldn't get over was how my intuition that his affection for me had grown had been right. How did I know? Well, I just *knew*. Funny how that works.

A few days passed, and Chuck picked me up to pay a friend of his a visit. Almost the whole time, Chuck kept his arm around my shoulders, me at ease with the affectionate gesture.

Later, Chuck and I went for a walk alone. He wrapped an arm around me and gave me a squeeze. "You know, Linda, I really love friends. Good close ones," he said, smiling at me.

Was he hinting at our closer relationship? Of course he was.

"Oh, I so agree. Good close friends are hard to find."

I leaned into his hug. I agreed with him to prove my good faith, and because that was what I really wanted, too: To be his good friend. I trusted and believed in him. Everything between us would be just fine.

Parked at the curb in front of my house late that evening, before I got out of his truck, impulsively, I asked, "Can I kiss you goodnight?"

He smiled, and laughed gently. "Sure you can. But only if you let me kiss you."

After a quick kiss on the lips, we parted. *Why shouldn't good friends be able to kiss each other without wanting anything more?* This all felt delightfully comfortable.

The next few days before Chuck left for Colorado, I felt happier and more contented than I'd been in a long time. On Friday, the day before his departure, we drove out to my favorite spot on Wolf Creek to talk. Such a beautiful night, too . . . stars flooded the sky, the Milky Way's veil directly overhead. Our conversations, always varied, and often philosophical, were no different on this evening. We covered marriage, Roy, Ben, Chuck's ex-girlfriend, writing in our journals, hitchhiking, friendships—you name it. My heart overflowed with an abundance of affection for him.

When we parted, he said, "I'm sorry I have to leave, but I will be back, and I will stay in contact."

My faked smile hurt. Life without him for three months was inconceivable. Still, he'd always be there, somewhere, when I needed him. And I'd always be here when he needed me. I knew I was not in love with him, but I loved him in a very special way—the love between two close friends. I hoped I'd always feel this way, no matter where I ended up, or who, if anyone, I ended up being with. It was then I realized how much I loved and needed my freedom. I would never let anyone tie me down so tightly that I couldn't keep Chuck as my friend.

Chapter 9

IN MID-MAY, MY dad stopped me as I passed by his recliner, saying, "Take a seat."

Puzzled, I perched on the love seat close by.

He lit his pipe, the familiar cherry-scented smoke curling from the bowl.

"I'm giving up on Med-Evac. We are moving to Tucson. I've found a job with an ambulance company there."

I couldn't speak. *What? No! This is home!*

When my parents made the decision to move to Arizona, my dad had already set his dream in motion: starting Prescott's first ambulance service, Med-Evac. Our family joke, often told at the dinner table to guests, was that prior to my dad's company, the local funeral home had quite a racket going. Because they also transported the sick and injured to the hospital, there was no need to rush: they'd get paid one way or the other. Only two years in, my dad had to face the reality that insurance companies were taking forever to pay up, and he didn't have the cash flow to wait. He would have to sell out.

In a weird, ironic twist, especially considering how desperately I'd wanted to get away from here a year ago, I no longer hated Prescott. In fact, I loved it here. If anyone had told me when we first arrived that I would learn to love and appreciate Prescott, I would have told them: "Over my dead body." That's because I didn't yet know that I would eventually adore the ponderosa forest that surrounded the city, the dry, clean mountain air, solid blue skies, the gushing, boulder-strewn creeks, cattail-lined lakes, narrow, winding old mining roads, exploring those mines with Chuck and Roy, panning for gold (and being overjoyed with finding three flakes), our annual live Christmas tree hunt (taking all day, resulting in a wild, asymmetrical, unruly thing—which was half its charm), collecting glittery rocks (that never quite glittered in the same way once home), pine cone gathering to make Christmas wreaths, our

Sunday outings to discover new places ... and more. Even if I got out on my own, this would no longer be "home."

These memories hit me hard enough to cease my chest and made me want to burst into tears.

My dad said he would rent an apartment in Tucson until our house sold. Despite my opposition to the move, it didn't take me long to admit that I should join my dad in Tucson to look for work. Talk about a difficult decision—I did not want to go, but knew I should go anyway— I'd never find a real job here.

EMPTINESS FILLED MY heart on a lonely Sunday evening. My one candle flickered, creating soft shadows. Tabitha slept soundly on my bed. From my record player, Linda Ronstadt's voice drifted around me. I took out my journal to write.

> *What will happen between Ben and me? I write him several times a week, but he writes once a month, if that. When I do get a letter, all is grand for twenty-four hours, but then it all falls apart. Even though he says he will come see me, I've all but given up that he will—mainly because in the five long months that have passed, he hasn't. Every time I open the mailbox and find no letter from him, my heart hits the pavement. My body literally aches to be with him. What good does it do to live in such a beautiful place when there is no one to share it with? Not being able to find work here in Prescott ruins everything I want from life.*

Angry and fed up, I slapped my journal shut, and tossed the pen across the room, where it hit the wall, leaving a mark. *Shit. I'll go to Tucson and get a damned job.*

A FEW DAYS later: a glimmer of hope. The phone company, Mountain Bell (Ma Bell, as they were known), advertised a job opening in Prescott for an operator, paper shuffler, phone answerer—whatever. I slipped on the two-piece mauve knit dress I'd sewn in anticipation of finding a real job, pulled on pantyhose, and stepped into suede clogs that were worn so infrequently, I could've returned them to the store and gotten a refund.

At Ma Bell's, I asked for an application at the front desk, and took one of the two seats against the wall. With the clipboard positioned on my lap, I carefully printed answers to their questions.

"Experience: Detail your customer service and phone skills."

Let's see . . . I took orders at Sandee's, answered phones at the print shop for that lecherous old man . . . what else? My jewelry experience didn't seem to fit, so I left that out. I stared at the skimpy summation of my work life, and heaved a heavy sigh. *I won't get this job.*

On the drive home, the whole futile experience festered like a splinter in my finger that I couldn't for the life of me find. Once in my bedroom, I kicked my shoes off into the closet, yanked off the pantyhose, tossed my outfit into a heap on the bed, dressed in my Levi's and work shirt, and tied on my Chukka boots. Now I felt like me. Noticing the postman leave, I dashed across the street to our mailbox. Inside: a letter from Ben. I didn't get psyched or anything. After all, it'd been ages since I'd heard from him.

With my guard up to prepare myself for potentially bad news as to why all that silence, I shut myself in my room and hopped onto my bed. One sentence in, a dark cloud formed.

"Sorry I haven't written, babe. No good excuse. I'm just feeling lazy."

What? Here I'd been waiting and waiting to hear from him . . . and he'd been too lazy to write?

I kept reading. *"There's nothing in the world I want more than you."*

My heartbeat skipped. *I want you, too, Ben. Nothing will keep him from me if that's how he truly feels.* My spirits plummeted at the next paragraph. He didn't get weekends off at all, and the only time he'd be free would be one week before he sailed overseas for nine months. Reality check. I may not see him until next summer. I let my hands and the letter drop to my lap. How would I prepare myself to not see him for another whole year?

THE LAST DAY of June. My dad left for his new job in Tucson. My mom kept her secretarial job with a Prescott attorney. The real estate agent had free reign to walk potential buyers through our house. At least that's what I assumed happened. I timed my exits to avoid seeing strangers in my room.

A few days later a call came from U.S. Electrical Motors. They wanted to set up an interview for tomorrow. Cautiously optimistic, I dressed for the part.

The sterile waiting room had a number of interviewees. Taking a seat in a metal chair with a vinyl seat, I caught the eye of a girl about my age, and we exchanged shy smiles. Nervous, I let my eyes wander. Not one single thing adorned the walls. The clicking of the receptionist's typewriter echoed in the room. Other applicants stared at the floor. I joined them, counting linoleum squares to pass the time.

The subsequent interview was brief, and I walked out without one iota of confidence left.

Within twenty-four hours, they called.

Granted, the woman who delivered the bad news was polite. "Thank you for your interest, but the position has been filled. Good luck in your search!"

Disappointed? Yes and no. I'd figured that would be the case.

I MET BARBARA through one of my dad's employees. His girlfriend became my friend. Barbara and I had guitar in common, and we played together once in a while.

"I'm going to the Fourth of July street dance on Friday," she said. "Want to come?"

I hesitated. These kinds of events didn't interest me much, but maybe it would be fun.

Throngs of people filled the town square. We made our way through the crowd, walking sideways, or stepping aside, to let people pass. Bands were playing in various locations. Groups formed around them, and people danced spontaneously to the music where they stood. Barb and I found a break in the crowd, and eased through. And there . . . coming toward me . . . Roy.

He recognized me and stopped. "Oh, hey . . ." he said, turning to a noisy group of teens laughing and talking as they passed us by.

What to say? My brain didn't seem to be working.

"Quite the crowd," I said, raising my voice to be heard over the loud music.

Distracted by the commotion, he turned back to me when I spoke. "Huh? What?"

"I said there's quite a crowd out tonight," raising my voice again, hating what I said even more the second time.

"Uh-huh." His eyes scanned the faces of the people around us, and never once connected with mine.

My smile faded. *Please God, kill me now.* "Well, um, it was good to see you, Roy."

"What? Oh, yeah, you too."

And off he drifted into the crowd.

For a few moments I didn't notice there were dozens of people skirting around me. All I saw was his form walking away, feeling the pain of his indifference. Did he still resent me for not returning his feelings? *Dammit.* Why couldn't I let go? It was as though I was trying to make our relationship puzzle pieces fit using a paring knife, only to find the subsequent pieces didn't fit either.

"You okay?" Barb asked.

I blinked back tears. "I've had enough. Can we go?"

The celebrations continued into the weekend. On Saturday, Barb talked me into going to watch the parade. No doubt Roy would be playing guitar on a float; I remembered him telling me he usually did. Could I handle this? Reassuring myself that if I did see him, I could ignore him like he did me. I agreed to go.

When I recognized Roy up there on the moving stage, I brimmed with pride. How handsome he looked in his vest, Levi's, and felt hat tipped slightly askance. I grinned until my face hurt, waving and nearly calling out his name. But he didn't respond, either because he didn't see me or didn't want to. A huge hole formed in my chest. I'd missed him. It didn't take much for me to drown in a flood of nostalgia as I remembered the times things had been good between us.

Always better with the written word than with verbalizing my thoughts, two days later I tried to write Roy a letter to explain how I felt. Afterwards, I reread what I wrote, tore it up, and called him.

"Linda! Nice to hear your voice."

I paused for a second to come up with what I needed to say, which ended up being: "I've been worried that you resent me."

I heard a sharp intake of breath. "No! I swear I've never resented you in any way! I've never said a single bad word about you to anyone. It's just that I was shocked to see you the other night. So much so, I was at a loss for words. And then I thought I saw you with Ben. That really freaked me out—made him real to me."

He thought Ben was here? No wonder he'd acted so strangely . . . I assured Roy that Ben had not been here. Maybe he was jealous? Tingles went down my spine, and made my tummy leap.

"I was thinking of heading to Granite Basin Lake tomorrow to take Yankee for a swim. Want to come?" he asked.

Of course I did.

Roy picked me up early. Among the giant boulders, we again played fetch with his boisterous black lab.

"You're beautiful," he said, glancing at me, and then to his dog. "But don't worry, I'm completely and totally over you. I just felt the need to tell you that."

I supposed he meant it, although I still didn't see any beauty in me. Aside from that, I wasn't sure I believed he was "completely and totally" over me. We had fun, though, making the day go way too fast. I hoped Roy and I would be able to do more together before I left for Tucson.

WHEN THE PLAN to join my dad in Tucson got postponed, I inwardly cheered. I kept looking for work, hoping I'd find something in Prescott and not have to leave. Later that week, with another job application completed, I waited for the phone to ring. It did, but the job was not mine.

Friday, Roy called. "My buddy Dave and I are going exploring. Want to come?"

Having someone else with us struck me as a steadfast friendship kind of plan. I could handle that, and besides, this sounded like fun.

"I know this really cool abandoned mine, wait 'till you see it!" Roy said after I slid into the front seat next to Dave, who sat in the middle.

If it was okay with Roy to explore an abandoned mine, it was okay by me.

After parking, we made our way through an oak and juniper woodland, the midday sun glaring and uncomfortably warm, with the trees not tall enough to provide shade. Good thing I'd thought to bring a canteen of water.

"It's right over here," Roy said, waving us onward.

Once I saw the narrow opening in the side of the hill, my confidence wavered. Would this be safe? Although I wasn't claustrophobic, that opening was a mere crack. We would have to crawl in.

Roy noticed my hesitance. "Don't worry. Once we get past the opening, you can stand up."

Apprehensive, but not wanting these guys to think I was chicken, I agreed to go inside. Roy went in first, slithering on his stomach, his hiking boots the last to disappear. "C'mon down!" his muffled voice said.

"Go ahead, Linda," Dave said. "I'll be right behind you."

I paused. Did I want to do this?

"If you get stuck, I'll pull you out." He grinned.

I laughed, and peered into the opening. Total pitch-black darkness. Squeezing through the opening, a split second of terror seized my stomach. Seconds later Roy grasped my hands and pulled me down the slight incline to join him. Dave followed.

Inside the arched tunnel, Roy shone his flashlight in an arc to illuminate our tiny space. "It's carved out of solid granite. I don't think we need to worry about a cave-in."

With the majority of my fear gone, a major dose of curiosity switched on, I followed Roy deeper into the tunnel. Damp, cold, and stale air greeted us. Behind me, slim rays of daylight from the opening winked-out. My throat constricted with a touch of panic. *Oh, stop it, all will be okay.*

Roy aimed his light at the tunnel wall and ran his hand down the rough surface. "Feel this."

I touched the wall, and found it to be wet, if not a bit slimy.

"I've never found pools of water down here," he said. "But in some spots the walls seep."

When we turned to continue, Roy took my hand. I let it go, confused. A bit later, he put his arm around me. I let him, but freaked a little. *Why is he doing this?*

At one point, Dave recorded us on his movie camera as we staged silly poses as though we were miners digging for gold. Corny, but fun. After more exploring, we found a dry place to sit. Roy positioned the flashlight to illuminate the area around us. I leaned against the tunnel wall, wondering about its stability. Not that it would have mattered. If the walls threatened to collapse, we were too deep to escape, anyway.

Dave sat next to me. He pointed to the necklace I wore. "What's with the four-leaf clover?"

I fingered the silver charm; a duplicate of the one I'd made for Ben last year, and a romantic symbol commemorating our clover search at

Nottingham. Unsure of how much information I wanted to share with Dave, I decided to not share much at all.

I fingered the smooth, polished silver. "This? Oh, it's in memory of someone."

Dave nodded. "Ben."

I sat up rigid. *He knows?* Roy must have given him an earful. What else had he shared with Dave? And there sat Roy, pretending not to be listening to this conversation, but of course hearing every single word. Roy supposedly told no one about me, and was "completely and totally" over me. Right? Why would he lie? Why should I let this get to me? I shouldn't have, but I did.

After another hour, we started back—and not too soon for me. By then we'd been underground for a few hours, and the claustrophobia I didn't think I suffered from began with a tightening in my chest, and quickly bordered on sheer panic. When I saw the shaft of light streaming from the entrance, I scrambled out of there first.

Heading back to Roy's truck, I couldn't stop chattering about our adventure. Proud of my bravery (even though I'd wavered at the end), my step, and my mood, were light. I didn't want to try to figure out Roy. The whole day was an experience-and-a-half. I didn't want to spoil it by over-thinking.

MORE GOOD NEWS: My Tucson trip had been postponed once again. This time because of car problems. An omen? At least I was granted yet another week in Prescott. My dad and I wouldn't leave until Sunday.

"Dave is here and we're hanging out and listening to music," Roy said over the phone the next Saturday night. "Come on over if you'd like."

"Okay, I'll be there in a bit."

Roy's mom answered the door. "Linda! So good to see you. How've you been? What's new? I thought of you the other day . . ."

Before I could answer, she turned around and called out, "Roy, Linda's here."

I smiled. Roy's mom was the sweetest woman on the planet, but I rarely could get a word in edgewise.

Roy and Dave were sprawled-out on Roy's bed when I entered his tiny room. The bed, dresser, a table for his record player, and a chair, filled the space. Roy jumped up, and gave me his spot. "I wanted to change records anyway," he said when I protested.

Roy selected a Waylon Jennings album. With his eyes zeroing in on mine, he said, "I want you to hear this one."

We often shared favorite songs, so I smiled and nodded. He positioned the needle on a track, and sat in the chair beside the bed.

While he and Dave talked, I read the album cover, half listening to the song. Then the lyrics drew me in. I leaned toward the speaker. The most romantic, but sorrowful words to "We Had It All," could have been written about us by Roy . . . the wind in the pines, the touch of my hair, our dreams . . . we had it all. I almost started to cry. So close. The only thing that stopped me was the fact that Dave was there. The song ended and the next one began. Roy did not look at me, nor did he say anything. But he didn't need to. No matter what he said to the contrary, he was still in love with me.

An hour later, I managed to drive home safely, despite the fact that my soul was crying in gut-wrenching sobs. What if I picked Ben, only to discover that I let Roy's love go when I shouldn't have?

OFF TO TUCSON in the morning, my dad and I leaving my mom to hold down the fort. The four-hour drive gave me plenty of time to think about Roy and that song. Was this really how he felt? Had I been the best thing in his life? I'd have to borrow the record from him soon, so I could hear it again—because I wanted to, and needed to, hear it again.

By the time we reached Phoenix, my thoughts switched to the upcoming work search. Until I found a job, I would return to Prescott with my dad every other weekend. *All I need to do is survive twelve days until I can see my friends again. Twelve whole days . . .*

Once at my dad's studio apartment, I unpacked my suitcase, tucking clothes into the empty half of the dresser my dad saved for me. Because of my dad's affinity for frozen TV dinners, I volunteered to be in charge of cooking meals. I drove the suburban to the grocery store with significant terror, negotiating more traffic than I'd ever faced in Prescott. Once I loaded up a week's worth of food into the cart, I bought the afternoon newspaper to search the classifieds. More scary driving on the return, but at least I didn't get lost. With groceries stored away, I pored through the want ads, circling any job with potential.

By Thursday, I'd applied for several jobs, boosting my mood and my confidence.

Mail time: the best part of the day. There, amidst the forwarded letters, I found a letter from Ben. Beautiful, but sad. He shared some very personal thoughts, which he had never done before. *"I've been thinking a lot about that summer I came to Syracuse, and when I knew you in high school. When I say I love you, I'm trying to say that I care about you very much. I need you because I love you. If that is what love is, then my love is real."*

Who's to say what love really is? Is it only what we think it is? Ben said he was not good enough for my love. He thought I put everything I had into loving someone. He's right. I did. But then again, if that was true, loving two people couldn't be possible, right? If you gave all of your love to one person, there wouldn't be any left for another. Love confused me. Not just the emotion, but the stigma behind the word— that love was reserved for only one person. I didn't buy that. I felt what I felt, and if I felt love for more than one person, who was I to question it?

All this came down to the concern that with Ben so far away, and our correspondence less than frequent, how would we ever work out? Roy was present in my everyday life; a constant reminder of someone who loved me deeply.

In my return letter to Ben, I disagreed with him not being worthy, and said that he meant a great deal to me. At the end I wrote that I hoped someday soon he could find a way to come see me. In the meantime, life went on without him.

AN ENTIRE WEEK went by with not one word from anyone. Then, finally, a letter arrived. It wasn't from Gail or Ben, which I'd been waiting for, but from Roy. Scanning the half-printed and half-cursive scrawling, I searched the entire letter before fully reading it to see if he wrote about love or feelings. But no, the letter was quite casual and friend-like. When I reached the end of the letter, I forgot all about what Roy didn't say. Chuck was back from Colorado! I needed to find something to do for three days or Saturday would take forever to get here. I cleaned the apartment, made dinner ahead of time and put it in the fridge to reheat later. Went for a swim at the apartment complex's pool. After that, I watched TV for a while. Bored, I turned it off. The phone rang. I stared at it. The phone here never rang.

"Hello?" I said tentatively, assuming it was probably a wrong number.

"Linda? It's me."

"Ben! Oh, Ben, where are you?" My hands quivered. Was he here, in Tucson?

"I'm still in San Diego, babe, but I'm coming to see you. In two weeks."

Two weeks! How in the world would I last two whole weeks? Agreed, it was nothing compared to the year since I saw him last . . . but still.

"I'll be shipping out in September, so this will be my only shot at seeing you for a while," he said.

My mind scrambled to find something to say, but it came up blank. Several moments of silence passed.

"I'll call you when I'm at the airport," Ben said.

"Okay!"

We said our goodbyes, and I placed the receiver in the cradle. Pausing with my hand still on the receiver, many thoughts raced through my head—so many that I didn't know what to grab onto to make them slow down. Ben would be leaving September 16th for nine months overseas. Nine months was too long. Much, much too long. I wondered if we'd work out. If we didn't, how disappointed would I be? Ben must be wondering the same thing. What struck me hard during our brief conversation was that I couldn't think of anything to say. Not one thing. This proved how well I knew him—which was not well at all. Letters were easy. How would it be when he was sitting in front of me? As of now, I loved him for what I knew about him. When he was here in person, I'd have to start from scratch, as though we'd just met. That only made sense.

The rest of the day seemed surreal after the letter and unexpected phone call. Good thing my dad had the night shift. It gave me the privacy I needed. Stretched out on my bed, I started reading my journal from beginning to end. When I read about ex-boyfriend Tom, I faced a very unpleasant reality—one that I'd been stowing away on a shelf because I didn't want to think about it. Making love with him had been a mistake. I'd been warned by friends about going all the way with him, and I ignored those warnings. I now knew that I had never loved him . . . an accusation he'd thrown at me when we broke up. But there was nothing I could do to change what I'd done.

After finishing rereading my journal, I tucked it under the mattress. Pulling up the covers, I hugged my pillow. With my eyes closed I could hear Ben's voice in my head, and I could almost, but not quite, feel his presence—like the shadows that candles make—soft, quiet, mysterious—barely there. Comforted, I drifted off to sleep, imagining the weight of Ben's body next to mine.

Friday night my dad and I headed to Prescott. Over and over I played out in my head what I would do after we pulled into the driveway. Sure, I'd give my mom a big hug, but then I'd run into my bedroom and call Chuck. I wanted to share with him the news about Ben's visit and everything else that had transpired since we'd spoken last. Would he be home? *Oh, please be home.*

Just as I'd planned, after giving my mom a hug, I went straight to my bedroom and called Chuck. My heart sank when his mom said he was out. He didn't return my call until noon the next day.

"I want to see you! I'll come pick you up," he said.

"I'll be waiting!"

Once inside his truck, we hugged tight.

"I missed you," I said, barely able to contain my enthusiasm.

Chuck smiled at me. "I missed you, too! I thought we'd check out the swap meet."

That sounded good to me.

At the swap meet, we walked and talked, sharing what was new in our lives, and rarely stopping to look at anything. I kept smiling at him, filling my eyes with how great he looked. Later, we decided to make a trip to Jerome. Although we rode in his truck instead of on his motorcycle, memory snapshots of the last time we went flashed as an internal slideshow. That was a great time, and so it repeated now.

On the way home, he said, "I'm going to Alaska next year. Will you come with me?"

Obtaining parental permission didn't cross my mind. "I'd love to!"

He looked pleased.

Riding high on the great day with Chuck, after dinner, I gave Roy a call, thinking he, too, would be delighted to hear from me. "Hi! I'm back for the weekend. What's up?"

Roy paused before speaking. "Oh yeah? That's nice."

His flat response delivered a sharp pang. *He doesn't want to talk to me. Should I end this call?* Instead, I stumbled around the awkward moment, trying to keep the conversation going. Something *must* have been wrong. But he wouldn't tell me what. After untold minutes of uncomfortable silences on his part, I said goodbye, and hung up. A few tears formed, and I brushed them away. Would we ever be able to confide in each other like we used to? I feared not. That hurt.

It seemed like I'd only just arrived in Prescott when I had to return to Tucson. Chuck had asked if I could stay longer, but I needed to ride with my dad. The drive south seemed twice as long, my "home at last" good mood evaporating with every passing mile.

Chapter 10

MONDAY'S TUCSON NEWSPAPER had something promising in the job department. A picture framing store needed help.

"Prefer someone with an art background," the ad said.

Hey, that's me! I knew how to matte and frame. I'd done it with my own paintings. Hope soared that maybe I'd found the right job. I had to drop my dad off at work so I could go apply. Afterwards, at the apartment, I daydreamed about working there. *I'll make enough money to rent an apartment. Not in a multi-storied complex like my sister's place . . . no, something quaint and homey. What kind of furnishings should I buy? I need to save up for a car. I hate busses. It would be nice to have some new clothes. Would I make new friends?*

My hopes ran high.

All of the fun daydreams ended the next day when I found out I didn't get the job. Devastating. Shortly thereafter, my older sister called to bitch at me. "Why don't you go to school? Why don't you start a career? Why don't you find a job? Why don't you do this and why don't you do that . . ."

Geez, get a career? Like you walk down the supermarket aisle and pick one off the shelf? What anyone failed to mention was how I might go about doing that, considering my parents were in no financial shape to pay for a college education, and my dad had refused to complete the paperwork required for financial aid. My sister's unwelcome "advice" fed my guilt, my self-doubt, my insecurity . . . all of them. I hated myself, hated my messed up situation, and hated that I couldn't just drop dead. Lately my entire world revolved around Ben coming to see me, which I recognized as a problem. What in the world would I do after he left? I'd be in the same awful rut. *The same rut I've always been in.* The framing store had turned me down. Two other jobs I'd applied for also didn't work out. I'd never been so torn up, and so miserable. I didn't know what to do with my life, and I didn't care.

Friday night. My dad left for Prescott without me. Ben was supposed to be coming tomorrow, but I'd not heard from him. Was he still coming? I turned on the obnoxious overhead light, and removed my journal from its hiding place underneath the mattress to write.

> *I wish I could go for a walk in the woods with Chuck. I wish I could lay by Ben's side in a warm, breezy field. I wish I could stand on top of a mountain and touch a star. I wish I could run and run down a beautiful snow-covered hill and never stop until I wanted to. Never. I wish I could find peace outside of me and most of all inside of me. I wish for once in my life that I could be at ease with things around me—sincerely content.*

I replaced my journal, switched off the light, and hoped for sleep. Instead, I ended up shedding a boatload of tears. If I slept, it was brief.

Daylight had broken a long time ago, but I was still curled-up in bed, trying not to cry anymore. No word from Ben. Pain throbbed behind my eyes from the lack of sleep and the hours of crying.

The phone rang. I grabbed the receiver, fumbling and almost dropping it.

"Hey, babe! I'm in Phoenix! I'll be there in a couple hours."

Two hours! Everything I'd hoped for and wanted would come true in two hours! Oh, those true feelings of suspense, of the unknown . . . seeing Ben again . . . what would we say? Would I love him more when he left? Or less? Or not at all? Maybe this reunion would just add to my confusion. Were we compatible, or too different? Guess I'd find out shortly . . .

A few hours later, I had to tell myself that Ben sitting next to me in the apartment was not a dream.

"Can I see your journal?" he asked.

Unconcerned, I said, "Sure, okay."

Without reading a word inside, he turned to a blank page and wrote something. He handed it back to me. I read:

> *Here I sit with the woman that I love. It's like a dream. If it is I pray to God that I never wake up. Because, Linda, I love you more than anything in this world. —me*

I didn't know if I should shed a tear or smile, so I did both.

Hand-in-hand, we walked to the grocery store to buy a bottle of wine. With my favorite Mateus Rosé purchased, we returned to the apartment complex. On the damp grass, we sat cross-legged opposite each other, drinking the wine from glass tumblers, talking about nothing particularly important or noteworthy. This didn't matter, because nothing we said registered. No . . . all I wanted to do was assess the gorgeous man sitting in front of me. For one, how touching to see the silver four-leafed clover that I'd made and sent to him hung on a leather cord around his neck. Although his long blond hair—which I'd adored— had been cropped short, the new cut accentuated his sharp features in an appealing way. He had great news, too. He'd quit cigarettes! All in all, it was as though I needed to etch his handsome face, muscular and tanned body, and gentle smile into my brain permanently in order to recall later that *this* man actually came here to see me, and that he was in love with me. *Me*—of all the girls he could have chosen. I knew now that I loved Ben more than anything in this world. And I knew that he shared my feelings. There would never be anyone else. Never. He was all I'd ever dreamed of, and more. He would marry me when he got out of the Navy. I wanted to marry him because I'd never loved anyone this much, and I doubted I could ever love anyone else this much again.

Ben did not attempt to make love to me that night, which was quite okay—I didn't feel ready. Instead, we snuggled, kissed, and talked. Drowsy and contented, I lay in his arms, and asked a bold question. "What kind of future do you see for us in three or more years?"

Ben squeezed me tighter. "I see pretty clearly where things will be when I'm out of the Navy."

"What will you do?"

"I will follow you everywhere you go . . ."

About three-thirty on Sunday afternoon, Ben and I waited streetside for his cab. With one arm wrapped around me, he sang John Denver's "My Sweet Lady," wiping tears from my face. There was no point in telling him that I didn't want him to leave—we both knew he had no choice.

TWO WEEKS LATER, I went to Prescott with my dad for the weekend. The first thing I did was call Chuck. His mother said he wasn't home. I called Roy to say hi, and to ask if he knew where Chuck was.

Within a few minutes I become suspicious that he was again hiding something from me. But what? He wouldn't say. Not interested in prying it out of him, I let it go. Chuck eventually returned my call, and we spent a few glorious hours catching up while walking around the edge of Willow Lake. Sunny yellow wildflowers held their heads high above the grassy shoreline. This small, quiet lake didn't attract many visitors, which suited us just fine. Time flew, and too soon we had to leave.

When Roy wanted to see me the next night, I accepted, glad that he was over whatever the heck it was that was bugging him yesterday. As always when we were apart, I'd missed him. It didn't matter that I'd just seen Ben. Roy's draw always overpowered anything and everyone.

He wanted to cruise, so we cruised, with a Bob Dylan cassette plugged into the tape player.

"I want to tell you something," he said.

Okay, good. Maybe now he'll tell me what's wrong.

Roy turned to me, and with a serious and determined expression, said, "I've decided that I can't be your friend unless you have sex with me."

Oh God, here we go again. "Roy, we've been through this," I said patiently. "I want us to be friends, I do, but that's all. I'm with Ben now."

Roy slapped the steering wheel, hard. "But you see, Linda, I can't be your friend."

I rolled my eyes. "Roy, don't you think love should be a part of it? For me, sex is something I prefer to share with someone I love. What you're asking . . . I could never do that."

He let out a loud and humorless laugh. "Bullshit. Love has nothing to do with it. There is no such thing as love. It's all a joke! All these games you've been playing. I see through them. I used to love you, you know, but I don't anymore. I'm so over you. Ha! You think that *I* think you're some kind of goddess . . . that you're Miss Perfect . . . well, I don't."

A goddess? Me? Most days I didn't even *like* myself, and I most certainly didn't for a minute think that he had been idolizing me, for crying out loud. And perfect? There was nothing about me that was *perfect*. He'd hit a very tender spot—the one that doubted the very essence of who I was—or was not.

I gripped the door handle and squeezed it. "I most certainly do *not!*"

"I thought you wanted to be my friend," he said, clenching the wheel.

"*I do!*"

"Yeah, well, if you really did, then we wouldn't be having this discussion. Am I that repulsive? Would you rather have sex with someone else?"

"Roy, you just aren't getting what I'm trying to say."

"Then what *are* you trying to say?"

Frustrated beyond belief, I couldn't reply. But even worse, the whole time I argued about wanting to be only his friend, I *did* want more from him, but didn't understand why. I had Ben! To have a sexual attraction come up again for Roy felt like a betrayal to Ben, who was now quite real. But besides all of that . . . a *conditional* friendship? Based on sex? I'd never heard of such a thing. How dare he suggest such a thing!

I couldn't stand one more minute of this. "Take me home."

Before his truck came to a full stop, I opened the door, poised to flee. I turned to him, my body and voice shaking. "We are done. I don't want your friendship. I don't ever want to see you again."

I jumped out, slammed the door shut, and ran into the house with tears pouring down my face.

Once in my room, still shaking, I wiped my face and blew my nose. A deep breath calmed me a little, and I got out my journal. I wanted to write down everything he said to ease the crushing pain in my chest.

> *He does not care about my feelings. He's so certain I'm on an ego trip with him and that I've used him. He never wants anything to do with me again.*

Why did I keep contacting him? Why didn't I just leave him alone? *I'm such an idiot.* I reread what I'd written. For a split-second I wanted to rip the page out and pretend it all never happened.

The long night led to a day of me replaying the awful conversation over and over in my head. Chuck's call came at the perfect time, distracting me from my self-inflicted torment.

"Want to go somewhere?" he asked.

Did I ever.

In about an hour, we sat near Willow Lake's shore. Rains had been plentiful that year, filling it to the brim. I pitched a stone into the water and watched the ripples echo. Still upset, and needing reassurance that I was right, I sadly told Chuck a little about what was going on with me and Roy. He listened patiently to what reverberated in my ears as some terrible thing that had happened to someone else, not me.

Chuck tossed a pebble into the lake, which plunked and sent up a few droplets before it sashayed into the murky depths. "Don't worry. Roy probably didn't mean what he said. He's being immature. Just wait, he'll call and apologize."

Yeah, I got that Roy could be incredibly immature—like proposing the conditional friendship crap. I usually believed Chuck, but not this time. Roy would not be calling me.

Before Chuck dropped me off, he turned and smiled. "I hate to see you go."

I hated to go. I hated living in a big city. I wanted to live in beautiful Prescott, with pines, hiking trails, and places to explore right outside my back door. I wanted to be near my mom.

"Can't you hang around Prescott a while longer?" he asked.

I shook my head. I had to keep looking for work. In addition, I wanted to keep my distance from Roy. Hanging around Prescott just begged for us to connect again.

Roy called in the morning wanting me to forgive him, proving that, once again, Chuck had been right. However, I couldn't do this anymore. "God, Roy, this is not working. I give up."

After a long pause, Roy said, "I made a mistake."

"I will not accept an apology this time. You should have thought of the consequences of what you were going to say beforehand," I said, calming down. But still, inexplicably, I decided to not completely cut him out of my life. I hedged. "Look, maybe in a few years we can figure out the friend thing, but there's no way anything can work out now."

After we hung up, I folded my arms on the table and rested my forehead on them. *Why did we have to end this way?*

BACK IN TUCSON Sunday afternoon, that evening, after my dad left for work, I reflected: Here it was, already the end of August, and no job yet. To sort things out, I lit a candle, and started writing in my journal:

> *Just when I thought I had my head together, thought I knew*
> *what I wanted—Roy had to go and wreak havoc with my head*
> *and heart. Why can't I let him go? It's like he fills a void in me,*

one that no one else can fill. How long will it be before I can make sense of this . . . and life? I want a job but I hate looking. That brings me down worst of all.

I paused, and then wrote: *It's not wise to lie in bed at night and ask yourself questions you can't answer.* I paused again, and laughed a little. *Same goes with writing in your journal asking more questions you can't answer.*

I closed my journal, closed my eyes, and fell asleep.

ON FRIDAY, I applied for a secretarial position with an agency that focused on connecting the young with the elderly. Different, that's for sure. I liked different. *Please let this work out.*

With this being our Tucson weekend, my dad and I took a Sunday drive up the road that snaked to Mount Lemmon, high in the Santa Catalina Mountains. Who knew a ponderosa pine forest grew so close to the city? So glorious, it rivaled Prescott, and certainly brightened my day. I wished I'd known sooner that this place existed. If I had, maybe I could have found a way to bring Ben up here when he'd visited. At an elevation of nine thousand feet, you can imagine how cool, piney, and luscious it was.

After lunch at the Summerhaven Inn, we headed down the mountain and back to city life. My thoughts meandered along with the road. What if I met someone special in my new job? I'd never made any promises or commitments to Ben; nor he to me. We both knew the distance between us was a big problem. Although I couldn't see myself in love with anyone but Ben . . . realistically, in three years, his time in the Navy, I recognized that it was possible I could fall in love with someone else. The same dilemma reappeared. How would I know if it was real love, or if this person was a temporary substitute until Ben returned?

Chapter 11

MY DAD MUST have mentioned my fruitless job search at work. Karen, whom I'd met at a company picnic, called me. "Hey, Linda, I've got a connection, and I hear he's hiring . . . let me see what he says."

What a surprise to have her call me back within a few hours.

"I got you an interview with the U.S. Forest Service," Karen said proudly.

The Forest Service? Had I heard her right? "When?"

"Today!"

Today! It will be fantastic if I get that job!

Ever since my lack of a driver's license made me miss out on the Prescott National Forest's patrol job, I'd hoped for, but had given up on, another opportunity with the agency. Now, Karen said I would work on Mount Lemmon. The fantastic forest where I'd just visited with my dad. The position would only last for a month or two. That didn't bother me. I'd be living and working in the middle of a National Forest instead of a big city. When I looked out windows, I'd see a forest instead of steel, concrete, and pavement. I'd hear birds sing instead of the drone of obnoxious traffic. I could sit outside underneath a pine instead of eating lunch at my desk. She didn't say exactly what I'd be doing, but so what? If they gave me that job, I swore I'd work harder than ever to prove what a great employee they'd hired. *Yes, I sure will.*

After the interview and filling out an unbelievable amount of paperwork tied up with enough red tape that it could go around the block and then some, I returned to the apartment. It was there everything mentally turned to dust.

Why get my hopes up? They aren't going to give this to me. I want it too much.

When McKelsey, my interviewer, called in the morning, I almost dropped the phone. Not only had I gotten the job, but I would start tomorrow! This job front turnaround came just when I needed it most.

After dinner, Karen took me shopping. I needed an alarm clock, but I also wanted to treat myself. In Ben's tape, he'd referenced the group, America's, song, "Glad to See You." I bought the album.

At eight, I reported to the district office with a suitcase in hand. I smiled at the few people I met, feeling shy and self-conscious. What did they think of me? Would I make any friends? That guy who'd said, "Hi," was kind of cute, would he talk to me again?

After filling out more paperwork, I joined Billy, one of the fire prevention technicians, for a lift up to Palisades Ranger Station, an hour's drive, and my home for a month or more, depending on funding and the weather. Billy dropped me off in front of a compact camper in the employee trailer park behind the station.

"If you need anything, I live right over there." He pointed to a twenty-footer slipped between slender pines.

Grateful for the friendly offer in this strange place, I smiled and waved as he drove away.

The door was unlocked, and I stooped to enter the 1950s abode. This place was way small, especially if I had a roommate, which McKelsey had said I might have. But still, not bad for ten bucks a month. The bunk bed and an ancient refrigerator took up most of the living room-bedroom combination; the tiny hall led to a tinier kitchen with yet another refrigerator, which struck me as odd. *Two refrigerators? What a waste of space.* I unpacked, and then stored the two sacks of groceries Billy had stopped to let me purchase before leaving Tucson. I rummaged through the cupboards, found a saucepan, and heated up a can of soup for dinner. When I went to stash the leftovers in the kitchen fridge, I discovered that it wasn't working. When I opened the door of the fridge next to the bed, the light came on and out came a swoosh of cool air. I set the soup inside, wondering why the working one wasn't in the kitchen.

Unable to sleep, I lay awake for a while, listening to the refrigerator hum, buzz, and click. I must have just drifted off when a loud *ka-bang* jolted me wide awake. *What the hell was that?* With the exception of the humming refrigerator, only silence replied. *I must have been dreaming.* It took me a while to fall back to sleep. Another *ka-bang* made me bolt upright, nearly whacking my head on the upper bunk. This time I decided it was not a dream. It was the fridge. What was wrong with it?

Would it explode? It sure sounded like it. And so went the rest of the night, the trailer-shaking noise waking me every couple of hours.

The next morning, a Friday, and the start of my workweek, I awoke a bit tired, thanks to that stupid fridge. I poured a bowl of cereal, and sat at the small kitchen dinette, crunching mindlessly. No need to worry about dressing-up here—based on what I'd seen, the jeans and the cotton pullover I'd packed would be fine. In the chilly morning air I walked up the path to the office for my first day.

"I expect you to be meticulous in your data entry," Inez said, her lips in a tight smile—if you could call the slight uplift at the side of her mouth a smile.

I nodded obediently at my immediate supervisor, studying her starched Forest Service uniform. She'd secured the top button of the shirt, which made me want to run my fingers around my top and pull it away from my throat. I hated anything tight around my neck.

"Your primary task will be entering work hours onto T & As for all of the fire personnel here," she said. "Every project will have multiple management codes. There is a separate one each for regular hours, overtime, Sundays, holidays, and hazardous duty. Each fire has its own designation code, too. You must use a Number Two pencil," she said, reaching for one from the pencil can on her desk and handing it to me. "All letters and numbers *must* be printed inside the allotted squares— nothing outside the borders—and you must make sure that your entries imprint through all of the carbon copies. And if you make an error, you must start over. The carbons don't erase well."

My eyes glazed over at the overload of information for filling out the Time and Attendance forms, but I nodded confidently to show her that none of this would be a problem.

Inez reached for the large stack of blank timesheets on her desk, and plunked them in front of me. "These need to be completed by ten o'clock Monday."

"Okay!" I said., but thinking, *Oh. My. God.*

Early Monday, deadline met, a finger on my right hand blistered from pressing through all four carbons, my mind frustrated with how many errors required me to start over, and a dozen pencils now a good inch shorter from sharpening them so they *would* imprint all of those carbons, McKelsey called me into his office.

"I've got an assignment for you," he said. "Have a seat."

A bit anxious—this was the "big guy" here—I dropped into the leather chair in front of his desk, my eyes wide, my back straight, and my hands gripping the edge of the cushion. *An assignment?*

"I need you to make a map of all of the lightning-strike fires that occurred up here over the past five years."

A map? I loved maps. Every summer, my family took a trip. My dad would carefully plan our route, puffing on his pipe, highlighting the roads we would take, the sights we would stop to see, and the campgrounds where we would spend the night. The road maps were more than meandering colored lines on paper; they were routes to a potential adventure.

"You will need to go through all of the fire incident reports back to 1970. There, you'll find the official cause of the fire, and the legal description, which you'll use to locate it on the map. Code each year with dots of a different color. Remember, though, I don't want you to map all fires, just lightning-caused ones," my boss said.

What he failed to mention was that most fires were lightning caused, but I wouldn't figure that out until hours later.

"Do you know how to read a legal description?" he asked.

I didn't even know what one was. "Umm, no."

"I'll teach you."

By early afternoon, my desk was piled high with incident reports to map. My stomach rolled. *Can I do this?* Soon, I found myself totally engrossed. As I located each fire, I discovered, to my surprise, the old adage that lightning never strikes the same place twice is wrong. Some of the dots would have to overlap. Focused on my work, I didn't notice at first when a few guys from one of our fire crews strolled into the office.

One approached me and asked, "Hey, what're you up to? Looks interesting."

Pleased that not only someone noticed me, but a cute firefighter at that—I smiled. "I'm mapping lightning fires."

Cute Firefighter grinned. "Hey, guys, look at what . . . sorry, what's your name?"

I smiled shyly. "Linda."

"Linda is mapping lightning fires!"

Seconds later I had a crowd around my desk.

The rest of the afternoon flew by. I looked forward to more days working on the map, and maybe getting a chance to talk to the fire crew again . . . it was nice to be noticed.

AFTER HEATING YET more soup for dinner, I sat at my four-foot-square Formica table, and nibbled crackers between spoonfuls. With no TV, no stereo, and *drat*, no book either . . . I now faced several hours before bedtime filled with . . . well . . . nothing.

Someone knocked on my door.

Upon opening it, there stood the nice-looking guy I'd seen around the complex. Instead of his green uniform, though, he wore blue jeans, a denim shirt, and a friendly smile.

"Hi, I'm your neighbor, Gary," he said, adjusting his wire-rimmed glasses. "I saw you move in the other day. Up for a game of ping-pong?"

Heck yes! We drove up the Catalina Highway to the retired World War II radar base, which housed the hot shot crew.

"They're an elite team of firefighters," he said. "Work from about May to August. Right now, all we have running are a couple tanker crews, and fire prevention techs like me. We'll stay on duty until the forest is wet-down, when we are no longer needed until spring."

After playing ping-pong for an hour, or rather after I chased the ball around the room for most of the hour, Gary returned me to my trailer.

In the stillness of the night when I should have been sleeping, I lay awake. *Until no longer needed.* Now that had Gary pointed out how quickly rain ended employment up here, I worried that my temporary job might be even more temporary than I'd originally thought. It was only the third week of September, and it seemed to be raining an awful lot. I liked it here, and didn't want my job to end. But it would end. To drive that depressing thought into my brain even more, it was now pouring outside. A familiar emptiness opened inside of me. Homesickness had been a debilitating problem when I was a kid, ruining Girl Scout camping trips, and sleepovers with friends. For homesickness to show up now when I thought I'd outgrown it, triggered additional emotions. I missed Ben to the point that the hollowness in my chest threatened to cave in. It didn't help that I'd mailed him many letters, and had received, so far, no replies. For the first time since I'd been up here, I wanted to cry my eyes out.

Chapter 12

NIGHT AFTER NIGHT the evil refrigerator ruined my sleep. No matter how much I tried to anticipate the vibrations that accompanied what sounded like a metal trash can being dropped from two stories, it didn't help. I pleaded with Inez to see if someone could remove the dead one in the kitchen, and replace it with the live one. At least the spastic vibrating version wouldn't be right next to my bed. Finally, two of the fire crew came over to do just that.

"There's a problem," one said. "The front door isn't wide enough to get the broken one out. Even if we take off the fridge door. Plus, the hallway is too narrow to switch them."

Thinking he was joking, I laughed. Then I realized he wasn't joking. I stared at him in disbelief. "Then how did they get in here?"

The guys shrugged. Both refrigerators would have to remain.

RUMORS FLEW LIKE wind scattering fallen leaves. Most jobs, including mine, would end soon. Despite that, the Forest Service still invested in me taking their driver's test so I could run errands for the district office in Tucson a couple days per week. Additionally, with fire season coming to an end, they no longer needed me to work weekends. Next Saturday I'd be able to go home with my dad. The excitement was palpable with the thought that soon I would see my mom, Chuck . . . and I had to admit, Roy.

Friday morning, the personnel clerk called me into her office.

"You won't be living at Palisades anymore," she said. "We can keep you busy for two weeks, but then we have to lay you off."

Even though I'd expected the layoff, the news destroyed my outlook not only for the immediate future, but for my entire life. What would I do now?

My sullen mood changed when I stopped to pick up our mail. A three letter jackpot! Ben's, that I'd prayed for; Roy's, that inexplicably made my hands tremble; and one from Gail. Propped by a pillow on my bed, I set Roy's letter aside to read last, and started with Ben's. Just what I needed to remind me that he still existed and he still loved me. Gail's letter would require a long response, as usual, because although she didn't write often, when she did, she wrote pages with lots of questions along with updates on her life. To begin Roy's letter, I needed a deep breath. As I read, I found myself surprised, in a good way, at what he wrote. The level of maturity he showed was impressive, and welcome. Sighing, I knew; it didn't matter if it was right or wrong, I would call him when I got home. Ironically, a year ago I worried about Roy being too serious about me. Now I wondered if I was getting too serious about him. I'd noticed my feelings for him were growing deeper and more complex . . . even with Ben back in my life. Even though I'd told Roy we were done, he'd captured a piece of my heart—and it appeared there was no getting it back.

Once in Prescott for the weekend, I called Chuck first. When I saw him park at the curb, I dashed outside. I opened the truck door, hopped in, and hugged him across the gear shift.

"Great to see you," I said.

And with a smile that made my day, he said, "You, too."

An hour later, we sat on the ponderosa-edged shore of Lynx Lake, peacefully observing a few rowboats gliding silently across the surface, catching up on what was new in our lives. How gratifying to see him, to know we were such good friends, the kind you could count on, who you knew liked you no matter how many stupid things you did or said. I began to understand better what Roy had been getting at when he said members of the opposite sex couldn't be friends. So far, only Chuck and I had managed to keep it that way. I considered myself quite fortunate.

That night, in bed, I came to a conclusion. I decided there were two kinds of love a normal human-being needed: mental love (knowing someone loves you) and physical love (holding, kissing, touching, and making love.) Ben could only give me mental love right now. That was nice, but not enough. How long could I accept and live with only the one kind? Did Roy offer me both? It didn't help my confusion much when my one phone call with Roy that weekend amounted to a brief conversation and no visit.

EACH DRAGGING DAY of my last workweek in mid-October bore a sad reminder that I'd soon be unemployed again. To complicate everything, my parents' plan to move to Tucson had changed. My dad decided to start yet another business in Prescott: selling and installing home and business security equipment. My plan? Continue to look for work in Prescott, but also reapply with the Coronado National Forest in Tucson for the next summer.

On Friday, one of my coworkers was passing by my desk when he abruptly halted. "You look miserable," he said. "What's wrong?"

Even though I barely knew this guy, his question made me choke up. I managed to hold back tears. "Today's my last day."

"It is? Well, we must do something for you!"

Within moments he was taking orders for a Dairy Queen run, dashing out to fill the requests. I'd not made any friends at the district office, so his enthusiasm to make sure I had a proper farewell cheered me up considerably.

Our Suburban loaded that evening, my dad and I returned to Prescott.

This time, I thought and hoped, *maybe for good*.

DESPITE AGAIN BEING unemployed, I couldn't help but be overjoyed to be home. Not only because I didn't want to leave in the first place, but because it was autumn. While most people think of spring as rejuvenating, a rebirth of sorts—for me it was fall that filled my heart full of hope and joy. Autumn lit a fire in me to explore and travel, instilled a burning desire to tap into my creative side, and made me giddy with anticipation of the upcoming holidays. Nothing could be better than the crisp mornings that required a jacket. Slim, white-barked aspens with sunny yellow leaves fluttering against a solid blue sky, and the air carrying the scent of those on the ground that had started to decay. My thoughts whirled with plans to visit all of my favorite places, including my special aspen grove.

Even though I recognized that every time I contacted Roy, I opened myself up to more hurt, the draw to see him was always more powerful than any logical thinking. When I called him, he wanted to meet after dinner, and we did. After a walk in the forest, we played guitar at his house. I sensed something between us had changed—as though we both feared saying the wrong thing. Maybe he was thinking about the last big argument we'd had, where he'd proposed the conditional friendship garbage, because I sure was. Now I wondered why he thought he could walk all over me and get away with it. Why did I let him?

Four days later, Chuck and I went out around seven-thirty, and got a table at Sambo's. When Roy wandered in soon after, he came over and said "Hi," but refused to make eye contact with me. No doubt about it—something happened that I couldn't explain whenever I saw him, not just magnetism—no—there was more to it than that. What would happen next between us?

After Roy left, Chuck scowled. "What's his problem?"

I shrugged, not wanting to get into a discussion I wasn't prepared for. I'd no clue what to say anyway. I couldn't help but wonder if Roy had lied to me more than I thought—for example, when he said that he didn't love me anymore. Was it possible to stop loving someone if at one time you really did?

Chuck and I took advantage of another perfect October day; his faded-red jeep carried us deep into the forest on barely passable roads to visit one of his favorite places. I loved being privy to his "secret" spots. After our adventure, he invited me to see a movie about Alaska. Sitting in the dark with him, watching the screen filled with dramatic mountains, icy glaciers, gushing rivers, and amazing wildlife, I knew that someday I would go there. Chuck had planned an Alaska trip in May, and said he'd stay a long time. This news left me hollow. How would I fill the void of him being gone? I'd reapplied with the Forest Service for next year's fire season, and I hoped to get the job, unless, of course, I found something in Prescott. Either way, I decided to save my money, and head to Alaska to visit Chuck in the fall.

"MY GIRLFRIEND IS here from California," Roy said when he called a few days later. "In a couple weeks I'll be going there for a while."

Girlfriend? I didn't know he had a girlfriend. Or, rather, more accurately, I didn't know he'd replaced me. Was that twinge in my chest jealousy? If it was, I challenged it with skepticism. I wondered if this was an attempt on his part to get to me. Why else would he call me to say this? Anything with him was possible. Anger flared. *Fine, then! I'm done. I don't care.*

Chuck phoned that evening. "Hey, do you want to go to Spook Night next week?"

Chuck picked me up after dinner, and when we meandered down a crowded Jerome street an hour later, he said something that made me wonder if he could read my mind.

Linda Strader

"I saw Roy the other day. Lately he's been acting distant, but then, I've always thought he could be cold and emotionless."

First the acting distant comment registered . . . because I'd sensed that, too. And next the cold and emotionless comment sunk in. Really? Chuck must be seeing a completely different Roy than I did, because I never thought of Roy being emotionless—which made me feel oddly disconnected to both of them. How could I be emotionally close to these guys, share as much as I did with them, only to discover that *they* didn't see themselves, or each other, as I did? How was that possible? Although I didn't know for sure that Roy acted differently around Chuck, the undeniable fact was that I didn't understand Roy's behavior toward me, just like I didn't understand the magnetism I felt toward him, either. Now that Chuck had brought up Roy, the whole rest of the evening in Jerome, I scanned faces, searching for his. Although Roy's absence left me empty, I also figured it was probably a good thing we didn't see him. The last thing I needed was more confusion had Roy not responded the way I wanted him to.

In the morning I awoke with lingering feelings of hopelessness— that empty, all-consuming ache inside. Where did I belong? My life had no direction. Why didn't anyone want to hire me? There must be something wrong with me. I wished I could travel. I wished I could go to Colorado. The urge to explore the west tugged at me with an invisible string. The confusion over Roy, not hearing from Ben, the pressure at home to find work in a town that didn't want me—all told me that I should leave. Not to Tucson, though. I decided to go to Colorado as soon as I'd saved enough money, and as soon as Chuck had too. We would both go after his Alaska trip. He could give me a ride to Durango or some other such town or city, and I'd see what happened from there. My jaw set tight. *I am going. Yes, I am going.*

"WANT TO GO hiking?" Roy asked when he called the next day.

This made me pause. What happened to his California girlfriend? Maybe he never had one . . . regardless, turning him down had never been an option. We went for a walk near Thumb Butte. Throughout the entire time, I held back from saying what I wanted to say, afraid of his reaction. When we sat on a sun-warmed boulder for a break, I had no idea where the courage came from to say this, but I found it.

"You confuse me, Roy. There are times when I can't tell if you care about me, or what the hell is going on."

After spilling those words, I steeled myself for the worst. Roy said nothing. I got the impression he wanted *me* to say more, but I didn't have more to say. We continued our walk, and the topic never came up again. But all was not lost. This day he was the guy I always thought he was. Himself. No pretentious behavior, no aloof and "I don't care" crap, no talk of his girlfriend in California, no pressuring me with sex—I really liked him this way. He even admitted to having pretended to act like someone else around me at times. I didn't know why, and I didn't know in what way, but no wonder I'd been confused! Although we were having a good time, I couldn't wait to go home and process this new information. My heart lightened at the thought that maybe we were finally on the same page—except for one thing. Did I love him, or was I just sexually attracted to him? Having sex with someone you didn't love wasn't a good idea, right? But that didn't stop me from thinking about it.

EVEN THOUGH LYNELL had stopped consigning my work a while ago, I continued to make jewelry. I'd sold a few pieces at the swap meet, and landed two special orders. One night, I had a vivid dream about an earring design. I awoke inspired, and later that day went out to the garden shed where my dad had set up a work station for me, and made a pair. Pleased with how they turned out, I wanted to make more.

Proud of my turquoise knowledge (thank you, Lynell), I purchased stones at the jewelry and supply store, Sawdust and Silver, where they would let me pore through their quality inventory. To make more earrings, I'd need more cabs, and went to the shop to see if they had anything nice within my price range.

The owner presented me with a tray of lovely sky-blue, and greenish-blue stones from the Kingman and Bisbee mines of Arizona. I preferred ones on the greenish side, so picked out two matching sets, and added a few singles for necklaces, rings, or bracelets.

"I could use a part-time designer," the owner said as he rung up my order. "Can you show me some of your work?"

Exuberant, I zipped home, and returned an hour later to share my designs, including the earrings I'd just made the other day.

"Very nice," he said, inspecting my handiwork. "Tell you what. Come make a dozen pair of earrings, using my supplies and equipment. If they sell, I'll have you come make more. I'll pay you five dollars an hour. Does that work?"

It was all I could do not to shriek. That was a phenomenal amount of money; twice the minimum wage. Maybe this would turn into a real job. Once in the car, with hands clasped, I stared up at the sky and pleaded: *Oh, please, please, please let this work out.*

JUST DAYS LATER, Roy and I went out cruising around eight p.m. My intuition had been telling me for a while that something drastic was about to happen between us. It was in the cards. It had been in the cards for a long time. There was no more denying that I was sexually attracted to Roy. Maybe it was time to toss my cards on the table. So I did.

"I've been thinking," I said. "I know we've talked about this before, and I have told you that we should stay friends. But I've changed my mind."

Roy turned to look at me, puzzled. "You have?"

"Well, yes, I believe I have. I think I would like you to make love to me." I paused. "There is one problem, though. I also believe that love should be a part of it, and I'm not sure if I love you the way I think I should . . ."

Roy found a place to pull over, parked, and shut off the engine. "Okay, I can do that . . ." He leaned over, pulled me close, and then kissed me, hard—full of longing, passion, all of which I returned in earnest. His hands slipped under my jacket, untucking my shirt. But something about his actions didn't feel right. They were mechanical, if not forced.

No, I can't do this.

"Wait," I said, pressing a hand against his chest. "I need to know if you care about me, or if this is just about sex."

Roy shifted back into his seat. "Well, I used to be very much in love with you, but I'm not anymore. The only reason I came onto you is because you seemed to want me to."

Just like a dream does when you wake up to reality, desire evaporated. I knew at that moment that sex with him would be just that—sex— without any love to back it up.

To make the whole moment even more humiliating, he ended it by saying: "I've met the right girl, but I barely know her."

"Okay. Fine. Take me home."

Once in my room, I grabbed my journal from my desk, flung myself onto the bed, flipped on the light, and wrote:

I think that his finding the right girl will be great for him. Now that I know he doesn't care, I feel so strange I can't begin to explain it. I'm hurt; I'm let down; I feel TERRIBLE.

When my intuition had told me that something drastic was going to happen between us, I must have thought that Roy and I would make love, all would be wonderful, and that would be that. Instead, it turned out that he didn't want me, and I didn't want him either. What a rude and painful awakening.

With sleep not an option, I decided to write him a letter. I lit the candle on my desk, and opened the drawer for paper and pen. The flame flickered for a moment, caught, and wax soon drizzled down the neck of the wine bottle.

Dear Roy,

You know, I was right when I predicted that something drastic would happen between us. But there is no way I could have known how I would be caught totally by surprise.

I decided not to grovel, nor would I let on how much he'd hurt me. I wrote more.

Now I know that we have always been meant to be only friends—and maybe not even that—but I hope not. It's my turn to say I'm sorry, sorry for every bit of pain I've ever caused you. Maybe now things can be cool between us. So, Roy, I hope we still have some good hiking and talking days left to enjoy. Call me if you want someone to walk with you, or talk, or whatever. Let's just continue to be the friends we were meant to be.

Pen capped, I read what I wrote. I'd said my peace. Carefully folding the paper into thirds, I slipped it into an envelope. Out of my desk drawer, I selected the blue sealing wax and my "L" stamp. I lit the stick, let it drip onto the back of the envelope, and pressed the stamp into the molten wax. A sharp breath snuffed my candle, and I crawled into bed.

In the morning, I awoke with a body feeling so heavy, I couldn't get out of bed. I cried for a half hour, but then had to regroup. The owner of Sawdust and Silver had called me into work again, and I needed to report and somehow tap into my creative side, even though I felt like I'd died during the night.

Chapter 13

AFTER A LONG nine-hour day of pouring every ounce of energy I had into designing and making earrings, once at home, I found Roy had called twice looking for me. I knew it couldn't be about the letter I'd just mailed yesterday. I stared at my bedroom phone, debating on whether or not it made sense to return his call. Regardless, I called him, but decided to maintain at least some dignity, if that was possible, by keeping my voice nonchalant.

"Hi. My mom said you called."

"Yeah, I was just wondering how you were doing."

Why would he care? He had found the right girl, and she wasn't me. I pulled a pillow to my chest. "I didn't sleep much last night."

"Oh? Why?"

As if I was going to tell him. "I wrote you a letter. Mailed it this morning."

"What's it about?"

"You'll see."

"Well . . . probably not for a while. I'm heading to California on Saturday. Not sure when I'll be back."

My voice stopped working for a moment; my throat tightened. *Leaving?* "Oh. Okay."

After we hung up, oddly, I felt better—at least he called.

Roy had offered to loan me his Waylon Jennings album. In the morning, I stopped to pick it up. Thank goodness it involved nothing more than a brief exchange at the door, which prevented him from saying something I didn't want to hear.

After dinner, I shut myself in my room and slipped the record onto the spindle. With the volume turned up, I lay on my bed, hugged my pillow, and listened to "We Had It All." Tears started to fall as each word hit home, and by the third time I'd played it, I was sobbing until my chest hurt, and my eyes were swollen. How he could have shared that deeply touching song with me then, and be so damned indifferent now? I couldn't understand, or maybe I did. I'd hurt him too much and too often. After all, it was me who led him on, only to pull out the Ben card when we got too close. And yet I kept hanging onto Roy, and he, apparently, to me. My entire relationship with Roy had spun out of control, and the more I tried to fix things between us, the worse they seemed to get.

NOVEMBER 3, 1974—my nineteenth birthday—fell on a Sunday, and I definitely felt nineteen. Maybe because I had to deal with being more adult today than I wanted to. Chuck called to say that Roy didn't go to California because Roy's dog, Yankee, had disappeared on Halloween. Roy was offering a fifty-dollar reward for his return. An image of that poor German Shepard I'd found popped into my head. *No . . . that's not what happened to Yankee. No!* Despite the fact I had no idea where I stood with Roy, I immediately went into action, spending most of the morning making and posting flyers offering Roy's reward on bulletin boards and power poles. God, if Yankee wasn't found, it would break Roy's heart. It was already breaking mine, and Yankee wasn't even my dog.

I called Roy after lunch to tell him what I'd accomplished.

"Someone took him," he said sharply. "I refuse to believe he'd run off."

I wanted to make him feel better, but didn't know how to. I refused to say, "It'll be okay." For me, such hollow words meant nothing when you were in the middle of something truly painful.

Later in the day, Roy offered to pick me up so we could search for Yankee. We rode across forested dirt roads, thinking maybe his dog had ended up in places where Roy had taken him for hikes. Roy flagged down passing vehicles and showed them a photo. He smiled and thanked drivers despite no lead. At least he showed an effort to be more hopeful about the dog's return, making it more bearable to be around him. So much so, I found myself enjoying his company, although I couldn't tell if he felt the same about me. If I believed what he'd said, that he had no romantic feelings for me anymore, I supposed I had my answer.

Two days passed with no word about Roy's dog. On Saturday, my family made a Phoenix shopping trip. We got home around five. Shortly after dinner, Roy called and asked me to join him for a hike the next day. It was good to hear a lighter tone of voice. He seemed to being doing better. I agreed to go.

When Roy pulled up in front of my house in the morning, I scampered out the front door, and hopped into his truck. He greeted me with that captivating smile of his.

"I thought we'd go to the Verde River," he said, steering away from the curb, "but I had a call last night. The boy said there's a black lab hanging out at the school bus stop in Chino Valley. It's on the way, so I want to check it out."

Chino Valley? That was thirty miles away. But then, Yankee had been gone for nearly a week now, so who knew how far he might have wandered. We rode in silence, apprehensive about the possibility of finding his dog.

On the main drag in Chino Valley, Roy slowed when we approached the tiny community's only school bus stop: a sign next to a bench. In the distance, kids played ball in a field, where the sun highlighted blades of grass, emphasizing the greens and tans. Roy decided to pull over and show them Yankee's photo. I sat in the truck, watching him make his way towards the boys, who were calling out to each other, engrossed in their game. *He looks good today,* I thought, with him sharply dressed in a button-down shirt, suede vest, and Levi's. *But don't you dare make this day into anything more than it is.*

The boys saw Roy, and gathered around him. Roy took the photo out of his shirt pocket, and showed it to them. One of the boys nodded and pointed down the road.

Roy returned with a huge grin on his face, which lit up mine. He hopped into the truck.

"What'd they say?" I asked.

"One of the kids felt sorry for the stray dog, and put him in their backyard! I bet it's Yankee!"

Roy was so full of hope that it made me hopeful, too. We followed the boy to his home, and there, in the fenced yard, was indeed Roy's Labrador.

Roy called out: "Yankee! Here boy! Come here!" The dog came running up to Roy with tail wagging and tongue lolling.

Positioned on one knee, a grinning Roy held Yankee's head in his hands, "Where have you been, boy? Good dog, good dog . . ." he said, rubbing and petting Yankee's head and stroking his broad, silky ears.

What a wonderful sight. I grinned until my cheeks hurt.

With the black lab riding happily in the truck bed, Roy and I laughed and talked nonstop about the events that led to Yankee's return.

Yankee safely home and fed, we took him for a walk in the woodlands near Roy's home. Sitting in the warm sun under the pines with Roy's arm securely around me, beautiful Yankee right at hand, I felt happier than I'd been in a long, long time.

"You know," Roy said, stroking his lab's fur, "I consider Yankee half yours."

Roy considered his beloved Yankee part mine? I didn't know exactly what he meant, but that didn't matter. It made me realize how much I loved Roy. Why deny it any longer? Why try to make it just a friendship? Today, he acted like he felt the same about me. I sure hoped that flying on the ground wasn't wrong, like in Buffalo Springfield's song, because even though my feet were planted on the ground, inside I was indeed flying.

The next day, with reward paid to a very thrilled boy, Roy and I drove to Sullivan Lake, and hiked into the deep canyon below the dam. Here, the soil gave off a strong scent of wet earth mixed with heavenly scents of lush broad-leafed trees and willowy grasses. After exploring there, we climbed out of the canyon and walked the lake's edge. Something caught my eye.

"Oooo, Roy, look. Cattails." I beamed at him, pointing to the tall, fascinating plants. "I want one. But they're out of reach. Aren't they beautiful? They even look like cat tails . . ."

"You want one? No problem."

Roy inched his way to the water's edge, climbing over rocks, and wading through thick undergrowth. When he leaned rather precariously over the lake to pick some, he had me worried. "Gosh, don't fall in!"

Deep in concentration, he broke the stems of several, and brought them to me.

With the stalks clutched in my one hand, and Roy holding the other, we walked up the path back to his truck. At that moment, I didn't have any room for confusion. It was all too good to be true! But Heaven forbid, I didn't want to ruin anything between us by asking him if this all meant more than friendship.

In bed that night, I realized that I'd not heard from Ben for two months. Whatever it was I'd been harboring for Ben, I knew nothing about our relationship situation would change overnight. But right now, my thoughts reeled. How much I wanted to travel with Roy. Just thinking about what an adventure it would be, what a great time we would have, made me giddy to the point that I couldn't make my insides settle down. It must have been over an hour before I fell asleep.

Dawn crept into my room with its golden rays, waking me after only a few hours of slumber. Memories of last week's conversation with Roy chipped away at all of the euphoric feelings I had from yesterday. He had NO feelings for me anymore? How could we have had such a connection—and by God we did, didn't we?—if he didn't feel a damned thing? Did he lie? Why would he? What a messed up situation. What a messed up *me*.

That afternoon Roy called, his mood subdued, like mine. It sounded like he didn't want to talk, so I babbled some nonsense about hanging up and getting back to "whatever."

"Oh, don't go. I *do* want to talk to you. I'm just in a listening mood," he said.

A listening mood? That was a first. Roy always had something to say. "Okay ... it's perfect camping weather," I said, to keep the conversation going. "I think I'll go next weekend."

"Oh, can I go?" he asked, like an excited little boy. A second later, he added, "Guess that's a no ..."

"Sure you can."

Roy's tone turned serious. "Do you mean that?"

I did. Would he show up? I doubted it. In fact, I doubted everything now. What he said, what he felt, what I said, what I felt ... Roy's words were glued to my brain. Were my words glued to his?

I'd like to say and believe "whatever happens, happens." But that was something I hadn't learned how to do. Chuck believed it fully, or so he put on. That was probably the one and only thing that bothered me about Chuck. He didn't want to believe that people are human, and emotions are something that shouldn't be hidden. When I felt emotions, I felt them strongly. It never occurred to me to hide them within my dark side.

AS USUAL, WHEN the afternoon newspaper arrived I dove straight to the want ads. Finding nothing, I checked my horoscope before reading the funnies and Ann Landers.

It's a challenge to be a Scorpio.

A strong character, willpower, and deep emotions are your positive attributes. Secrets attract you like magnets. You keep your own, but always try to find out other people's. This isn't idle curiosity; you need to really need to know what makes them tick. Whatever you do you do it fully. You are a searcher, and a digger into life's mysteries. You do your own thing, no matter what. It's great to be able to stand alone, but don't become a loner. Once you set a goal you go after it with courage and determination. So set your goals high!

I read it again. Was this me? For sure my emotions were intense, but wasn't that true of everyone? Maybe not. I sure didn't believe in hiding them, while at the same time, I never thought that having strong emotions were a positive trait. How could suffering be a positive? And as for secrets, I did find those intriguing. Is that what attracted me to Roy? Ben? Both of those guys were incredibly hard to understand. Then there was the reference to life's mysteries. No doubt love was a mystery. Did my wanting to do my own thing ruin my chances of finding work? I'd never thought about doing anything *but* my own thing. Could I change? Should I change? I clipped out the horoscope and tucked it in my journal to study later.

Friday evening, Roy came over. Our guitar playing was interspersed with conversations about life, but not about love. What a relief. I didn't think I could handle anything more at the moment, especially if he brought up how he didn't care about me anymore. We'd just put our guitars into their respective cases, when a harmonica in my case's storage compartment caught my eye.

"Do you want this? I thought I'd learn to play, but it's just not me."

"Thanks," he said, slipping it into his shirt pocket.

My parents and sister had long since gone to sleep when Roy and I moved to sit on the love seat in front of the fireplace. The fire snapped and crackled, filling the room with warm, flickering light, the only illumination in the room. We didn't talk. For me, the moment was too perfect, too everything, to be ruined by our voices. Roy woke me when I dozed-off by placing his hand on my knee. I took his hand, and laced my fingers through his.

"Come closer," he said.

I did, and he kissed me—tenderly at first, and then with intense passion. My thoughts raced . . . wanting to believe this was all about love. When we paused, he stroked my hair, which made tingles course down the back of my neck. As nice as the moment felt, I had to ask something to clear my confused mind. "I need to know. Do you care at all for me? Last week you said you didn't."

He did not answer, and because I wanted to believe he *did* care about me, I let him continue kissing and touching me everywhere, lighting my soul until I became breathless with want and need.

Roy paused, took my hand, and said, "Do you want to go all the way?"

He didn't say this in a way that made me think he loved me and wanted to make love to me. It was more like him asking me if I'd like to go get a pizza. Feeling degraded, I wanted to hide; to tell him to leave. But no, I didn't really want him to leave. To save face, I pretended that I didn't care either. It seemed like the best choice at the moment. "No, I don't think that's a good idea."

Roy's grip on my hand went dead, and he leaned away. "Yeah, you're right. How do you feel about *me*, then?"

I dove in and told him the truth. "Roy. I care deeply about you, more than ever. I love you."

"There's no way I can accept that," he said, his tone bitter. "Besides, I don't care about you in that way anymore. We can only be friends."

The night deteriorated into more talk love versus friendship . . . or whatever it was that held us together.

Roy sighed deeply, and lowered his eyes. "I'm not good enough for you to love. I want you to forget me for your own good."

Forget you? Forget us? This made no sense, but I feared he meant it.

I took a deep breath. "I know all of the apologies in the world can't make you feel less bitter about the stupid things I've done, but I'm truly sorry for not knowing what I wanted back then. The fact is I don't want to forget you; I don't want to stop seeing you."

Little more was said, probably because it was now two a.m., and we were too tired and emotionally exhausted to continue. After he left, I discovered the harmonica I'd given him on the end table, thinking he must have forgotten it.

After breakfast the next morning, I scrambled into the small boulder outcrop that composed part of our backyard. I nestled into a private, sunny spot, leaned against a large rock, and let the sun warm my face. A slight pine-scented breeze kept me comfortable.

It was there that reality punched me hard.

Roy had forgotten the harmonica on purpose. It meant nothing to him, because neither did I. The only reason he'd hung around last night was for the possibility of sex. I hugged my knees to my chest, and rested my forehead on them. I wanted to stay in that secluded spot forever. Or take off somewhere—anywhere—and not return for a long, long time.

That evening, Chuck called. "Want to go cruise around?"

I sure did.

When I opened Chuck's truck door, Roy's eyes met mine, and we both lowered them at the same time. *Great.* Determined not to let that awkward moment ruin the evening, I quickly started up a conversation with Chuck. Soon the three of us were engaged in a deep discussion about the universe, our purpose in life, whether there was life outside of our solar system. Hard to believe the awful night with Roy had been only the night before.

Several hours later, we ended up at Roy's house listening to records in his room.

"Well," Chuck said after an hour, standing, "I need to head home. Ready, Linda?"

I jumped up, but Roy said, "I'd like you to stay. I can take you home later."

Why did I stay? Because, as always, when he wanted to be with me, I wanted to be with him. Chuck left, and I sat on the bed, with Roy in the chair next to me. He crossed his legs and arms. "I felt vibes that you wanted to talk to me."

He was half-right. I guess I really did. "I don't think you understand what I feel for you . . ."

Roy held up his hand to stop me. "I think you spread the word love around too freely."

Why couldn't you say you loved someone you cared deeply about? Was caring for someone in that way the same as loving them? If not, what the hell was so horrible about that? Everyone knew how good it felt to be loved. Didn't it make sense that knowing someone cared deeply for you also felt good? At that moment I never felt so unloved.

I fought breaking into tears. No word from Ben—Roy all but wished me harm ...

"You know what really did us in?" Roy asked, now staring straight at me. "Last Christmas. When I dropped off my gift at your job, and I saw that guy, Tom, put his arm around you."

My mouth fell open. *You were there?*

"You didn't notice, did you? I was still in the parking lot. When I saw you with that guy, I hated you. I hated *him*. I wished you two no good."

My thoughts whirled to recall that day. We'd gone to lunch. Cathy, Tom and I were goofing around, and Tom gave me that casual hug. Tom and I weren't even dating yet, but obviously Roy assumed we were. What made his assumption worse was the fact that I now believed Tom was not worth losing Roy's love.

Roy stood up, paced his room and ranted. "You know what I did after I left the parking lot? For the next week I hooked up with every girl I could find. Just to prove to you I could. And another thing. You and Ben aren't going to work out. You won't work out because it wasn't love at first sight."

I stared at him in disbelief. Maybe Ben and I *wouldn't* work out, but I doubted that would be the reason why. What was love at first sight anyway? Maybe it had happened for Roy, but it had never happened for me. It took nerve for him to say that in the same breath he said how he'd hooked up with a bunch of girls after seeing me with Tom.

I'd had enough. "I want to go home."

Chapter 14

DAYS PASSED. I had to get some normalcy back in my life. Time to look for work again.

I hadn't heard from the owner of Sawdust and Silver, and decided to stop in to see if he needed me to make more earrings. I figured it couldn't hurt to be proactive. Maybe he'd been busy.

A bell tied to the door tinkled when I walked in, and a voice from the back room said, "Be right there."

"No hurry."

I stood at the counter, peering into the glass display case at the jewelry for sale while waiting for him to come out. My eyes landed on dangly chandelier earrings that were dead-ringers for the ones I'd made for him—but that were not my creations.

The owner appeared, wiping his hands on a towel. "Can I help you?"

My voice didn't want to work because the reality was just starting to sink in: he had someone copy my designs. Even though I knew he would not be saying yes, I said, "I was just wondering if you needed me to make more earrings."

"Well, I've sold some," he said, shifting his eyes away from mine. "I'll let you know if I need your help."

I faked a smile, and walked out. He'd stolen my designs. My face burned with anger and embarrassment. How naive could I get? Even worse, I'd let myself get my hopes up. *I should have known this wouldn't work out.*

That huge disappointment, tacked onto the last emotion-packed night with Roy, kept me up all night.

In the morning, my heart was broken, and I couldn't seem to keep it together. I knew I was being very selfish wanting more from Roy. I tried so hard not to feel that way. I hurt because Roy didn't love me anymore—and I knew I loved him. I should have been contented and completely satisfied with the fact that he wanted to be my friend. Wasn't that what I'd strived for all along? So what the hell was I doing wanting more?

I'd figured out this much about Roy: Whether he was being honest about his feelings, or not, I'd never know. I vowed to not say one more word to him about how I felt. Not one, single, solitary word.

I vowed to stop caring.

The Saturday before Thanksgiving, a beautiful sunny day, had a chill in the air, which helped me tap into the holiday spirit—something I'd found hard to do ever since we'd moved to Arizona's warmer climate. Although I liked the weather here, the Thanksgivings and Christmases of my childhood in Syracuse were typically gray, cold, and sometimes white, and therefore ingrained into my memory bank as weather befitting The Holidays. Inspired, I spent half the morning sewing Christmas gifts, and the other half shopping. Roy called at noon.

"I'm going out to the poultry farm in Humboldt to pick up a turkey for a friend . . . wanna join me?"

Of course I did . . . but gave myself a stern reminder: *DO NOT read more into this than is there.*

Roy wanted to first make a detour to Lynx Lake. "There's this cool tree stump out there I want to see if I can get," he said, grinning at me. "It would make a great table."

Sounded like an adventure. I liked adventures. Especially with Roy.

After pulling off on a side road, Roy backed his car into position.

"It's down here," he said, walking to the shore.

Ten minutes later I stared at the large stump, bearing a close resemblance to an octopus.

"I guess I should have brought the truck," he said, rubbing the stubble on his chin.

I laughed. "So how do you propose we do this?"

"Well, how about we roll it end-over-end until we can heave it into the trunk . . . easy, don't you think?"

While that sounded simple, the stump's configuration prevented it from cooperating with Roy's plan. The darned thing kept twisting and turning, sending it sideways without gaining much ground. One time a root slapped Roy in the face, and another time it painfully rolled over my foot. The whole time we were laughing, eventually with tears streaming down our faces. Finally, though, we had it aligned with the trunk of his car.

"Okay," Roy said, "get on the other side, and when I count to three, we'll lift it inside."

Skeptical, I said, "If you say so."

After a number of failed attempts, we finagled it into the trunk, more or less, but there was no way the lid would shut.

Roy opened one of the car's back doors, saying, "I've got a rope in here somewhere . . ."

Once the lid was secured to the bumper, we stood back and stared. "Tentacles" stuck out in every direction.

"It looks like it's trying to escape a kidnapping," I said.

Our burst of laughter echoed across the lake, sending birds in nearby trees off in alarm.

Mission accomplished, turkey picked up and delivered, we played Frisbee at the elementary school near Roy's house until dusk. What a blast! I've always been a total klutz catching that stupid thing, but Roy and I laughed whenever I missed . . . which was every single time. The day rivaled the spectacular one when we'd found Yankee.

After sunset, when it was too dark to play, we went to my house, and listened to music in my room.

"Soooo . . . when're you gonna let me read a page out of your journal?" Roy asked with a sly smile.

I don't know what possessed me to let him, but he'd been bugging me about it off and on, and for whatever reason, at the moment I didn't see the problem. As I stood there and watched him read, though, I grew more uncomfortable by the second, and snatched it from him before he could turn the page.

His head snapped up. "Hey!"

I closed my journal, and put it away. "That's enough."

He frowned. "Well, I guess I could've read it all night."

I smiled. That's what I was afraid of, considering all of the juicy tidbits that were in there. How fun to tease him, though. Today we shared a great connection. One that at times was shaky, but in reality could not be broken. How I wished this wonderful feeling of elation would last forever and ever . . .

A few days later, Roy called and dropped a bomb. "I'm leaving Prescott in February. I'll probably be gone a long time."

Leaving? I knew and felt deeply that if he left, it would end everything between us. It was hard enough pretending to be friends when he didn't give a damn about me. Hard wasn't a painful enough word for what it would be like without him. No more talks. No more hilarious and fantastic times. Right when I thought I could handle our relationship, he leaves. Later that night he made it worse by calling to say he'd decided we were too different to even maintain a friendship.

"We don't like the same things. And you take life too seriously," he said.

What the hell? I took life too seriously? What if he didn't take life seriously enough?

Well, no more meek and mild-mannered me. I raised my voice. "That's a lot of bull! First off, I do like the things you do, and the only reason you don't like the things I do is because you don't *want* to."

"We are completely opposite—"

I stopped him dead. "No, we are far from opposites."

"You only show up when you're feeling down."

"That's not true!"

After more arguing, and sick of it, I said, "Look, I need to go."

We hung up. I covered my face with my hands and sighed deeply.

It never fails. Every time I get my spirits and hopes up something happens to let me down. HARD. More like dropping me on the pavement. From thirty stories.

But I kept picking up the pieces. Yes, I kept picking them up. And as long as I could—I'd be all right. I sure would. But how much more could I take? It'd been over two months since I'd heard from Ben. He was becoming an illusion. I could no longer conjure up a picture of him in my mind. What if Roy was right that Ben and I weren't meant to be together? Then what? The twinge of hope I used to get when I went to the mailbox didn't come anymore. Sure, I said to myself, "Ben please write," thirty-thousand times a day, but I'd almost all but given up.

THE NEXT FEW weeks plagued me with a bad cold and cough that wouldn't go away. Despite feeling like crap, I managed to make some jewelry to sell at the swap meet, sew up some Christmas gifts, and make a little money working for Sawdust and Silver—doing production work only. No more creating original designs they could steal.

Barb, the girlfriend of my dad's employee, called one rainy afternoon. "I'm making taffy, want to come help?"

I'd never made taffy before, but figured it might be fun. "Okay, I'll be right over."

When I arrived at her apartment, she'd already started.

"I've got it ready to pull," she said, pointing at the glossy mixture in a bowl.

We laughed ourselves silly at the sticky process. My mood perked up and even my cough improved. However, at the end of the day I was so down I couldn't find any tears, unsure of what specifically to cry about. Roy called to express concern about my lingering illness. I thanked him for calling, and hung up the phone. Why would he care? Numb, I stared at the ceiling of my bedroom.

Two days before Christmas, I awoke to snowflakes gently seesawing to join the light dusting already on the ground. And while it improved my Christmas spirit and overall mood, it also made me feel nostalgic for Syracuse Christmases. Not that my family was the kind to throw big parties, or that I attended special events. No, the Christmases I recalled were the ones where I stenciled our front window with Glass Wax Christmas scenes—which required major elbow grease to remove, carefully selected gifts for my family and a few close friends—wrapping and rewrapping them at least twice to make them perfect, where we cut our tree at a farm and decorated it with family heirlooms while munching on popcorn, and where we all watched TV specials such as *A Charlie Brown Christmas*, *Rudolph The Red-Nosed Reindeer*, and *A Christmas Carol*. Although the Glass Wax tradition went by the wayside, I still watched TV specials and spent a considerable amount of time wrapping gifts "just so." Our Christmas tree hunt had changed to scouting for a wild one, but fun just the same. The only downside was that I had to mail gifts to friends back east.

At long last, I heard from Ben. After ripping his letter open, I found one small piece of paper with only a few sentences. I sank into myself. *That's it?*

> *Just a short note, love, as I don't have much time to write. I want you to know I love and miss you, and think about you every single day. Soon we will be together. You can count on it.*
> *Love, Ben*

I sighed. At least he wrote, which put him back into reality.

Christmas morning, 1974

I ROLLED OVER to check the clock, thinking it must be time to get up. *Eight o'clock? Where's the sun?* Climbing out of bed, I parted the curtains and shrieked. *It's snowing!* The Universe must have known I needed something magical like a White Christmas in my life. Anxious to experience it first hand before the family gift-opening frenzy, I dressed in warm clothes to rush outside to dance among the flurries, feeling the sting of crystals on my face, and reveling in the peaceful, all-encompassing hush that accompanies snowfall.

When I came back in, everyone was up and settling in around the tree. My mom passed out gifts, insisting that we open them one at a time so she could see each person's reaction. It took forever that way, but I had to admit it was nice to slow down and watch people open gifts. So much so, I neglected to open my own presents until my mom pressured me to do so.

A SURPRISE CALL from Roy a few days later included a casual request:

"Want to go see a movie?"

If I'd been thinking about how absurd this date-like invitation really was, I would've said no. Like a complete fool, though, I said okay.

We stood in line waiting to buy tickets, hands in pockets, stomping our feet occasionally to stay warm, our breaths forming white puffs.

"So what's new?" he asked.

I paused for a second before responding. "Not much," fully aware that I didn't mention hearing from Ben.

Because the movie he wanted to see was sold out (Fate?), we drove around for a while. I kept quiet. Roy he kept glancing over at me, as though expecting me to speak. Did he sense something was bothering me? In truth, I didn't know what to say to him, or even why I was there.

"I need to pick up some throat lozenges for my mom," he said, turning into the Stop N Go parking lot.

While he visited the cold-care aisle, I flipped through a bin of albums on sale for half-price. Don McLean's album caught my eye. I pulled it out, and flipped it over to read the song titles.

"Do you want to get that?" Roy asked from behind me.

"Yes, but I didn't bring my wallet." I put the album back.

"I'll buy it for you," he said, retrieving it from the display.

"Okay, but I'll pay you back."

"No, you don't have to. Let this be your Christmas gift."

I didn't know if I should accept this, but I did want the album. I said, "Thank you," and let him pay.

With new music in hand, we drove to his house to listen. Sitting on his bed—him closest to the record player, me leaning against the headboard—I thought it strange for us to be here like this. After all we'd been through, I was unsure how to act, unsure of what he wanted from me. He moved closer, and fingered my hair. Every nerve ending sparkled; anticipation made my hands tremble. I sat perfectly still, wanting his touch, but afraid of it, too. What would he say this time? That he liked me, but did not love me? That he wanted to be friends with sex, or friends without sex? Or that we had nothing in common? He attempted to kiss me. I pushed him away. *Not again.* "I thought you said we couldn't be close friends, much less lovers. I thought you didn't love me anymore."

"I never said such a thing . . . well, at least not quite like that." His eyes lowered. "If I did, I lied. I do love you, in a way."

In a WAY? What the hell! In what way? Certainly not in the way I wanted him to. How in the world could I believe someone who admitted to lying?

"You know, I'd been doing pretty good in trying to forget you, until you called." Angry tears filled my eyes; my upper lip trembled. "Why *did* you call? Was there no one else to turn to? Did you have to scrape the bottom of the jar? Were you that desperate?"

"No . . . that's not it," he said with a deep sigh. "I'm so messed up. I don't know what to do, or which path to take."

We were both weary of this game. And yet, why did we still play it? I played it because Roy had the key to my heart. And the key was the last thing in the world I wanted Roy to have. Did he know he had it? He must. Otherwise he couldn't get me to go to him every time he called. I just wished I could forget him. I just wished he'd *let* me.

Neither of us knew what else to say at that point. He leaned in again to kiss me, and I let him. I wanted to believe that he kissed me because he loved me, but who was I kidding?

"I'm sorry, but you are just so beautiful, I had to do that," he said, smoothing my hair behind one ear.

I frowned. *"Beautiful?"* No way. *I must get out of here.* With my eyes focused on the floor, I stood, and took a deep breath. "Please take me home."

When I opened the front door, I stood in awe in front of a winter fairyland. While we were inside our confusing, painful world in which we just couldn't figure out how to be in love with each other at the same time—four inches of fresh snow had fallen, covering everything with a thick layer of what resembled powdered sugar, coating tree branches, blanketing rooftops and his truck. The one streetlight made the scene twinkle as though stars lay scattered on the ground. Caught up in the magical scene, I stood there wishing that Roy would put his arm around me, and really mean it. Not just "in a way."

Chapter 15

New Year's Day, 1975

THAT NIGHT WITH Roy pretty much did it for me. No more games. I had to stop letting him torture me. Could I begin the New Year without him? That was my goal, to edge him out of my thoughts and my life. And what about Ben? No word from him since well before Christmas. All of this silence . . . maybe I should forget him, too. Time to move on.

This guy strolled solemnly by my house every day after school with hands in pockets, head down, and long, dark hair almost hiding the shadow of a mustache. I wanted to meet him. Bravely, I'd staged a couple of encounters where I smiled and said, "Hi," and he returned the smile and greeting. Nice smile! A nice, deep, masculine voice, too. Now—how to really meet this mystery guy, beyond passing him on the sidewalk?

My friend Kim, her friend, Robert, and I, ventured out to Wolf Creek for a day hike, and then to Sambo's for tea. I mentioned Mystery Guy, sighing and saying that I doubted we'd ever meet formally.

"I know him," Kim said. "He's in my homeroom, and lives two doors down from me. His name is Marc."

Now I had a name, but I also had his age: Sixteen. Well, okay, not ideal, but he did look much older. When the waitress brought more hot water for our tea, I just happened to glance up at one of the restaurant's windows. Roy saw me just as I saw him. He smiled and waved. I raised my hand in acknowledgment, trembled a bit as he and a couple of his friends took a booth in another section.

Be strong, I thought. *You need to let him go.*

It was time to shake up my life.

My conversation with Kim and Robert got a bit lively, with both of them tossing out suggestions of how Marc and I could meet up.

"Write him a letter. I'll put it in his locker," Kim said.

I nixed that idea right away—what if someone saw her?

"Next time he walks past your house, stop him and ask for his phone number," Robert said.

"Too obvious," I said. "And what if he says no?"

None of their suggestions worked for me. Once alone, I plotted the romantic idea of secret notes and signals. I decided to mail him a note, asking him if he would take a chance and meet me. How to have him let me know if he wanted to? Have him tie a string on the stop sign at an intersection near my house. Silly, but romantically effective. If it was there, fine. If not, he wasn't interested, and I'd quit thinking about him. No need to see his reaction; therefore, no embarrassment or hurt. Kim gave me his address. I slid the envelope into our mailbox, and raised the red flag. That done, I decided to take care of one more thing. Now that I planned to stay away from Roy, I needed to fill the guitar-playing void that decision would create. A sign at my favorite music store offered lessons. I called them, and scheduled one with the owner's son, which would take place at the store on Friday evening.

All day Wednesday, with that night being the string-tying deadline, I paced the house, nervous and apprehensive. What time would he tie the string, if he would do it at all?

Eight p.m.: *What an idiot I am. What the hell was I thinking?*

It was quite apparent that I hadn't been thinking. Marc would probably laugh hysterically, and share my letter with his buddies, who would probably tell him that I was some desperate *dog* who couldn't get a guy to notice her if she stamped "easy" on her forehead. I covered my face with my hands.

Oh, God, what did I just do?

After everyone had gone to bed, I lit a candle in my room, flicked on my portable black-and-white TV, and hopped onto my bed. But I couldn't focus. I got off the bed, changing channels until I found a movie. I must have fallen asleep, because when I glanced at the clock it was one a.m., and the TV displayed nothing but fuzz. Outside my bedroom window, the streetlight shined blue on the snow, and twinkling and silvery on the frosty stop sign. Did it hide the string? Or was it not there? I had to know. I tiptoed to the hall closet, put on my fleece-lined jacket, turned up the collar, and dashed outside to check. With the temperature in the teens, the snow crunched and squeaked underfoot as I approached the sign. The frigid, cedar-smoke scented air from neighborhood chimneys pinked my cheeks, making my breath visible. I kept squinting at the sign, wondering where the string would be should it actually be there. Then I saw the small piece of white cotton string carefully threaded and tied through the perforated metal post. I resisted the urge to squeal with delight.

He wants to meet me!

The joy that the string was there lasted until daybreak, when I got slapped in the face with the reality of what I'd started. The hardest part was yet to come. That was finding out how compatible we were—or not. It was almost as though I never took into consideration that he was a real person—with his own personality, thoughts, and dreams. He always looked so solemn when he'd walked by . . . and now, with him actually doing what I asked, what would he be like when we met?

The next night, Kim and I nursed along cups of tea at Sambo's, using the original tea bag and many refills of hot water provided by the waitress. She probably detested cheapskates like us.

"Marc wants to meet me," I said, keeping my voice low to prevent the elderly couple next to us from overhearing.

"Wow, the string was there! Call him. Here's his number. I'll even give you the dime," she said, gesturing toward the payphone.

I cringed at her loud voice and whispered, "I can't."

"Why not? I thought you wanted to meet this guy."

After an hour of coercion, I took the dime, and placed the call.

My body and voice trembled when I asked his mother if he was home. Static filled my ear during the receiver transfer. A deep voice said, "Hello?"

After a brief conversation, Marc suggested we meet about eight-thirty that evening. He would pick me up at my house.

Tonight? Don't you dare chicken-out. I started to give him my address, but he said, "Oh, I know where you live."

A huge smile crossed my face. *He knows where I live!*

I rushed home, and the second I walked in the door, my mom said, "Roy called for you earlier."

"Oh, okay."

Tough, Roy. I'm ready to forget you.

Rather than have Marc come to the door, leaving me with the uncomfortable task of explaining to my parents who he was and how we'd met, I told my mom I was going out with Chuck. I sat on the front steps, shivering in the cold, full of trepidation. What if he didn't like me? What if I didn't like him? Fifteen minutes later, a beat-up VW bug stopped at the curb. I dashed out to the car, and opened the passenger-side door.

"Hi," I said, climbing in.

He smiled. "Hey."

We drove around, not really talking about anything important—which shouldn't have been surprising considering we knew nothing about each other.

"Kinda cold out today," I said, for lack of anything else to say.

Marc nodded. "Really? Didn't notice."

I began to wonder if I'd made a huge mistake. At last, though, he brought up the letter.

"At first I wasn't going to do it," he said, with a quick glance my way. "But a buddy told me that you must really have your head together to have approached me like that."

Hilarious. *Me? Together?* This was the exact opposite of what I'd envisioned his friends saying, making it even funnier.

"I'm glad you did," I said, trying hard to sequester a laugh.

I gazed out the window at the warm glows of lights from homes as we drove around Prescott, talking more as we relaxed. A light snow began to fall, and Marc chuckled. "This is kinda a pain . . . but my windshield wipers don't work. We'd better head back."

Every few minutes, Marc had to pull over to brush the snow off the windshield, which made the trip home rather long, which by now was fine with me.

"You should probably get those fixed one of these days," I said, giggling, when he hopped back into the seat after another window clearing.

He laughed. "Yeah, I know. I keep saying that . . ."

What a smile he had—it made his eyes light up. When Marc dropped me off, he said, "I work nights at a restaurant, so between school and homework it doesn't give me much free time, but I'll call you soon."

The next morning I couldn't wipe the stupid grin off my face. I'd actually pulled our meeting off without screwing up and saying something stupid. And when Marc called at noon, he added to our surreal introduction by asking, "Is it okay if I stop by later?"

And sure enough, he did. We didn't talk for very long, but the whole time I couldn't stop smiling, unable to shake the humorous notion that he did this because he wanted to see me "for real" in broad daylight.

AFTER DINNER ON Friday, I loaded up my guitar and headed to my first lesson from the music store owner's son, Jeff. Okay, to be honest, the fact that Jeff was cute *had* influenced my decision, but I told myself that I was there to improve my guitar skills, period.

Jeff greeted me with a smile, and we removed our guitars from their respective cases. When he reached into a cooler and produced two beers, I was caught off guard. Always calorie conscious, and also uncomfortable at the thought of drinking alcohol during a lesson, I politely passed. Jeff twisted off the cap of one, and took a swig. He played some amazing music, and sang along. I was completely mesmerized, both by his skills and his original lyrics. About fifteen minutes later, he set his guitar down, and picked up his beer.

"So who's your favorite musician?" he asked.

"Jackson Browne," I said, more than willing to expound on why his amazing storytelling lyrics were at the top of my list.

That led to him jumping up and gathering albums from the back room to play some far out music. How much I wished I could buy new music. But that required having a job, which I didn't happen to have. What a surprise to find out we had many other things in common besides guitar and music: hiking, camping, and photography. Not that I had a fancy camera like he had, but I still enjoyed taking photos. Soon I forgot all about the reason I was there. I also didn't know how I'd missed the gold wedding band that shone brightly on his left hand tonight. Even though I didn't really get much of a guitar lesson, I agreed to another next Friday.

A week later Marc called on his night off from work. "I'll come pick you up in a bit."

It was after seven when we drove out to the Wolf Creek area and parked. It didn't seem like we were rushing things when he put his arm around me.

"My last relationship didn't work out for a variety of reasons," Marc said. He didn't offer more, and I quietly debated on what to tell him about my past relationships. I'd made a promise to myself to not bring up Roy, but ended up doing so anyway. I figured it would come out sooner or later. Just get it over with.

"So what happened between you two? Was it serious?" he asked.

I started to dive into the details, but then determined it wasn't necessary. Why go into all the drama? "We dated for a while, but we aren't together anymore."

That was true ... or was it? I'd lost track.

"I'm glad you contacted me," he said. He reached into his back pocket, pulled out his wallet, and opened it. "I've got your letter right here ..."

In his wallet? I didn't think he could've done anything sweeter. Speechless, I just smiled, and no doubt glowed, that my letter meant enough to him to keep close at hand.

Marc returned the letter and wallet to his pocket. He took my wrist, pulled me closer, and with one hand on the back of my head, kissed me gently, but deeply, sending tingles down my spine.

SMALL TOWN LIVING had its drawbacks, in the sense that the odds of running into someone you knew ran high, and seemed to run higher when you didn't particularly *want* to run into a certain person. It wasn't a surprise to see Roy pass by me the next day on the road. He glanced my way, and then averted his eyes without acknowledgment. I flinched, and felt my eyes water. No matter how hard I tried not to let him get to me, he still did.

The next day the phone rang, and because it was usually for me, I grabbed it on the second ring.

"Hey, what's happenin'?" Marc said. "Want to get together later?"

"Sure," I said. "What time?"

"I'll call you when I get off work."

It was after nine-thirty when he called and offered to come pick me up. We drove around, ending up out the quiet Senator Highway. How disappointing that along the way I discovered we had little in common. All he talked about was his love of big cities like Los Angeles, and how important it was to have the coolest hot rod to make his friends envious. These were problems because, one, I despised big cities, and two, I had no interest in stupid, macho hot rod cars. What really hit me in a way that I hadn't expected, was that I didn't sense that he was trying to impress me. Instead, I picked up on an irritating arrogance that he didn't feel the need to. This did not sit well. On top of that, because he didn't give me a chance to talk, I mainly listened. The temptation to give up on him was strong, but then I reminded myself: *You've only known him four days. Opinions could change—give it time.*

Marc dropped me off at home after midnight, and before I fell asleep I thought about him and the evening. Okay, overall, he was nice. I wished he was older, but I knew you couldn't rush years on someone. It bugged me that he was so worried about status. This made me reflect back to when I was sixteen. What a different world. Sure, I'd wanted other kids to like me, but I didn't want to be popular. Now, I believed kids were growing up faster than they did before, at least so it seemed. Was that a good thing? I couldn't imagine how.

The next day's afternoon paper had an article that grabbed my attention: Ben's ship, the USS Enterprise, was heading for the Indian Ocean. It scared me to think of him so far away. I also felt as though our relationship was much like his ship, sailing away to a distant place. What our future may hold was becoming increasingly vague with each passing day.

ON TUESDAY, WITH it a glorious day, I sat in the sun on the front steps and strummed my guitar. Marc saw me on his way home from school, and walked over. "Hey."

"Have a seat," I said, moving over to make room.

He sat and stared at the cars whizzing by.

Apparently, I'd have to do the talking today. I mentioned that I'd started taking guitar lessons. "I'm looking forward to learning more."

He yawned. "Good. You need them."

What? The pain on my face must have clicked.

Marc stared at me. "Geez, I was just kidding. You take my jokes too seriously."

I had no idea how to respond to that. After a few minutes, he went home.

No longer interested in playing, I went into the house and shut myself in my room. His comment made me feel a bit sick. I curled up on the bed. Was I being overly sensitive? Was Roy right when he'd said that I took life too seriously? Why wasn't it important to take someone's feelings into account before you said something potentially hurtful? I began to question relationships with guys, period. I wondered about loneliness, about marriage. My guitar teacher, Jeff, brought marriage into a whole new light. Because he was married, we could never be friends. We could never call each other once in a while just to talk; we could never do anything other than get together for guitar lessons. I couldn't imagine why I would ever want to get married. Besides not being able to have guys as friends, what if I fell for someone after I'd made a formal commitment? Then what? Marriage made no sense.

IN LATE JANUARY, the wind howled, making trees dance and sway while wispy clouds streaked across the full moon. I loved evenings like this. Why, then, did I want to crawl into a hole somewhere and not come out? It'd been ages since I felt happy inside and out. When was the last time? I couldn't recall. I had this very empty spot inside that was shedding tears. I was lonely. Yet, why should I be? I had many people in my life. Not too long ago, Kim's friend Robert had said, "Everyone needs somebody on their level that they can talk to." It made me think. Did I have someone on my level around here to talk to? No, at least not enough to help me.

Snow fell all the next day. It didn't stick, but by evening I had a great time walking amidst the swirling flakes. A wonderful memory arose of the time Roy and I went sledding at Thumb Butte—dragging his rickety sled up the snowy hill, struggling and laughing hysterically when the darned sled wouldn't slide because rocks blocked our way . . . would things ever be so carefree between us again?

At dinner that night, my dad started pressuring me to go to Los Angeles to work as my uncle's housekeeper for an unspecified amount of time. Okay, I understood that his brother needed help after my aunt had passed away, but no way did I want to do this. I hated big cities! What perfect timing for the phone to ring.

"What to go out?" Chuck asked.

Rescued! I needed this. Besides, I'd been worried. No contact with Chuck for two months was rare. It seemed like we were drifting apart, which was exactly what I'd dreaded.

I paced the living room, anticipating his truck pulling up in front of the house. When it did, I bounded out the front door, unable to control my enthusiasm.

"How 'bout Sambo's first?" he asked after we hugged each other tight.

Over cups of tea, I listened to him fill me in on his news, and then I did the same. Next we headed to his family's old, abandoned house in the fascinating area known as the Granite Dells. Located on the outskirts of town, with gigantic boulders for a backyard, the house was purported to be haunted. Chuck had insisted he'd heard ghostly noises on more than one occasion. One time he swore someone in high-heeled shoes paced the attic. We often hung out here, talking and waiting for something spooky to happen. Funny how we always used hushed voices, as though we thought someone was listening. I wanted to believe, but the spirits never cooperated in my presence.

Although the house had a fireplace, we had no wood, so we huddled close on the dusty old couch, the only piece of furniture, and talked about ghosts. Our conversation faltered for a moment, allowing me to dive into my concerns.

"I've felt like we've been drifting apart," I said, resting my hand on his arm. "We don't talk or get together like we used to."

He placed his hand over mine, and patted it. "Yes, I noticed that too. I was also worried, and didn't know what to do. I hadn't brought it up, because I knew it would all work out."

We then reminisced about times we'd shared. I told him about Marc, and not hearing from Ben yet, and he told me about a few girls he'd met recently. We talked about what would happen to our friendship if one of us ever got married. We both agreed that the most horrible thing that could happen was if we drifted apart for good. I hoped and prayed it would never, ever come to that. After the evening ended, it seemed like we were back as we should be. I hadn't felt that close to him in a long time.

DAYS PASSED BY slowly, with me continuing to scan the want ads daily. I'd not heard anything from Ben, although the newspaper did mention his ship was now docked in Kenya. Africa . . . a distant place I couldn't remotely fathom.

My older sister, Cindy, came up from Tucson in late February for a weekend visit. It occurred to me that maybe I should try again to look for work down there. That would get me away from Roy, too . . . maybe I could stay with her. I asked.

"No," she said, without explanation or discussion.

Gee, thanks. I marched into my room, and slammed the door. Here I'd thought that since she was always lecturing me about finding work, she'd at least be willing to give me a helping hand.

Five minutes before she was about to leave, she knocked on my bedroom door and said, "Okay. You can come."

Did I want to go? But I really needed a place to stay if I was serious about finding a job in Tucson. I threw some clothes into a suitcase, and in ten minutes we were on the road. With the whole plan a spur-of-the-moment thing, buzzing down State Highway 69 to connect to the Interstate, I realized that no one but my parents and my other sister knew I'd left—which felt freeing somehow. Let everyone wonder where the heck I'd disappeared to . . . and why.

In the morning, I walked to the Forest Service's Santa Catalina District Office to check on the job situation. McKelsey told me I'd have a pretty good chance of returning to Palisades. *Yes!* Instead of walking out of there, I floated a foot above the ground.

The next day my sister let me borrow her car, and I applied at several department stores—just to be on the safe side. My dad's former coworker referred me to a phone answering service where I'd apply tomorrow. Things were really looking up! Maybe I'd find a job soon . . . but in all honesty, the only one I wanted was on Mount Lemmon.

On a warm sunny day, with several job applications pending and a forwarded letter from Ben in hand, I allowed myself some time to relax, and took a bottle of Diet Pepsi to Cindy's back stoop to read Ben's letter and work on my tan.

"I miss you! I love you so much," he wrote. *"I'm out at sea, and have no idea when I'll be back, or when I can see you. It's so lonely out here."*

A million miles spread out between us, or at least it might as well have been that far. Thinking about our distance apart reminded me of some strange reactions I received whenever I told someone about Ben being overseas. They all thought I should be upset because he might be with another girl. Some were amazed, others just plain didn't believe me when I told them it didn't bother me. With him so far away, it made no sense to expect a commitment.

ONE NIGHT, AS Cindy readied for work at Tucson Medical Center, she told me to take her to work. When I swung up to the employee entrance, she insisted that I come in and apply for an admin job in her unit. Not particularly thrilled about the idea of working in a hospital, or in the same place she did, I still felt obligated to go in.

After parking, I followed her into the employee entrance where she dutifully marched down the hall, while I scurried to keep up with her brisk pace. We took the elevator up to her floor, and again I shadowed her as she made for the Intensive Care Unit. Cindy pushed the double doors open, and they swooshed behind me as I entered the room, where the ice-cold air conditioning raised the hair on my arms. Rows of beds with patients covered in white flannel blankets lined both walls of the large room smelling of urine, bleach, and antiseptic. My sister walked purposefully down the aisle toward the door at one end, while I slowed down, my wide eyes flitting from patient to patient: Pale faces with oxygen tubes snaking from nostrils, IVs growing from arms like vines, heart monitors beeping, respirators whooshing, vacant eyes staring, open mouths gasping . . . death hung in the air like a dense fog, triggering the deepest, if not smothering, empathy, I'd ever felt. Every single molecule in my body wanted to leave—*now*.

Cindy left me in an office where I sat and let the clerk tell me about the position. I said I'd think about it.

That night, waiting for sleep, I knew that seeing people on their deathbed daily would damage my psyche. I could not, and would not, apply for the job. Curled up into a ball, I let tears fall. *When am I going to find the right job?* I wished I had Ben's tape to listen to. His voice would calm me. I wondered where he was at that moment . . .

ONE OF MY job applications finally generated an actual interview later that week. Nervous and apprehensive, I sat in down in front of a forty-something woman with reading glasses hanging from a gold chain around her neck.

"We can offer you a part-time position," she said. "We pay two dollars an hour."

Could I get out on my own working less than forty hours at two dollars an hour?

I tossed and turned all that night. Scared about being on my own. Scared that I couldn't survive on my own. Knowing I couldn't possibly be on my own with part-time work at two bucks an hour, I decided to pass on that offer. To make the decision harder, my sister now let me know I wasn't welcome in her apartment anymore.

Depressed and defeated, in early March, I returned to Prescott. Even though I wanted to get out on my own, I also loved being home. My mom welcomed me with hugs, and my bedroom provided me with both familiarity and privacy.

After talking with my mom for a while, I called Chuck, who promptly came to pick me up. I didn't want to bring up the subject of Roy, but maybe I did . . . because it didn't take long for me to ask how Roy was doing, and for Chuck to fill me in. As Chuck told it, Roy had confirmed that he'd finally met the girl he thought was "the one."

"She's supposedly crazy about him," Chuck said, his face scrunched with skepticism. "Roy says she is all he thought she would be—but I get the impression he wants *out*."

Although hearing that I was not the one anymore cut me open—a big, gaping, bloody wound—I also felt slightly vindicated. Hadn't I heard this before? I didn't believe Roy for a minute. Besides, somehow I *knew* Roy couldn't handle a girl being crazy over him. Call me jealous (yeah, I was), but it also seemed to me, based on our past, that the more I'd told Roy I didn't share in the love he had for me, the more he wanted me. When I finally said I loved him, he didn't want me anymore. That's why it made sense to me that if this girl was indeed crazy over him, Roy would lose interest in her. However, I hated to admit it, and felt sorry that I had to admit it—but he still got to me. It would take time, but I would have to gradually let go of everything I'd ever felt for him. *The circle is broken. The game is over.* Although I told myself this was a good thing, my heart didn't believe so, and dammit, it hurt.

Chapter 16

MY HANDS TREMBLED when I ripped into the letter from the Forest Service. *It's a job offer!* What I read, though, made me stare at the words as though they were written in a foreign language.

> *Thank you for applying with the Coronado National Forest. Unfortunately, your qualifications do not meet with the position you applied for.*

What the hell did that mean? How could I not qualify for a position I'd already held? It took thirty minutes for the news to sink in. Thirty more and I sat in my room nearly catatonic. *Why is life just one disappointment after another?* Until this rejection letter arrived, I hadn't realized how much I'd counted on getting that job. Now what? Should I call McKelsey and ask why? But that wouldn't help. It didn't matter why. They didn't give me the job. End of story.

Three days later, I received a phone call.

"Don't give up on the job," McKelsey said. "I'm workin' on it."

Bad mood? What bad mood? I could've danced around the kitchen . . . *He's on my side!*

"HEY," MARC SAID, a few days after I'd gotten home. "What a shock when I called you last week and your mom said you'd gone to Tucson!"

That my disappearance shocked him pleased me endlessly, but I played it cool. Let him chase me for a change.

"I kinda missed you," he said. "Let's get together next week. I'll call you."

I frowned. "Kinda missed me" didn't cut it. "I'll call you" didn't either. How many times had I heard that line? After we hung up, I shrugged. *I'll believe it when I see it.*

Thursday, my mom and I loaded up the Suburban with lunch, water, leather gloves, a bow saw, and dog, Peanuts, to hunt down and cut firewood. Even though April days were warming up, nights were cold, and we used the fireplace often.

After driving awhile on backcountry roads, we came up on a large dead tree.

I slid the Suburban into a spot where we could load easily. We picked through the branches for the easiest to drag. Even after cutting, some required both of us to load. Soon we had all the weight the suburban could handle, and I drove home. The hard work did wonders for my mood. It didn't hurt that McKelsey was trying to get me that job. When Ben came, my life would be perfect.

However, my good mood deteriorated after dinner, despite how hard I tried to not let it slip. I recognized that I may be depending on Ben too much to make everything better. Ben had been gone way too long—with all of the crap going on in Vietnam, he most likely would have been sent off for only God knew how much longer . . . which scared me, although I figured it must be tough on him, too.

Out running errands in the morning, my heart flip-flopped when I thought I saw Roy's truck. But no, it was not his. Then I could've sworn I saw him playing guitar in the town plaza—but no, that wasn't him, either. I gave myself a stern lecture. *Stop this. He has that girl now.*

Chuck's prediction that Roy wanted out of the relationship had not materialized—and the chances of seeing Roy where I used to were extremely remote. Yet, I still searched—searched the faces of people on the street, faces of people driving, looking for a familiar face, a familiar smile—his.

MARC NEVER DID call me, which suited me just fine. Well, not really just fine—actually I was furious with him. When my bedroom phone rang at eleven p.m., I grabbed the receiver on the first ring to prevent the racket from waking my parents. Only Marc called so late— he worked at a restaurant, and was just getting off work.

"Hello?" I said, keeping my voice low.

"Hey, whassup?"

"Nothing."

I let him do the talking, mainly because my head was swimming in the relationship pools of Roy and Ben—one bottomless, the other with no shore.

"You must think I'm a real jerk," he said after my cool response.

Close. I mean, after all, he always promised to call and didn't, he promised to come see me, and hadn't. We'd never even gone on a real date.

"Well, Marc, there are times when I think I don't matter to you one way or the other."

"I never meant to hurt your feelings by flaking out on you," he said. "Plus, I'd never take advantage of you. I mean, I'm attracted to you, but I'd never force myself on you. You're probably thinking I'm just after your body, but I'm not."

Why wouldn't I think that? Weren't all guys on that road? I really admired guys and the way they handled their sex drive. They didn't get hurt much, if at all, when they found out a girl had been using them for sex. But what happened when you turned the tables? Girls felt like dirt, and hated the guy if she thought he'd used her. I sure hated the thought of being used. I'd begun to wonder if Marc was just stringing me along for his entertainment. Many times I thought to cut off communications with him—although I hadn't so far. His attention, even if short-lived, fed my fragile ego.

"And," he said, "I'll have you know, I really don't like to hear you say you don't matter to me, 'cause that's not true. You do."

A big surprise. In fact, the whole conversation surprised me. Before he hung up, he left me with his typical ego-centric-kind-of-comment for the evening, contradicting everything he'd said so far: "Well, it seems to me that you are too serious, and I'm not serious enough."

I hung up, and sighed. What was that supposed to mean? Had I just been insulted? What, if anything, would I do about it? Nothing. Deep down, at some level I still liked Marc. Maybe he'd change.

After a string of cloudy days, a rare event in Arizona, I awoke to a beautiful sunny Sunday. Kim and I sat in Sambo's later that morning, drinking multiple cups of tea so weak, it was nothing more than tinted water—but we weren't there for the great tea. We were there to talk, away from the prying ears of family.

"My parents don't communicate well," Kim said. "They rarely talk to each other, and when they do, it turns into an argument about something that could have been avoided had they just talked to each other!"

I understood. I'd seen similar problems with mine. And then there were the times when my dad would yell at my mom, and she'd just take it—not defend herself, even when he was dead wrong. Not that I thought they'd divorce, but I worried what it said about marriage. Shouldn't communications always be open, without fear of reprisal? It made sense to me, but I wondered if it was possible after five, or even ten years of being together. I feared I'd become bitter about marriage, or lose interest in living, or a million other things. Maybe marriage would never be right for me.

With Kim and I talked out, I headed home to give my mom a hand preparing our usual big Sunday dinner.

Monday, I ran a few errands. I'd barely gotten home when I noticed the mail truck pull away. I waited for traffic to clear, and dashed over to see if there was anything in our box to make it worth the trip. The familiar handwriting I wanted to see was there.

I ripped open the envelope.

"I'm planning on coming to see you for two weeks in June," Ben wrote.

Two whole weeks!

"Let's go camping when I come. Can you do that? It would be great to have you all to myself for a week or so."

It would be great to have him all to myself, too . . . but there was no way I could pull that off as long as I still lived at home.

All logistics aside, every time Ben wrote, I fell in love with him all over again. I knew he loved me, too. Sometimes I couldn't imagine life without him. But then I worried. Was I deceiving myself that our love was the real thing, like I had deceived myself with Tom? I didn't think so, but then there were my confused feelings for Roy. It didn't matter how much I tried to justify, dismiss, or explain away those feelings, they were always there.

In the meantime, I hoped to hear from the Forest Service, because working was still a priority.

Saturday, I cut firewood with my mom in the morning, and in the afternoon, she headed out to the garden.

"Can I help?" I asked her.

"Sure, I need to clean up for spring planting . . ."

She pulled weeds, pruned the raspberry bushes, and mulched the strawberries. I turned over the soil with the pitchfork, tossing an occasional rock out of the planting bed. We didn't talk other than to coordinate our efforts, but I really enjoyed gardening with her. I also enjoyed the scent of freshly-turned earth, and looked forward to planting tomatoes and zucchini—two of our favorites.

In mid-April, I got the phone call I'd been waiting for.

"This is the Coronado National Forest in Tucson," the man said. "We are pleased to offer you a timekeeping position on the Santa Catalina Ranger District."

McKelsey came through! After accepting the offer, overjoyed, I wanted to dance around the house, but instead my thoughts whirled with plans to be made. They needed me to work at the district office in Tucson the first three weeks before I'd move up to Mount Lemmon. That meant I'd need a place to stay. Renting for three weeks was probably not feasible, or even possible. My older sister had been lecturing me for a long time about finding a real job. Well, hadn't I just done so? Would she help me out? This wouldn't be the same as when I stayed with her to look for work. This would be for a specific amount of time, and I'd help with rent and groceries. It would be for only three weeks. I swallowed my pride and called her.

Her reply: "No."

You'd think I'd asked her if I could use her car to commute from Earth to Mars. Afraid she might start lecturing me about the "unreasonable request," I slammed the receiver down in tears. *Now what?*

Five minutes later she called to say she'd changed her mind. After that exchange, I would've much rather gone somewhere else, but there wasn't any place else *to* go. But even with the problem of where to stay solved, I was scared and apprehensive as to what the future held in store for me. However, I recognized there wasn't one damn thing I could do about it—the future would be what it would be.

Chapter 17

THE CHORE OF packing for the three-week Tucson stay was easy; but I also had to plan for the move to Mount Lemmon, where I'd want my record player, albums, and guitar. Oddly, it wasn't leaving that had me all tied up into knots, nor was it the new job . . . it was not knowing when I'd be coming back. I mean, of course I wanted this job, and was excited about it, but it was hard to leave the familiar. How long would I be away from my friends? My mom? I would sure miss everyone, but especially my mom, since we'd grown much closer lately. I was afraid that I'd be lonely in this new job. Shouldn't I have been?

Sunday, my parents deposited me at my sister's apartment. I'd be sleeping on the couch, but I didn't care. It wouldn't be for long. Lucky for me, my sister lived close enough to my new job that I could ride my clunky three-speed bike the four blocks, thereby avoiding taking a bus, my least favorite mode of travel. I liked the freedom of coming and going when it suited me.

In the morning, I selected bicycle-friendly and office appropriate clothes—my best navy cords and a button-down white blouse—for my first day. A half-hour later I chained my bike to the rack outside the Santa Catalina District Office, and walked up the exterior staircase to the main entry. New job jitters—how I hated them. Transferring to Palisades in a few weeks couldn't come soon enough. At least up there I knew a few people.

I stood at the empty reception desk for ten minutes before someone noticed me. Once they figured out I was a new employee, a bushy-haired guy with a toothy grin escorted me to my supervisor Pat's office, where she explained what my job entailed.

"Mostly you'll be answering the phone. When you aren't doing that, you'll be filing and typing letters. Do you know how to use a multi-line phone?"

I'd never even seen one before.

"I'll show you . . ."

And off the day went.

What a day, I thought, pedaling my bike in the late afternoon heat to Cindy's apartment. Wiped out, I ate cereal for dinner, and sacked out on the couch early.

On Thursday, I overheard talk of a big goodbye party the coming Saturday in Sabino Canyon, a recreation area on our district. The flyer in my inbox had outlined the details of the Forest-wide picnic. I thought to go . . . until I read the cost to attend: Five dollars. I'd been saving my money to see my favorite musician, Jackson Browne, and there was no way I could do both. Jackson won.

At quitting time, I again pedaled to Cindy's apartment, feeling low and without a friend in the world. With everyone in the office excited and talking about the upcoming bash, I couldn't shake the feeling of being left out, even though it was my choice not to attend. The dark cloud in my head was so thick, that it took me a full hour to notice the letter from Ben on the counter, and two seconds to rip it open.

> *Hi Linda! I'm sorry for not having written sooner. I want to ask you something. What do you think about me reenlisting for another four years? With the job situation not looking so good, this would really be good for me, and us. You could go to the ports I go to . . . we could make it work. What are you doing for Christmas? I would love it if you could spend it with me at my mom's house in Syracuse. What do you think? I've been meaning to ask—what is your ring size? You like white gold, right?*

It was time to resume breathing before I passed out. His asking about white gold and my ring size must be a precursor to a marriage proposal. I floated around the apartment for hours . . . until a dreaded reality check, the kind that never bring good thoughts. I guess I'd figured the day would come soon that Ben would bring up engagement—but not this soon. Was I ready for this? Was I *really* ready for this? After stressing for over an hour, I decided to hold off making any decisions until he was here with me, when they'd be easier to make.

TELEPHONES. FOR THE first time in my life, I hated telephones. In this busy office, they never stopped ringing. I mean, *never*. It all started at 8:01.

I pressed the lighted button, saying, "Santa Catalina Ranger District, may I help you?"

"Yeah, I want to know if there are any campfire restrictions before we go up to Rose Canyon Lake to fish."

I had no idea.

"Let me check."

I pressed "hold," and punched Pat's extension.

"Are there any fire restrictions?" I asked her.

"Not right now."

I pushed "hold" again. "No, sir, there are no restrictions."

Next call: "I'm taking my scout troop up for a day hike and picnic. Are there any fire restrictions?"

"No ma'am, there aren't."

Three hours later, after answering the phone nonstop, my brain and mouth stopped coordinating with each other.

"Santa Catalanger Ristrict Dostrict may I halp you?"

Dead silence. "Uh . . . I thought I was calling the Forest Service?"

I gulped, and my cheeks warmed. *Oh, God.* "Yes sir, this is the Forest Service."

Desperate for some peace, at lunchtime, I found a quiet place without a phone so I could have thirty minutes of silence. Not that it helped. The sound of the phone ringing in my ears never let up—even when it wasn't ringing, and even when I wasn't at work.

I dodged five o'clock traffic by using a longer route through residential neighborhoods, pedaling slower than in the morning because of the afternoon heat. I locked up my bike, and trudged two flights of stairs to the apartment, tossing my daypack onto the couch. I sat down next to it and stared at the wall. My brain spun, but my body was too tired to move. The room's silence screamed at me. With only mail contact between friends and my mom, the loneliness was suffocating. Could I ever live alone and not be lonely? Okay, I wasn't quite living alone, but because my sister worked nights, we rarely saw each other. But maybe that was also a good thing. She wanted me out of the apartment. I hated living here. I wished I could leave—forever. Go to where I felt wanted. A couple of times out of desperation I'd asked McKelsey if I might be moving to Palisades sooner than planned, but he'd said no. I'd have to lay low until I could be out of her place.

A week later, which in truth felt like a month, Ben wrote with an update on his visit. The USS Enterprise would reach San Francisco soon, and he'd requested two weeks shore leave in July to come visit me. First San Francisco registered. *He's so close!* Then two weeks registered. *We'll have two weeks together!* And then July registered. *Oh. Not until July.* That was months away. I sighed, and reread the letter a few times to make sure I'd not missed anything. I had not.

How horribly those weeks dragged—but thank God my stint at the district office was finally up. Early Saturday morning, I packed up my belongings and paced the apartment. My parents had said they'd be along late in the day to transport me up the mountain, but I wanted to be prepared in case they arrived early. That left me with plenty of time to think. I hoped to have some time alone with my mom so I could tell her about Ben and me . . . and that we may be getting married. Of course I knew there was a huge difference between *thinking* about marriage and actually going through with it, but I'd only written to Gail about what he'd said about the ring, and thought I would burst if I didn't tell *someone*. I feared my mom's reaction because I hadn't said a word about Ben to her since he'd sent the tape. In a way I wanted to wait until Ben was here, but then again, I thought that wasn't enough fair warning to drop the marriage bomb, if there was one to drop. Now for the question I kept asking myself: Did knowing Ben loved me make me happier? Or was it simply because *someone* loved me? I began to fear that I was possibly in love with the idea of being in love. Why did love have to be so complicated?

At last my parents arrived to rescue my sister's carpet from my infernal pacing. My mom and I first went shopping for items I'd need, and then we all went out for pizza. As we waited for our order, I nabbed the opportunity.

"I'm heading to the restroom, Mom . . . want to join me?"

She paused for a second, and said, "Yes, I'd better go, too."

Thank goodness we were the only ones in there. I finished washing my hands, and waited for her to come out of the stall to do the same.

"Mom . . ."

She looked at me quizzically.

How to say this? Would she approve, disapprove, freak out, tell me I was nuts? It all came out in one big *whoosh.* "I think Ben may ask me to marry him."

Oh, God, there it is . . . I said the M word.

"Well, Lin, if that's what you want, then that's what I want. I only want you to be happy, dear."

What a relief she didn't fall over. Now another concern popped up. If Ben indeed came, would my mom like him? They'd never met. Would he be friendly and chatty, or silent and mysterious? She would not get silent and mysterious. Whether or not my dad liked him didn't matter . . . he always ignored my boyfriends. But I wanted my mom to love whomever I ended up with, and whomever I ended up with had to love her.

Chapter 18

MY GOVERNMENT QUARTERS on Mount Lemmon would be the same two-refrigerator trailer I'd had last year. Kathy, my new roommate, laughed when I told her the story of why the non-working one still occupied the kitchen, but scowled when I told her about the rude middle-of-the-night racket the working one made. Billy still lived across the way, and he gave me a ride up to the Radar Base to have dinner with the hot shot crew that evening. The warm welcome did wonders for my mood.

Wound-up from the busy day, I slept little that night. However, I didn't have a problem waking in the morning—I couldn't stand to lie there one minute longer, excited about going to work and seeing some of my friends on the fire crew again.

Now that all fire personnel were on-duty, I had over fifty T&As to fill out. Daunting, to say the least. After a few days, to help lighten the drudgery, I invented a game. I tried to imagine what each guy would look like based on his name. Would "Scott" be dark haired and slender? A beard? Someone named Harry most likely had a huskier build and short hair. Anyone named Charlie should wear glasses and have long hair. What fun to daydream . . . I couldn't wait to meet these guys to see if I was right.

Deep in a data mind-fog, at five, I headed down the short-cut path to my quarters. Lanky Billy caught up to me in a brisk trot.

"How 'bout a lift up to the Radar Base for dinner?"

Cooking and eating alone left much to be desired. "Sure! Give me five?"

After dinner, a bunch of us headed to the Mount Lemmon Inn for drinks. Blue cigarette-smoke haze filled the room, making it hard to see in the dim interior. Billy headed straight for the group of loud guys sitting at a long table in the center of the room, with me about three steps behind.

Twenty men made up the hot shot crew, and I'd met about ten of them so far. I recognized Scott, whom I'd seen around, but not yet been introduced to. Even though he didn't quite fit my imaginary version, I found him more than good-looking. The split second we made eye contact, a jolt of electricity zipped through me like I'd touched a bare wire.

"Here, Linda, have a seat," Billy said, bringing a chair over from another table, unfortunately too far from Scott.

I sat, and quietly absorbed the energy around me. It was hard to keep track of all the firefighting adventure stories going around, but enjoyable just the same. With everyone laughing, smiling, and occasionally teasing me about being the only single girl up here, I hoped to be invited to join them more often. It was easy to get caught-up in all of their attention. Besides, not one of my officemates offered anything like the camaraderie I'd found between these guys. I wanted to be included in their fun.

The lively conversations lasted until eleven. Billy dropped me off at my trailer, his headlights illuminating the way to my dark entrance. I'd be alone again tonight. Kathy rarely stayed, preferring to commute to Tucson to be with her fiancé. Fine by me—there really wasn't room in the trailer for two. Only one person could walk the narrow hall between the kitchen and bedroom/living area, and someone had to leave the kitchen for the other to cook.

Once in bed, I listened to the forest, its silence thundering between my ears. I'd never lived in a place so peaceful, quiet, and scenic. But I still couldn't sleep. It was all I could do to stop the whirlwind of thoughts and settle down. What a great time I had around here, to the point that it didn't feel like a job. Although cooped-up during the workday, at least all I had to do was open the door to nature. And then there was that chemistry I'd felt with Scott. Would he possibly get between me and Ben? *It's not like you haven't considered you and Ben not working out,* I thought, in an effort to justify my interest in getting to know Scott better. Besides, although Ben had asked me about my ring preference, he'd not said another word since. Was he having doubts too?

MY DAYS WERE filled with mind-numbing T&As, interrupted only by lunch and frequent trips to the pencil sharpener. I had to force myself not to clock watch, knowing that doing so would only make the day longer. My nights were spent either playing guitar with Billy, or hanging out with the hot shots up at the Inn. I'd never had a social life quite like this—in fact, until now, I didn't know what constituted a social life. Was this a social life? I guessed maybe it was.

Friday night, my roommate, Kathy, my supervisor, Inez, and I, went up to the Inn. We ordered drinks, and took them to an empty table. The jukebox played one of my favorite songs by Pure Prairie League, "Fire on the Mountain." The catchy beat made wish I knew Country-Western Swing dance. As soon as we sat, a guy I recognized from the Helitack crew plopped in the chair beside me.

"What's a nice girl like you doing in a place like this?" Duane asked, his expression deadpan.

I laughed. What a line. But I let it slide. Slender, with long dark hair and matching mustache, he looked a bit dashing, if not rogue. We talked over the loud music as best as we could, and eventually ended up outside, where somehow he convinced me to ride with him down to Sollers Point, the Helitack crew's base of operations. There, believe it or not, he also managed to talk me into sitting in the parked helicopter.

"Are you sure it's allowed?" I asked. After all, it didn't belong to the Forest Service. We must have been breaking every rule imaginable.

"No worries. Just don't push any buttons."

That was funny, so I laughed. "Okay, no pushing buttons."

Duane climbed into the pilot seat, while I hopped in next to him.

I'd never seen the inside of a helicopter before. Fascinated, I surveyed the complex instrument panel. Then I looked out the windshield, where the lights of Tucson sparkled in the distance. I imagined what it would be like to soar off into the dark sky—nothing short of fantastic, I figured.

"My job is far better than the hot shot crew's, I'll have you know," Duane said. "We fly to fires. Initial attack, first on the scene, man, that adrenalin rush . . . 'we stop 'em, you mop 'em.'"

I smiled. "Mop?"

"We don't stick around to put out hotspots. That's grunt labor."

He stared directly into my eyes. Self-conscious, I broke the connection by looking away.

The whole time, Duane did not let eye contact falter one second, making me nervous—but in a nice way. I knew he wanted to kiss me, but when he leaned over and did, I freaked out. *What in the hell am I doing with a guy I don't know?* I pressed my hands against his shoulders, and pushed. "No, please."

"C'mon, baby, what's the matter?" he asked, attempting another kiss. "Don't you like me?"

It wasn't about not liking him; I didn't like feeling pressured. "That's not the point," I said.

"Soooo . . . what is?"

Change the topic. "I didn't see you at the radar base for dinner. Do you guys cook for yourselves?"

He sighed and moved back to his seat. "I'm vegetarian. I make my own meals. Do you eat meat?"

"Sometimes. But not often . . ." I scrambled to say the right thing. "I mean rarely . . ." *Oh God, why am I worried about what he thinks?* In reality, I didn't care much for meat, but his accusatory tone irked me to the point that I wished I *did* eat more meat, just to annoy the heck out of him. But now, more than anything, I wanted to get out of this awkward situation and go to my quarters. "Well, it's getting late . . ."

Duane shook his fist as he said, "Do you realize how much eating meat destroys the environment? Not to mention the cruelty to animals. That's what's wrong with people like you. You don't care about the world. You should be more responsible . . ."

Not that I had an aversion to vegetables, in fact, I loved them, but I was developing an aversion to Duane. If it hadn't been so late, I would've walked home. Instead, I endured more lecturing while Duane gave me a ride to my trailer.

Once in my quarters, I gave *myself* a lecture about letting Duane kiss me. *You sure get yourself into some strange situations, don't you?* I took out my journal.

> *Oh, Ben, I don't know what to feel anymore. How I wish*
> *I had you to talk to, to help me understand my feelings about*
> *you. How much longer am I going to have to wait?*

AT MY DESK in the morning, slaving over T&As, I realized that all of my pencils were dull. Hadn't I just sharpened them? Inez interrupted my trip to fix the problem by handing over the phone. "It's for you."

For me?

"Hi Linda, it's Derek. We met at the Inn."

Derek . . . Oh! One of the hot shots. He was at least ten years older than the others; way too old for me. Puzzled, I wondered why he was calling me at work.

"Hi, yes, I remember you," I said.

"I'm going to Tucson Friday to run errands," he said. "I'd be happy to give you a ride if you need one."

As a matter of fact, it *was* hard for me to get to town to buy groceries and do laundry without a car. "That would be great!" I said, accepting this as a friendly offer to a car-less teenager.

Derek picked me up, and we chatted on the trip down the winding mountain road. Time went fast because we grocery shopped, walked around the University of Arizona campus, where I bought a couple of new albums at a discount record store, went to a movie, and ate dinner at McDonald's. Afterwards, we headed back up the mountain, continuing to talk for a while once in my trailer.

"Want to go up to the Inn?" Derek asked.

Why not? I loved hanging out there.

Friday night at the Inn was no different than any bar on a Friday night—the place was packed. Music from the jukebox competed with loud voices; people stood between tables, laughing and drinking. Derek wandered off. When I saw my roommate Kathy, I waved to get her attention. As she threaded her way toward me, I saw Scott, in animated form, talking to several of his crewmates. His eyes fleetingly met mine— our chemical connection still there and quite real—but oddly we didn't speak to each other. Thank God I only saw Duane once. When he approached me, I twiddled my fingers at him, said "Hello," and then turned my back saying, "Goodbye."

I didn't care what he thought.

In the morning, I awoke to a glorious summer day in the mountains, and decided it was time for a hike. Dressed in denim shorts and a work shirt tied at my waist instead of tucked-in, I laced my hiking boots, and headed up to the Mt. Bigelow fire lookout tower. I didn't climb up the stairs though, and returned the same way I went up. After the strenuous hike, and the late night, I took a much-needed nap.

An hour later, the sound of voices approaching the trailer woke me. Kathy, Billy, and his roommate, Ron, gathered in our combo living room-bedroom.

"We're hiking up to Bigelow Lookout to visit Wilma," Kathy said. "Want to come?"

It didn't matter I'd just done that hike a few hours ago. I laced up my boots yet again to go see Wilma, our fire lookout.

My first time climb up the seventy-five-foot-tall fire lookout tower scared me to death. In addition to the dizzying height, I feared the stiff breeze would blow me off the staircase. And holy cow, those metal-mesh steps made the ordeal ten times worse, because I could see through them to the hard, solid ground below—quite real and visceral. Partway up, though, I'd discovered that if I focused on the step directly in front of me, it wasn't too bad. Now, other than getting a bit winded, I climbed with ease.

The second hike differed from the first one in that I took my time, laughing and chatting with everyone. Ron was every bit as nice as Billy, but more boisterous, telling jokes that had us all in stitches.

Once at the tower, we climbed the steep switchback steps to where Wilma had laid out a spread of snacks, and opened a bottle of wine; all served in her ten by ten foot living space. After nibbling crackers, cheese, and apple slices, we sat on the catwalk with our wine to watch sunset, listening to night birds and the breeze rustling pines, talking softly to not disturb the tranquility.

If that wasn't enough for one day, Billy and Ron wanted to go to the Inn for more drinks. Tempted, but exhausted, I passed—which turned out to be a good thing in my crazy new world. If I'd joined them, I would have missed Harry, our Palisades Tanker foreman, who came over to play guitar for Kathy. Too shy to admit that I also played, especially around drop-dead adorable Harry, I simply listened as he filled our tiny space with great music.

After he left, Kathy rolled her eyes and crossed both hands over her heart. "Ooooo . . . that Harry. What a great musician. He has the most divine blue eyes I've ever seen. I swear, if I wasn't engaged . . ."

I smiled at her theatrics, but didn't admit to her that he affected me in the same way. However, what I saw, in essence, was a heartbreak time-bomb: gentle demeanor, kind blue eyes, dark, wavy hair, fantastic musician—way too "everything amazing" to bother with plain old me. Not to mention the fact he had a girlfriend in Tucson, making him totally off limits. Actually, I couldn't figure out why any of the guys up here bothered with me. All of this attention didn't fool me for a minute.

This was all about me being the only unattached girl at Palisades. The guys were bored. I couldn't imagine any other possible reason. Late at night I'd often wonder when I'd wake up and discover that nobody up here liked me after all.

AFTER DINNER THE next day, Kathy and I took the shortcut route through the forest to Sollers Point for a visit with the Helitack crew. Al greeted us at the door wearing an apron.

"We just finished dinner," he said. "I'm almost done with the dishes; c'mon in."

We took a seat in front of the stone fireplace, although on this mild night the hearth was cold. Duane was there, but I managed to sit between two guys I liked, thwarting his attempt to monopolize me by offering a chair at his side.

No way on this planet, Duane.

Last week, Al had asked me if I would be interested in cooking dinners for the crew.

"We were supposed to share cooking," he'd said, "but it's not working out. When it was Tim's turn, all he made was a giant pot of rice. That's it! Who wants to eat nothing but rice?" He fiddled with his handlebar mustache. "We'll pay you, don't worry 'bout that. We just need someone who can come up with something more interesting than rice. I'm a good cook, but I don't want to be stuck with cooking duty every single night."

Tonight I told him I would, thinking the extra money would be nice. The only thing that had me worried, though, was being around Duane. How would I be able to stay away from him, or rather, keep him away from me? I'd have to figure that out before starting.

Chapter 19

AT THE END of the month, I requested time-off to go home. Four whole days! My uncle and cousin would be visiting from California, and I wanted to see them. More than that, I missed my mom and my friends.

All caught up in this new, busy and thrilling life, I didn't have time to think about anything other than work, and after work, who would ask me out, and where they would take me. All of this attention was easy to get used to. Easy to get lost in. When I received a letter from Ben the day before my trip, my fun, carefree lifestyle screeched to a halt—much like I'd bumped the needle on my record player. *Oh. Ben.* It was at that moment I realized I'd not thought about him all week. This scared me into believing that I might not really be in love with him after all. Or maybe I was scared about letting my freedom go. What if I went ahead and dated the guys up here I had an interest in, and nothing worked out? Then I could say that Ben and I were meant to be together. Didn't that make sense?

From the office phone, I called Greyhound for their Prescott itinerary. The bored man on the line recited his reply as if he'd repeated it a thousand times that day: "We have one leaving at eight a.m., another one leaving at noon."

I paused. Why would I take the bus leaving at noon, when I could take the bus leaving at eight, and be there all the earlier? Billy, who'd offered to drive me to the bus station, had no problem with the early departure.

It wasn't until I arrived in Phoenix at eleven a.m. that I discovered my connecting bus to Prescott didn't leave for *six* hours. Six! Distraught, I called my mom collect to tell her that I'd be much later than I thought. After hanging up, I sat in one of those God-awful plastic chairs that were, in truth, seating torture chambers, which cut into the back of my legs and formed a painful arch in my back. What the heck would I do to pass the time? For the next fifteen minutes I rehearsed what I would tell the Greyhound reservation clerk for not clarifying that the earlier departure time didn't mean I'd arrive in Prescott any earlier—and ten minutes furious that I didn't think to ask.

Internal rant over, I noticed tiny televisions attached to a row of seats. For twenty-five cents I could watch TV for thirty minutes. I checked my wallet. Eight quarters. I watched *Star Trek* for an hour, and part of a movie. A bored passenger, probably suffering from the same fate as me, smiled my way. We talked for a while, which passed more time. That person left, and another sat down. We also chatted for a while. When my bus finally pulled out of the station, I leaned back into my seat and closed my eyes, completely wiped-out. *Finally.* Three hours later, in my room and in my own bed, I knew it was true: There's no place like home.

My relatives arrived at midnight. I staggered out of bed to greet them. Everyone stayed up late, slept in late, and after a breakfast of my mom's homemade waffles, I holed up in my room to call friends. Chuck wasn't home, so I left a message. Kim was home, and we went for a walk. Afterwards, I joined my family on an outing.

In a remote area of the rugged and forested Bradshaw Mountains south of Prescott, we parked roadside, and walked to a creek to pan for gold. Who in the world ever thought this could be profitable needed to check their priorities. Not only backbreaking to scoop up sand from the bottom of a running creek with the gold pan, but if you didn't sluice the mixture just right, any gold that you happened to pick up would end up back in the water. However, that day, I actually ended up with four whole gold flakes . . . not worth a dime, but of course I kept them.

Chuck finally found time to come visit Sunday after dinner, and we spent a couple hours catching up—not nearly enough time. He'd just left when former Mystery Guy, Marc, called.

"Hey! I really want to see you. Can I pick you up?"

When I settled into the passenger seat, he leaned over to hug me.

"I've really missed you," he said, steering his car away from the curb.

My eyes grew wide. *You did?*

"I've grown up a lot, and I respect you more now," he said. Then he turned towards me, his eyes giving me a once-over. "Man, you look great."

I'd lost seven pounds and felt great.

With his eyes wide, he asked, "Do you really have to leave tomorrow? Can't you stay longer?"

Staggered at this sudden need to spend time with me, I stumbled for words, and eventually found the ones necessary. "No, I have to be at work on Tuesday."

"That's a bummer."

We found a place to park, talked a while, kissed a while . . . and although his turnaround sure surprised me, I didn't see our relationship going anywhere. We'd given it a shot, and nothing had happened.

HOW BRUTAL TO return to work after being spoiled with four days off. At least the day went fast, mainly because Inez hadn't touched a single timesheet and the deadline loomed. This bugged me because she'd said she'd help out while I was gone, but what could I say? I stayed an hour late to get as many done as I could.

When I stepped into my trailer a little past six, Kathy, neighbors Ron and Billy, and Heartbreak Harry, were there drinking beer. I really liked Harry, but he drank more than anyone I'd ever met. That worried me. In my experience, people who drank too much usually had a sad reason inside for doing so. I recognized right away that could've been why I felt an attraction to Harry. I often found lost, sad souls attractive. Maybe because I knew what it was like to be lost and sad.

The next day, everyone except me had to attend a meeting, which left me alone in the office. I didn't get a lunch break until one, making it a long morning and a short afternoon. As usual, I ate my sandwich outside, enjoying the fresh air and a pleasant breeze.

Derek had offered to take me down the mountain to grocery shop, but Inez said she was going and that I was welcome. I called Derek to thank him for his offer, but that I had a ride.

"I see," he said, in a tone that told me it was far from okay. "What about dinner?"

I already had a date.

"Sorry, I can't," I said. "Maybe another time?"

The silence on his end made my insides squirm.

"So you're going out with someone else?"

"I have plans," I said, refusing to give more detail than that. No doubt in my mind: he was getting *much* too possessive over me. That's all I needed: someone else who wanted to tie me down. However, I definitely did not want any hurt feelings while I was here. Derek and

I had a hike planned for Saturday, so I'd have to find a way to make it clear that I considered us just friends.

Motivated by the fact that Marc had noticed I'd lost weight, I wanted to lose more. Before work the next morning, I pulled on jogging shorts, T-shirt, and sneakers, and ran the two miles to the Boy Scout camp facility down the forested road from my trailer and back. Although winded and sweaty at the end, the high from the workout and a nature-immersion-fix put me in a great mood. I promised myself I'd do that more often.

After a shower, I walked to the office, only to see quite a bit of activity near the government quarters. Guys in hardhats and carrying chain saws milled about; red flagging tied around a few tall pines fluttered in the breeze. *What's up?*

With T&As completed, I spent most of the morning watching the guys clear trees for a new building. Rather neat to see them screw things up, almost destroying a couple of housing units when one of the trees they cut fell the wrong way. That added some excitement to the day.

Derek and I hiked the Butterfly Trail on Saturday, one I'd wanted to explore since moving up here. The trailhead sign, visible from the office, had beckoned me nearly every day.

At first, my mind floated elsewhere, thinking about Ben coming soon, and Derek's ridiculous jealousy when he had no right to it. But later, I relaxed, and I found the words to tell Derek what needed to be said.

"I enjoy your company, but you must know that I want to keep us casual."

He did not smile. "Sure, okay."

Unwilling to deal with the uncomfortable moment one second longer, I changed the subject to the task at hand. Derek had brought along the used 35mm camera, and every accessory imaginable, that I'd agreed to buy from him for an unbelievable ninety dollars. He patiently explained all of the fancy features: aperture, F-stop, light meter, as well as using the telephoto and close-up lenses. Over the six-miles hiking deep into a lush conifer forest, I used up the entire thirty-six-print roll. We had a nice time, and I was glad I'd cleared the air about us.

After work the next day, Kathy and I watched the guys play volleyball until dark. On the way back, I stopped at the office to call home. Because I called collect, I kept it short. Just as my trailer came into view . . . *Damn!* Duane's jeep was parked in front. Apparently, I had the only record player within fifty miles, or so I assumed, as he had been using the lack of options as an excuse to show up, unannounced, to play his albums. What nerve to think he was welcome! But not going to my quarters to avoid him was *not* an option, so with a deep sigh, I continued.

Once inside, the smile I gave Kathy was by no means the same as the plastic one I gave Duane.

"Hey, Linda," she said, glancing to Duane. "Look who's here."

I crossed my arms. "I see that."

"It's about time you came home," Duane said. "I bought a new album and wanted to use your record player."

Kath and I ended up talking to him for ninety minutes, our eyes meeting, and rolling, on a regular basis.

In no time, I formed a permanent opinion of him: Creep!

Both of us were delighted when Duane said he had to go. In fact, we couldn't show him the door fast enough, and we burst into laughter seconds after he drove away.

"Oh my God, what an egotist," Kathy said, giggling breathlessly, with tears rolling down her cheeks.

"Did you notice how absolutely everything we talked about revolved around HIM?" I said, swiping away my own tears.

Kathy held her stomach, nodding, and continuing to laugh hysterically. Then she froze and stared at something next to the couch. "Oh no, he left his album!"

I stopped laughing. *No.* There was not one single doubt in my mind that he'd done this intentionally in order to return at another time, hoping to find me alone. Well, I'd fix that problem. I'd take it down to Sollers Point while he was at work.

Derek offered again a week later to take me to Tucson to run errands. I appreciated him helping me out. I'd no idea how I would've got these things done otherwise. After groceries, laundry, and stopping at the bank to cash my check, he suggested drinks at the bar where my favorite local band played.

I ordered a Tequila Sunrise; Derek, whiskey on the rocks. When the band took a break, he looked up from his drink. "So. I hear you've been hanging out with Harry."

This sounded like an accusation. I had to compose myself before speaking. "Is that a problem?"

"Yeah, well, I happen to know you also went out with Duane."

Even though that was far from true, this was none of his business. But he'd made it his business and that made me furious. "Look, I'm not going to defend myself because I don't have to."

Storms brewed in his eyes, and his jaw went rigid. End of discussion. End of evening.

"Here, you drive," he said, tossing me his keys once we were in the parking lot.

Because he was now in a foul mood, I figured it was a good idea.

We rode in silence through Tucson until reaching the winding mountain road up to Palisades. Derek folded his arms across his chest, and stared straight ahead. "I think you should know there are two guys up here talking about how you'll come around and go to bed with them."

My arms went weak, and I swerved toward the edge of the road. Derek offered to take the wheel. I let him.

After a few minutes, I found the nerve to ask: "Who said this?"

Derek glanced over at me before negotiating a curve. "I can't tell you."

I opened my mouth to protest.

"Actually," he said, "it was Billy and Ron."

The ground shifted under my feet like an earthquake registering 5.5 on the Richter scale. They were my friends! Or maybe not. Had I missed their intent? *I am such a naive idiot.*

Once in my quarters, the glowing hands on the clock next to my bed read three a.m. This whole mess made me realize how special Ben was. For sure he didn't think of me as a conquest to be won. How silly of me to assume that all guys had his integrity. If Billy and Ron thought of me as easy, what did the rest of the guys here think? Was I on their conquest list too?

When I saw Billy the next morning, at first I thought to keep my mouth shut, but the more I thought about what Derek had said, the madder I got. With jaw and fists clenched, I marched over to Billy's trailer and rapped on his door.

"We need to talk," I said when he opened it. Before he uttered a single word, I forged on. "Derek said you made a comment about how, sooner or later, I'd go to bed with you. Is that true?"

Billy's eyes widened. "What? No. Absolutely not."

Did I expect Billy to actually admit to his guilt? Maybe, maybe not, but I definitely felt relieved when he didn't. So there I sat, in the middle, hoping Billy had told me the truth, wondering why Derek would lie, and whether I should confront him too. The whole mess gave me a stomachache. Everything was getting way out of hand. What happened to my new, fun social life?

WHEN THE HOT shots hosted a party the next week, I bummed a ride with one of the guys. Once we piled out of the car, the large crowd already there intimidated me. Would anyone here care that I came?

Not a fan of beer, I filled a plastic cup with jug wine and attempted to mingle—which amounted to standing out of the way and people watching. Many of the guys I'd met before came up to talk to me, and soon I relaxed. I caught a glimpse of Scott a few times, the hot shot I'd met at the Inn. Each time I saw him, his eyes met mine, jump-starting my heart just like the first time we'd met. He made his way over to me, and waited patiently for my current conversation to end.

"Need a refill?" he asked after Ted moved on, pointing at my empty cup.

My hands trembled. *He actually came over to talk to me.* "Sure, thank you."

Two drinks and thirty minutes later, as far as Scott and I were concerned, there wasn't a soul at the party but the two of us. By the time he kissed me, I wondered what took him so long. With the wine throwing any caution or propriety out the window, we ended up in his British MGB sports car, making out for hours, the chemistry between us more powerful than anything I'd experienced since Roy. If someone had walked up on us, I doubt I would have even noticed.

Exhausted from being up all night, I slept until noon. I probably should have felt guilty about what happened with Scott, but instead I felt guilty that I didn't. I wanted to explore my strong attraction to him. That complications could arise didn't concern me. *I've got this.*

Scott had told me he would come over in the morning, but he hadn't showed up. Turned out he'd been dispatched to a fire with his crew. An offer to head up to the Inn made up for the disappointment. A group of firefighters who'd remained behind were already there, and I joined them. I took a seat at the crowded table, and presto, a glass of wine appeared in front of me. I reached for my purse.

"Paid for," the waitress said, gesturing toward a bearded member of the crew, who nodded and smiled. I also smiled, and mouthed, *Thank you.*

The topic of discussion at the table? Fire! Getting the call. The anticipation. Hiking in, raging flames, dense smoke, mishaps, screw-ups, accidents, and most of all, the pride in a job well done . . . I'd never heard of such exciting work. Of course they teased each other relentlessly, as guys do, even about events that didn't sound remotely humorous to me. But that didn't stop me from wanting to hear more. I began to think that they, and everyone else up here who worked outside, had a far better and more interesting job than I did. Caught up in the fun, I stayed up late and drank too much.

Being a little too hungover in the morning promised a long day at work. At my desk, I stared at the blurry numbers on my timesheets. Whenever the two-way radio squawked or a voice spoke too loud, you'd think someone crashed cymbals next to my ear. My preoccupation with my self-imposed pain was interrupted when a man burst through the front door, his face flushed, and his eyes wide. "There's a fire!"

Chapter 20

THERE'S A FIRE! Alarmed, I turned to Inez.

"Where?" she asked the man, her eyes wide.

He pointed toward the door. "Right over there!"

Inez and I bolted outside.

Fierce winds that day whipped tall pines like palm trees in a typhoon. A cloud of smoke swept into the station, stinging my eyes and making me cough. Fire snapped and crackled through tinder-dry pine needles, heading straight for our office. Inez dashed inside. Bewildered, it took me a moment to do the same.

McKelsey glared at Inez after she delivered the news, his eyes blazing. "Where in hell's the tanker crew?"

Poor Inez cringed, and blinked hard. I felt her pain. "Checking out an unattended campfire?" she said, raising her voice at the end as though a question.

He scowled. "Well Goddammit, get 'em the hell back here."

Not only was the tanker crew unavailable, but the hot shots were still fighting that fire elsewhere. Unbelievable. We had a fire at the fire station, and no firefighters were here!

Several tourists, who had come in for information, stood frozen in disbelief as Inez flew past them to the two-way radio. Caught up in the urgency, I wanted to help, but had no idea how.

Inez pressed the call button to hail Harry and his tanker crew. "Five-two-oh; Oh-five."

She stared at the mike, willing it to speak.

"Oh–five; five-two-oh," it spoke.

"Harry! We've got a fire! At the station!"

"Oh, c'mon Inez. I'm in no mood for this."

"Harry," she said, her voice terse. "Get back here *now*. I'm not kidding."

After she ended the call, McKelsey told us to evacuate the building. I dashed outside with everyone, where winds swirled the smoke through employee cabins and garage bays of the complex, driving more people outside in panic and confusion. Lookyloo drivers stopped in the middle of the road. *Great.* The last thing we needed was a car wreck.

My thoughts tumbled over each other like rocks in an avalanche. Should I make a mad dash to my trailer to grab stuff? *Oh, God, yes . . . my albums! Guitar! Journal!* Just as I turned to leave, the Palisades Tanker roared into the parking lot. Harry and his crew jumped out of the truck. One unrolled the hose; another started the pump, the motor sputtering and spitting out a backfire before it kicked-in. Sweat beaded-up on the canvas hose as it swelled with water, drawn from the two-hundred-gallon tank on board.

Instead of rescuing my belongings, I watched the crew hose down the flames. The odor of wet charcoal replaced that of smoke, steam now rising from the blackened ground.

With the excitement over, Inez and I walked together, with others murmuring and shaking their heads in wonderment as we returned to our desks.

"There'll be a fire investigation for sure," she said. "I'll bet money some careless tourist tossed a cigarette out the car window."

I'd not thought about how it started, but it sure couldn't have been lightning because there hadn't been any. When I returned to my timesheets, I realized adrenaline must work wonders for hangovers— my headache was completely gone.

FRIDAY, AFTER WORK, McKelsey called me into his office. This was rare, and I wondered what was up.

"Sit down," he said, shuffling papers on his desk. "We need to have a little talk."

Worried that I'd screwed up something important, my mind ran Olympic circles around what I could have possibly done.

"I'm hearing that you're sleeping around, and that has to stop."

My face blanched. *Did he really just ask me that?* I could not believe he just asked me that. *That's not true!*

His dark eyes stared me down. "Don't you get involved with any of the guys here."

"I . . . but . . . it's not . . . I didn't . . ."

Tears brimming, humiliated, I briskly walked to my trailer. *What the hell does that mean? That I can't associate with anyone?*

After the kind of crying that purges your wounded soul, I felt differently. *How dare he accuse of something I did not do! How dare he accuse me of being*—and this made me cringe—*a slut*. Besides, it wasn't any of his or the government's damned business what I did on my own time. Who'd been talking behind my back? Did jealousy somehow play a role in this rumor? I had a hard time believing anyone could possibly get jealous over me.

DESPITE SLAVING ALL day long with only a fifteen minute lunch break, my workload continued to back up. How would I ever get this done? Something had to give. After dinner, I snuck back to the office to work for a few hours—hours that I would not charge the government for because I wasn't allowed to work overtime.

Huddled over my task, to my surprise, the door swung open, and in walked Inez.

She stopped and stared at me. "What are you doing here so late?"

Busted. I slapped a completed timesheet on top of the pile. "There's just not enough time for me to finish these during my normal hours."

"You *do* know you aren't supposed to work overtime, don't you? You could get in trouble."

Sourly I thought, *Yeah, well, I already am, for something I didn't even do.*

I shrugged; she left.

After managing to make some progress, blurry-eyed and weary, I flicked off the lights and headed home. My throat felt a bit sore, and I had that overall cold-coming-on sensation. *Rats. Just what I don't need.* After a bowl of chicken soup, my cold-care standby, I went straight to bed, hoping to sleep off whatever the heck I was coming down with.

When I awoke in the morning, I felt like crap, but I had too much to do at work to stay in bed.

A few minutes past eight, Derek called. "How about dinner tonight?"

Foggy, stuffy, and feverish, I explained that I'd come down with a cold, and would have to pass.

At lunch, instead of my usual outdoor fix, I heated up more chicken soup, and after eating, went straight to bed. I fell comatose for a solid hour. When I woke up, I felt like a whole new person, as though I was starting the day from scratch.

Back at my desk, I attacked my workload, and made significant progress.

About a quarter to five, I had another phone call.

"I know it's short notice," Scott said, "but would you like to join me at the big dinner bash the hot shots are having tonight?"

With no problem ignoring McKelsey's ridiculous attempt to control my social life, delighted, I said, "Sure!"

At seven o'clock, there we were, sitting at a table amidst the jovial group, when Derek knelt down beside me, and said into my ear, "Go ahead and tell me to go to hell."

It took me several moments to get a grip. What was he doing here? Then it clicked: His earlier invitation was for *this* dinner party.

Embarrassed all to hell that I naively thought what I'd done was no big deal, I now realized I'd done something awful. "Oh! I'm so sorry . . . I didn't realize . . ."

Derek refused to hear me out, and he made a scene by storming out of the restaurant, leaving a wake of confused faces at neighboring tables. Thank goodness everyone went back to their conversations, while I tried my best not to dwell on Derek's actions. I wanted to enjoy being with Scott.

Much later, I lie in bed, sorting my evening. Scott struck me as quite intelligent, but not arrogant. Warm and funny, he was the best company I'd found so far up here. Not that I didn't like the other guys, it was just that I found us pleasantly compatible. Amazing—I knew Scott very little indeed, but I had to admit—he was the first one in a long time to come even close to making me forget about Ben. My eyes widened. *Oh. Yeah.* Ben. He'd be coming soon. How in the world would I deal with *that?*

At three a.m., the pounding racket on my door woke me from deep, dreamless slumber. Derek's muffled, but loud, voice penetrated the thin metal. "I want to talk to you. Open the door!"

Confused and trembling from the rude awakening, I'd barely done so when he barreled in past me. I stood in front of him, sleepy, disoriented, and feeling rather exposed in my summer nightgown.

"You lying little cheat!" he said, stabbing his right index finger at my face. "Am I not good enough for you? You little bitch. Every time I turn around I see you with another guy. What the hell is wrong with you? One man is not good enough? You have to go and screw all of them?"

Now fully awake, with my fingernails embedded painfully into my palms, it was all I could do not to scream at him. "What the hell are you talking about?"

"You know damn well what I'm talking about," he said. "You lied to me, saying you were sick!"

My faced paled. *Shit.* "Look," I said, truly embarrassed, "when you called I *was* not feeling well, but I felt better later and decided to go."

"Bullshit!" he said, pacing back and forth.

When his tirade continued with no sign of letting up, I let him have it, pointing at the door. "Get out! Now!"

Derek's eyes narrowed at me, and he marched out, slamming the door with so much force, the trailer shook.

It took me a while to calm down. I told myself that he was out of line, that he had not asked me on a date that I knew of, and besides, how dare he barge in and act like he owned me. At last, when I'd covered all of the defensive bases possible, I fell asleep.

Pre-dawn, awake, I forced myself to not think about Derek's rampage, but instead revisited my pleasant evening with Scott.

What did he say when we'd finished dinner and sat in his car? Oh yeah— he said he worried I might reject him. And how he hoped I wouldn't, because although we barely knew each other, he thought maybe he was falling in love with me.

Reject him? No. I was afraid that *he* would reject *me* after I fell in love with *him*. What scared me even more was how could I explain to Ben that I was filled with doubts more than ever. That it wasn't because I didn't love him, it was because I needed more time to date others before committing—to be sure we were right for each other. How in the world would I find it in me to tell him this?

Chapter 21

SCOTT DROPPED ME off at my trailer in the wee morning hours after we'd shared two days and two nights together. We'd dined at fancy restaurants, hit up the bar where my favorite local band played, and drove out a remote desert road to make out. We had such fun. Scott could make me laugh until my stomach hurt and my eyes watered. A first for me, and I loved it. And while we did sleep together, we did not make love. This was important to me. What was the rush?

Those days would have been perfect, except that his car broke down. Not once. Not twice. But three times. The first time, with me handing him tools as needed, he fixed it on the spot. We were on our way in less than a half-hour. Only eight hours later, it happened again. He figured out the problem, and made the repair in about an hour. What patience he had—he never uttered a single curse word. True, I was a little annoyed at the inconvenience, but hey, stuff happens. The third time, I hated his stupid car. I hated his car, but adored his infinite patience, and found our whirlwind emotionally charged relationship exhilarating.

Now to sort out why I had such a strong connection with him. For sure part of it was genuine laughter we shared. And no doubt the sexual energy, too. He made me feel wanted, desirable, and even sexy. To think that somehow he thought he loved me. I didn't know how that could be, but that's what he'd said. Our relationship amazed me. Could this be real love? But dammit, what about Ben? Wasn't that real love? What if, after all Ben and I had been through, I'd been wrong? Right at the point in my life when I thought I knew how it felt to be in love, I wondered if I'd been wrong. Maybe with Scott it was just infatuation . . . I didn't know. But at least I could say I'd always been honest with Scott. He knew about my dilemma, and that Ben would be coming to see me soon.

At dinner one of those two nights, Scott's and my normally lighthearted, laughter-filled conversation turned serious. Scott reached across the candlelit table and grasped both of my hands. "Look," he said, "when Ben comes I want you to spend time with him. As much as it takes. That is the only way you will be able to make a decision about whether he is right for you. If he is not, I'm here."

I nodded. What an amazing guy. I'd never met anyone with this level of understanding. However, that didn't stop me from stressing. I didn't know for sure if Ben was coming the next Tuesday, or not. *Dammit!* I didn't want to end my relationship with Ben—yet. How would he react when I explained my uncertainty? Many questions with no answers . . . I would have to wait and see what happened.

FRIDAY WAS MY day off, allowing me the luxury of sleeping in. Late morning, I hiked to Bigelow Lookout to visit with Wilma, who, although probably had twenty years on me, had become a friend. I admired her job up there in the tall tower.

When I arrived, she held up her new belly dancing costume.

"Inez and I are taking lessons," she said, laughing and sashaying the tasseled bra by its straps. "Do you want to join us?"

I couldn't imagine prim and proper Inez, who always wore the top button of her uniform fastened at her throat, in a belly dancing costume. Nor me, for that matter. I considered myself too fat to dare wear anything like that, but I did toy with the idea of joining them. It seemed like such an outrageous, fun, if not sexy as hell, thing to do. I told her I'd think about it.

Still tired from two late nights in a row, I didn't visit very long, and went to bed early.

At half past midnight, Derek scared the crap out of me by flinging my trailer door open and yelling, "You liar. You cheat. I saw Harry come over here at lunchtime. You can't fool me. You've got something going on with him."

I leapt out of bed. Dizzy from the abrupt awakening, I placed a hand on the wall to hold myself up. "Jesus, Derek. Harry and I had *lunch* together. You don't own me. We aren't even dating."

"Give me back the books I loaned you. *Now!*"

With a body-shaking fury that I didn't know I was capable of, I grabbed the books and shoved them at him—hard. "Get out! Get the hell out right now!"

Derek glared at me, his face red and contorted. He started to say something, but maybe thought better of it, because he fled without closing the door. I immediately closed it and turned the lock, my hands shaking and my heart pounding. I sat down on the couch, trying to compose myself. Would he return? I'd never make the mistake of leaving the door unlocked again, that's for sure. *I should report him.* But then I thought, *What good would that do?* No doubt McKelsey would find a way to blame *me*. I decided I would have to handle Derek on my own.

By the time I'd calmed down enough to go back to bed, it was time to go to work.

AFTER A RATHER long and busy day, I thought to just go home and rest before having to head out again. Tonight would be my first stab at cooking for the Helitack crew, but Harry invited me to play volleyball with the gang, and that sounded like way more fun than my original plan.

Sollers Point, our Helitack's base of operation and its crew's residence, wasn't too far from the ranger station using the shortcut trail. I made my way through the trees, detouring around an outcrop of lichen-covered granite. Swarms of tiny gnats buzzed around me, gathering warmth from the last of the sun's rays. I approached from the rear of the house, skirting around to the front door. It stood open, and voices drifted from inside.

"Hello?" I said, unsure if I should just walk in.

Al came out of the kitchen and waved his arm. "Hey! I bought ingredients for tacos."

Yum! I *loved* tacos.

The crew hung out in the living room, nodding and saying "Hi" as Al escorted me to the galley-style kitchen. No sign of Duane, thank God. It must have been his day off.

"Man-oh-man, I'm starving! We just got off a fire," Al said.

Although Al had said he didn't want to cook, he hovered as though he wanted to help. I suggested that he fry the corn tortillas filled with meat in a gigantic skillet, while I chopped lettuce and tomatoes, and shredded cheese. The sizzling aroma of ground beef mixed with heady Mexican spices made my stomach rumble in anticipation for something other than soup.

Once everything was ready, we ate companionably seated on benches at a long wooden table. Tacos are a messy business, but that is half the fun. What a great way to share food and laughter with these guys. Al gave me a lift after dinner so I wouldn't have to walk home. On the drive, we planned the next meal I'd prepare: spaghetti and meatballs.

Early on Sunday, my regular workday, Inez handed me the phone. "It's for you."

Thinking it must be Scott, I gave a cheerful, "Hello."

"So," Derek said. "I'm going to give you one chance to defend yourself."

It was all I could do to not burst out laughing. He was *not* calling to apologize for being a jerk, but to ask me if I want to defend myself? I made my reply short, concise, and clear: "No. Get lost or go to hell." I slammed the phone down.

Take your pick, asshole.

The next morning, I found a letter from Ben in my inbox.

"I'll be there on July second," he wrote. *"I can't wait to see you!"*

Oh. My. God. That's tomorrow. I stared into space, decidedly not overjoyed at the prospect of seeing him, but instead thoroughly petrified. What the hell was I going to do about Scott? Bordering on a panic attack, all changed when the Forest dispatcher reported a smoke. Inez radioed Harry: "We've got a fire!"

From the window, I watched the Palisades tanker crew speed out of the complex with lights flashing and siren wailing. One ear tuned to the radio as I worked, I listened to conversations between the dispatcher and crew. Would a ground crew be needed? Harry didn't think so.

If that wasn't enough, just a couple hours later the dispatcher called in yet another fire. This time, the hot shots went into action. More radio chatter about the location, size, dropping fire retardant, and using our and another district's helicopter to bucket water out of nearby Rose Canyon Lake to help extinguish the blaze. When the talking became routine, I again hovered over my beyond-dull timesheets.

A panic-stricken voice spoke over the radio: "Dispatcher, this is helicopter six-two-five. We are experiencing engine problems. Do you copy?"

"Yes we copy, six-two-five. What's the problem?"

Silence.

"Six-two-five?"

The pilot responded, his voice shaky. "We're going down!"

My brain caught up with the conversation. The helicopter was going to crash! I turned to Inez. "Did you hear—?"

But Inez wasn't listening to me. She sat ramrod straight, her eyes wide and her mouth open.

"Inez! Is it ours?" I asked, horrified that some of the guys I knew might die.

"Huh? Uh, no, it's not."

Relieved that no one on board was anybody I knew, now I worried about the safety of those that *were* on board.

Forest Service air traffic dialog returned to the fires, as the accident now fell under another authority. Dread made it impossible for me to work. *Oh, God, please let everyone be okay.*

Not thirty minutes later, the sky turned dark and menacing, giving me something new to worry about. I did not like the look of this one bit. Thunder rumbled. The motionless air felt thick, oppressive, as though in wait. The wait didn't last long. In an instant, rain torrents fell in sheets, and lightning popped like giant flashbulbs. Ear-splitting thunder rattled the windows. Furious wind bent pine trees in half. I stood staring out into the fury, hugging myself as rainwater flooded the parking lot, chilled not only from both the twenty-degree fall in temperature, but from fear. *How bad is this going to get?*

Inez walked up next to me. "Well, this is good. Those two fires aren't going anywhere now, and I doubt with this much rain any new ones got started."

She returned to her desk.

I stared in disbelief. *How can she be so calm?*

I sat, but couldn't concentrate. For sure I'd never look at our Helitack crew in quite the same way again. Those guys were my friends, and the thought that they could die doing their job sent an uneasy chill up and down my spine.

Chapter 22

MY STOMACH CHURNED. My emotions a complex mix of anxiety, anticipation, excitement, and fear. Ben was coming today. When would he arrive? What would I say? What would happen between us?

When I answered the knock on my door, I opened it to see Ben's handsome face. I reached out to touch his cheek in order to assure myself that this wasn't a dream. We didn't speak, but embraced, his body firm and real against mine. After we kissed, Ben gathered my hair at the nape of my neck, searching my into eyes with his. His love bore straight into my soul.

"Is it really you?" I asked, resting my fingers again on his cheek.

He nodded.

Deep emotions of joy overflowed, preventing my holding back of tears. *He's really here!* We embraced again, holding each other tight, neither of us wanting to let go.

Within a short time, though, my insides settled down. I'd never been so elated one minute and so uncertain the next. There was no comparing this visit to the one last year. That summer, I was madly in love with him, and believed that he was in love with me. This summer, although I felt confident that he felt the same, I didn't know if I did. Or rather, I knew that I didn't feel the same way, but I also didn't know if those feelings would return now that he was here.

Ben and I sat on the couch holding hands for two hours, filling the time with both conversation and lulls of silence. How *do* you make up for a year's worth of time apart? To counter the awkward moments, I took in my fill of the man sitting next to me. He'd not aged that I could tell. His tan was a bit darker, accentuating his blond hair. The horrid buzz-cut had grown out a little, thank goodness, as I'd always thought his long, silky hair was one of his best attributes. Weren't his muscles more defined? *Maybe.* All in all, he looked fantastic. What did he think of me . . . was I pretty enough?

Because Ben had hitchhiked up the mountain, we did the same to reach the campground a few miles up the road, where he would sleep. We'd never discussed him staying with me, and after McKelsey's lecture, even though I still believed my love life was none of his business, I decided it was best that he did not.

No sooner did we pitch his tent, than dark indigo clouds formed overhead and thunder grumbled. The air took on that major rain-is-coming sensation.

I stared at the ominous sky and held a palm up. A few giant raindrops wet my hand. "Uh-oh, it's gonna pour."

"Is there a restaurant close where we can grab something to eat?" Ben asked.

"In Summerhaven. Let's hope we can beat the storm."

So much for beating the storm. We got soaked standing roadside with thumbs out for a ride. Our rescue driver had a towel handy, and I used it to squeeze out some of the excess moisture in my hair before he dropped us off at The Vyne.

Ben opened the restaurant door for me, placing his hand on my low back as I walked in. We stood next to each other, waiting to be seated. I gave the place a cursory once over. Wouldn't you know it? The very first person I saw was the last person I expected, or wanted, to see at that moment. Scott and I locked eyes for a second before I forced mine to the floor, my knees buckling. When I looked up, Scott had vanished. I swallowed hard, and glanced over at Ben. Had he seen my reaction? I couldn't imagine how he missed it, but his behavior hadn't changed.

The waitress led us to a booth, and we sat across from each other. Struggling to compose myself, I had to sit on my hands to stop them from trembling. *Calm down.* Our server took drink orders and left menus. God, did I ever need a glass of wine. With food the last thing on my mind, I scanned the menu, decided on a grilled cheese sandwich, and pushed the laminated cardboard to the edge of the table. Somehow, my glass of wine vanished. Ben ordered me another one. Calmer, and lightheaded, I relaxed, determined to focus on Ben here, with me, right now.

"How long can you stay?" I asked.

"Ten days."

"Great!"

An interminably long period of silence passed. Ben studied his hands folded in front of him. I sipped my wine. I twirled the paper coaster on the table. I scanned the room, taking in people, the view outside, the wall decorations . . . Here I was, with the man I'd dreamed about, and had wanted to be with, for years, but couldn't ignore that my fleeting connection with Scott had again drawn me to him like a magnet to metal. I could still sense Scott's presence in the room, even though I assumed he'd long since left after seeing me with Ben. How could I get through this evening? When our food arrived, I nibbled my sandwich, which in truth caused a pain in my chest akin to trying to swallow a rock.

In the morning, Ben joined me on a hike to Bigelow Lookout. I introduced him to Wilma. She gave me a knowing and compassionate smile—I'd told her about my dilemma—but I knew she couldn't help me with my decision. This was my problem to solve.

After a short visit, Ben and I returned to my trailer. I sat on the couch; he sat cross-legged on the floor opposite me.

"I've never told anyone this . . . I have a kid somewhere in the world. It happened a long time ago." He lowered his head, offering nothing more.

He has a kid? I'd never given having children a single thought. What would that mean to us if we married? Would I have to deal with this child? Did I want to?

He'd confessed something very personal. I decided to do the same.

"I need to tell you something," I said, tapping into bravery I didn't know I had until now. "I dated this guy, Tom, for a while. I may have written to you about him. I slept with him. He wanted to get married, but he wasn't right for me. We broke up after you sent me the tape."

He sat quiet for several moments. "I won't judge you."

More silence followed while I considered telling him about Scott. But then it occurred to me that how I felt about Ben really didn't have much to do with Scott, in the sense that I wasn't sure where Scott and I were going, if anywhere. Instead, I told him the truth—that I needed my freedom, his understanding, and *time*, before making any commitments.

He paused for a split second. "You've got it all."

I took a deep breath, and felt tears form. *I don't deserve this.*

"Linda, I want us to be together, always, and yet if we don't work out, I'll be disappointed and hurt, but I'll accept that's the way it's meant to be."

Ben left soon after, and I crawled into bed. *No! This is not how things were supposed to turn out between us!* But the way I felt right then? A long ways from wanting to be what I thought of as "overly attached" to him or to anyone. I cared about Ben, and Scott, and even felt some kind of love for both of them. I still struggled with what was the real thing— the kind you read about, the kind everyone wants. What was "real" love as opposed to, for lack of a better word, "not real" love? Certainly real love is not based on infatuation . . . but how do you tell the difference when you are deep inside of the feeling?

The next work day just dragged on and on. At five, still feeling down, I trudged back to my trailer. Curled up on the couch, hugging my knees to my chest, my record player filled my space with Jerry Jeff Walker's lonesome blues.

Six o'clock. *Where is Ben?* It had been a stormy day with keen lightning and earth-shaking thunder. I feared whether he was dry, warm, and safe.

My thoughts wandered to Scott. Something he'd said the other night had hit me hard. Despite all of his talk about feeling love for me, he'd said that when fire season was over, we would go our separate ways. Seriously? How could you say you love someone in one breath, and in the next say "let's chalk it up to a summer romance?" For the first time since I'd been on this mountain, I looked into the future and saw things I didn't want to see. Things that could hurt me. And I had begun to believe that Scott could really, really hurt me. He said he loved me, but how many girls had he said that to? More importantly, what if I fell in love with him, and he walked away? What if I let go of Ben, only to find out that I shouldn't have? What if neither him nor Ben were right for me? Who was?

At six-thirty, Ben knocked on my door.

"I was so worried," I said after we sat down.

Ben gathered my hair at the nape of my neck, and captured my eyes with his. "I went for a walk, but had to find shelter to wait out the rain."

More than anything, I wanted the moment to be perfect, but again I found myself struggling to fill the awful silence. Finally, I mentioned our time at Nottingham High School in Syracuse.

"I wanted you to like me," I said, "but I thought you liked Sheri more."

Ben smiled. "I looked right through her to watch you."

He'd written that to me a long time ago, and it still made my insides melt. But while our reminiscing was wonderful, it also added to my confusion as to what was the right thing to do.

After we'd decided to head up to the Inn for dinner, I remembered something I had to do. "I told my mom I'd call tonight. The phone is in the office. I won't be long."

Despite my inner conflict, Ben and I planned to take a bus next week to Prescott for a few days. Everything about this decision felt wrong. *Why in the hell am I doing this?* I felt like I was following someone else's life plan for me—even though I'd prepared the plan—to be with someone I wasn't sure I was *supposed* to be with. Even more unsettling, I knew I would have to tell my mom that I didn't think Ben and I would be getting engaged—for now, anyway. Or maybe never. I hoped she wouldn't be too disappointed.

I settled in at Inez's phone, and dialed "O." Once my mom accepted the collect call, I said, "Ben is here, Mom, and we'd like to come up next week. Is that okay?"

"Of course! What day?"

Plans made, Ben and I hitched up to the Inn, where we found a small get-together of my coworkers, with everyone laughing and having a grand time. Several smiled at me when I approached.

"It's Kathy's birthday," someone said, "Come join us!"

They made room at the long table for two more chairs. It was easy for me to jump into the lively conversations, and several times I turned to Ben to smile and include him in the fun. But he'd have none of it. He sat there, staring at his hands on the table, super-quiet and reserved. I wanted him to engage with my friends so that they, and I, could see what a great guy he was. There I sat, with the one and only guy I thought could cure my loneliness, and I was L-O-N-E-L-Y. The entire evening I bordered on the edge of a meltdown. However, I still managed to put on a good show of being happy and having a good time—my forte.

Later that night, in bed, I still wanted to cry, but Kath was home, and, well, I didn't feel up to telling her what was going on, or having her ask me what was wrong, making me feel obligated to explain. I wanted to talk to Scott, but he wasn't around either. What I feared the most was on the verge of happening: my love for Ben had not been real after all. So many things tore at me. I'd changed over the past year. I wasn't a lovesick teen. I no longer needed to make a long-distance relationship work—I had Scott. Didn't I? While that should have been freeing, instead it made me hate myself for not having the guts to tell Ben what was really going on. I couldn't help feeling that we had been apart too long—maybe too long—to salvage anything . . . or maybe we never had anything to salvage in the first place. A soul-gutting revelation.

When I got home from work the next day, all of the emotional turmoil I'd been dealing with did me in. I collapsed onto the couch and curled up with my knees to my chest. *What a disaster I've made out of my life.* Tears began to fall. Once they started, I dissolved into choking sobs, my chest heaving and my breath coming in gasps. I cried because I did not feel love for Ben anymore, and I dreaded telling him the truth. That and a million other troubles swept out of me like a tsunami. A knock on my door halted a sob. I pulled a few tissues from the box, blew my nose, wiped away tears, and opened the door. One look at my face, a train wreck with swollen eyes and flushed skin, and Ben wrapped his arms tight around me. I sobbed on his shoulder for at least five minutes. Tears finally spent, I tried to explain.

"How can we make this work?" I said, my voice quavering. "You still have three more years in the Navy. We'll be lucky to see each other twice a year, if that . . ."

Ben did not speak. Emotionally drained to the point of exhaustion, I could barely hold my head up.

Ben stood, and said, "Look, you're beat, I'm beat. I'll let you rest. See you tomorrow." He kissed my forehead, and walked out the door.

Grateful that he didn't quiz or pressure me for answers, I fell into bed. No way could I sleep, though. Ben and I were heading to Prescott in the morning. I had no idea why I was following through with this trip, other than desperately needing to see and talk to my mom. Maybe distancing myself from Scott would help . . . would make things clearer. Maybe that distance would make a decision easier.

Early morning, Ben and I caught a ride with one of the hot shots, who dropped us off at the bus station. Once in Prescott, I nabbed the first opportunity to talk with my mom alone after Ben had gone for a walk. I sat on their bed while she folded laundry. I took a deep breath to begin.

"Mom, I don't know what to do. I thought I loved Ben, but now I'm not sure. Scott is wonderful to me, but I've wanted to be with Ben for so long, and now he's here . . . but I don't feel the same anymore. I don't know what to do."

Tears spilled down my cheeks, and it hurt to swallow.

"I know this is tough, hon," she said, sitting down beside me. "It will all work out for the best, though."

Although she didn't tell me what to do, she must have trusted that I would do the right thing. I *did* know what to do. I just didn't want to do it.

After dinner, Ben and I took a drive. I pulled off onto a remote forested dirt road, and parked. The moonless night added to the isolation and privacy. I unbuckled my seatbelt, and leaned against my door.

"You have all of the freedom you want," Ben said, glancing at me, and then lowering his eyes, "no matter what you want to do with it. If you want me to stay, I'll stay. If you feel it won't work, say so, and I'll be gone."

To hear this stated succinctly, and quite honestly touching on what I wanted from him, should've made me feel better, made ending us easier—but it didn't. It actually made things worse. I hated myself. Why couldn't love be simpler? Why couldn't I love him, be happy, and call it good enough? But no matter how hard I questioned why it hadn't worked out the way I thought it should have, the same answer always came back around: *Because it just doesn't work that way.*

On the return trip to Palisades with my parents the next morning, we watched a torrential storm rage outside the car windows. I worried whether we'd even get there. I'd always associated rain with my own tears, and today was no exception.

After my folks dropped Ben off at his camp, his last night before he'd return to San Francisco and his ship, he said, "I'll stop by your office in the morning to say goodbye." I nodded, and we hugged briefly. My parents then drove me to my quarters at Palisades. I waved as they drove off. Once their car was out of sight, I let myself into the office to call Scott. The sound of his voice grounded me like an anchor, something I desperately needed to keep me from drifting away into open ocean. My time with Ben had left me uncertain, un-centered, out of touch with myself—maybe even out of touch with reality.

"So good to hear your voice," Scott said. "You have no idea how much I've missed you. Wondering how it's going with you and Ben . . . wondering if you still want me the way I want you . . ."

Every nerve in my body tingled. Scott always managed to seduce me, even over the phone. I wanted to crawl into his bed.

"We've been super busy," he said. "Already been to a few fires since we talked last . . . you wouldn't believe what happened . . . stupid Forest "Circus" antics, as usual . . ."

I smiled at his comical nickname for the Forest Service. Listening to him, and more importantly, listening to my heart, I realized that although his voice centered me, what I felt for him was infatuation, or maybe just sexual attraction—but not real love. Many people preach about the difference between love and infatuation, and how to tell the difference. But what happens if you know the difference, and you KNOW what you feel is not love—does that mean you should end the relationship? I just didn't buy that. How I wished Scott would take me away on a trip. Maybe a long time together would help me decide. I needed to go somewhere—it was a beautiful, beautiful dream. *But a dream is all that it is, so forget it, Linda.*

AT THE END of a day filled with the paperwork I hated, the radio squawked an emergency. A boy had become separated from his family during a hike. Kathy left to join the search. Lost hikers happened often enough, so I figured he'd be found safe. When she came home after midnight, she plopped down on the edge of my bed, crying, appearing haggard and worn.

"It was dark, so no helicopter. Rugged road-less canyon, so no trucks. We had to carry him out on a stretcher." She sobbed, wiping tears with the back of her hand. "He was alive when we found him"—more ragged sobbing—"and dead before we reached the road."

She leaned to cry on my shoulder, and I wrapped an arm around her. I didn't know what to say. At that moment I realized that everything about my life up here: hanging out with the guys, going out on dates, even the awful confrontation with Derek, were all trivial compared to the many dangers and challenges my coworkers faced on a regular basis. Including loss of life. My own tears fell in sympathy for her pain, and for that poor boy who had died while on a simple day hike with his family.

It was a long night for both Kathy and me. My mind filled with the images that she had shared, and my heart filled with empathy for that poor boy's family made it hard to sleep. It was all I could do to drag myself to the office in the morning.

At my desk, every time the office door opened, I anticipated Ben walking in to say goodbye. My timesheet ritual did nothing to alleviate the increasing level of disappointment as the hours passed. By two o'clock, I slumped over my desk with the sad realization that he wasn't coming.

All night long I cried, hating that I hurt him, and feeling like a terrible, terrible person for having let go of the man I'd dreamed of for the past three years.

ABOUT A WEEK later, summer heat blazed, even in the mountains. Two hot shots invited me to hitchhike down the mountain for a swim at a Tucson YWCA. Always game for an adventure *and* swimming, I added cutoffs and a tank top over my swimsuit, tucked a rolled towel under my arm, slipped on my calf-sculpting Dr. Scholl's sandals, and joined the guys on the side of the road.

Not long after sticking out our thumbs, we had a ride to the base of the mountain. The next ride dropped us a short block from the pool. Good thing it wasn't too far. By the time we arrived at the Y, I dripped with sweat, and my feet hurt.

A large crowd bobbed in the water that blistering afternoon. We claimed spots with our towels. I peeled off my shorts and tank top, kicked off those torturous sandals, and after finding a suitable opening, jumped in, holding in a shriek at the shock of cold water on my hot skin. After I'd had enough of the chill, bumping into other swimmers, and chlorine strong enough to kill every germ imaginable and turn my hair green, I sunbathed on my towel. I hopped back into the water on occasion to cool down until late afternoon. At four, we gathered up our belongings, and began our quest for the return trip.

An Oldsmobile pulled over soon after we assumed "the pose," and the three of us piled into the backseat. The dark-eyed driver studied me from the rearview mirror.

"Hey, aren't you Bill Strader's daughter?"

My mouth fell open. *You know my dad?* I studied his face. He looked vaguely familiar. Had I met him at my dad's company picnic? *Oh, good*

God, yes. What were the odds that I'd get picked up by someone who knew my dad . . . who'd kill me if he knew I'd been hitchhiking? Never good at lying, I stuttered: "Yes . . ." wondering about the consequences of admitting this damning information.

The driver turned to me and grinned. "Don't worry, I won't tell."

What a relief—but now we had another little problem. He wasn't going up the mountain. In fact, no one was driving the twisting mountain road this late at night. We stood on the side of the road with thumbs out, watching cars whiz by for two long hours. Finally, we gave up, and walked to a Quik Mart. Exhausted, hot, hungry, and cranky, I sat down on the curb while one of the guys made a phone call. After the promise of beer and pizza as payment—we had our ride. That fiasco, although an adventure of sorts, convinced me that my hitchhiking days were done.

The end of the week had me holding the plain white envelope from Ben in my hands for a few moments, studying it, turning it over a few times, hoping that just by doing so I would know what he wrote. I tore it open. Scanning each sentence, I looked for some kind of justifiable reason why he didn't come say goodbye that day. When I read his excuse—that he "hated goodbyes"—I stared in disbelief. I wanted more. I wanted some kind of emergency, something . . . well, catastrophic . . . that justified him leaving as he did. Or maybe deep inside I wanted to lay the blame on him for ending us, and not on me. The rest of the letter didn't even register. *Okay*, I thought. *Either he's lying or it's true.* Either way, I knew I would never see him again. I'd broken his heart. What caught me off guard, though, was I actually felt better not having to wonder about where we were going, or not going, anymore. More importantly, I no longer felt guilty about my relationship with Scott.

"LET'S GET AWAY for a while," Scott said one night while we were hanging out on the couch.

I sat up straight and shrieked with glee. "Really? Yes! Oh yes! Where to?"

"I've always wanted to hit up every mountain range in Southern Arizona. Let's see how many we can visit in four days."

Thrilled at the idea of traveling alone with him, something I'd thought about since we'd met, I forced myself to contain my enthusiasm. I had to be realistic. For him to get time off during fire season would not be easy, if not impossible. All it would take was one fire call anywhere near our planned departure day, and the romantic adventure wouldn't happen. Regardless, with a map spread on my teeny kitchen table, we planned our route. That done, we decided to visit Wilma, driving instead of hiking the trail.

"What brings you up here?" Wilma asked, smiling, as we emerged through the hatch in her floor.

"We decided to come up and visit. Is that okay?" I asked. I didn't want to impose.

"Of course! I love company. Have a seat. I'll open a bottle of wine."

Scott and I sat on her cot, the only place in the tower to sit aside from her glass-footed stool.

"Did you guys hear there's a fire in the Huachuca Mountains?" she asked as she unscrewed the cork and poured red wine into juice glasses.

I moaned internally . . . *Noooo* . . .

"It's not too big yet," she said. "Let's sit on the catwalk. We can see it from there."

The fire's glow on the horizon mirrored the warm colors of sunset. Despite knowing the destruction, I couldn't deny that flames at night were spectacular. We sipped wine, watched and conversed, listening to Forest Service radio chatter on the fire's status. Scott's anticipation about going to a fire was contagious, eating away at my stomach.

At work the next morning, I plunked down in my chair to begin the drudgery of data entry. Inez swiveled her chair to face me. "Did you hear the hot shots got sent to a fire last night?"

Well, that just figures. Would Scott be back in time? We were supposed to leave in three days. Well, nothing to do but wait and see.

Two days later, still no sign of Scott. I walked home after work, my head hanging, assuming our trip had been cancelled. A guy dressed in a yellow ash-smudged fire shirt and blue jeans sat on my doorstep. Scott stood up to greet me. "Hi beautiful, I'm back."

Delighted, I threw my arms around him as he wrapped his around me. Passionate kissing made up for the temporary disappointment.

After I'd made dinner for us, with it being a lovely evening, we decided to go for a walk. Strolling down the quiet dirt road behind my trailer park, we held hands, speaking in soft voices.

"What do you think about our future?" he asked. "I mean, we should probably discuss moving in together, don't you think?"

I had no qualms about exploring the idea of living with a guy instead of getting married, but this seemed premature to me. The truth? I was not ready or looking for anything more than I already had with him. And I felt quite lucky with what I had.

I smiled at him. "We'll see."

Right after work the next day I added my small suitcase to the camping equipment Scott had piled into the back of his compact sports car. We were both laughing and full of excitement about getting away from work.

All was good for about two hours as we motored along State Route 77, with Scott talking about the fire he'd been to in Idaho. What would it be like to travel to Western forests? To work outside? Far more interesting and exciting than sitting at a desk all day.

"You shoulda seen the forests up there," Scott was saying. "Pines over a hundred feet tall! Creeks everywhere. Too bad the smoke drove away all the wildlife—"

A loud *thunk* echoed from under the hood, and the engine died.

We coasted to the side of the road.

"What was that?" I asked, terrified that the car was majorly broken— as opposed to minorly can-be-fixed-in-thirty-minutes broken.

"I don't know," Scott said, frowning. "We're a couple of miles from the nearest town. It'll be dark soon. I'll check the problem out when it's light. We'll be fine. Don't worry."

There we were, stranded in the middle of nowhere, outside of Mammoth, Arizona, population of maybe a hundred, and now, temporarily, I hoped, one-hundred-and-two. With it being way past the bedtime of any small town resident, we opted to sleep in the car. If we were lucky, Mammoth had an auto parts store. If we were lottery-winning-lucky, they'd have the part we needed.

Considering that his car barely had enough room to sit in, much less sleep in, we spread our sleeping bags on the hot ground. But sleep? No, we did not sleep. At least I know I didn't. With the temperature over ninety and the humidity high, sweat tricked down my temples. I stared at the sky, wide awake, paranoid about biting ants, stinging scorpions, and venomous snakes. At least those worries helped me ignore the rocks poking my right hip.

At daylight, Scott raised the car hood and studied the situation. "Hmmm . . . it's no biggie. I've got the tools to fix it. We just need this "do-hickey" here."

Okay, he didn't say "do-hickey," but he might as well have, because I had no idea what he was talking about.

Before the sun threatened to bake us into a casserole, we walked the mile to town, where, lo and behold, we found an auto parts store. "Open 8 to 5," the sign read.

Scott looked at his watch, and then to me, "It's only six."

We sat down on the stoop to wait.

Scott whistled a tune. I leaned against the door, and closed my eyes. Not only was I tired and cranky, but I desperately wanted to use a bathroom, brush my teeth, and wash the stickiness off my face. At seven-thirty, we heard sounds coming from inside the building. A face in the front window seemed to notice us, and seconds later, the door opened.

"You folks look like you've got a problem," the old man said.

Although he didn't smile, I swore there was a hint of kindness in his eyes.

"Yeah," Scott said, "we broke down last night. I need a part for my MGB . . ."

"Well, well . . . c'mon in and let me see if I can help you young 'uns."

I have no doubt my eyes were pleading: *Please, please be able to help us.*

Scott and I sat on stools at the counter while the kind man flipped through a parts catalog. He scratched his graying stubble. "You lucked out."

Unbelievable. Kind Man actually had the part for a car that was older than me. Okay, maybe not that old, but for as many times as it had quit on us, that seemed about right.

Once on the road, I napped for an hour. When I awoke, we'd left the desert behind, and had begun the climb into the scenic White Mountains. Both sleep and cooler air tinged with the scent of pine improved my mood ten-fold. I smiled and laughed with Scott about last night's adventure, and took in the romantic scenery of evergreens, wildflower strewn meadows, and puffy cumulus clouds overhead.

Once at Hawley Lake, we pitched our tent on pine-needle covered ground, and ate the sandwiches we'd picked up at the town market.

Tired, we didn't talk much, and crawled into our sleeping bags early, falling asleep without even kissing goodnight.

Birdsong accompanied Scott's voice. "Good morning, beautiful," he said when I stirred.

"What time is it?" I asked.

"Five."

"Oh."

"If we're going to keep to our schedule, we'd better get up."

I agreed, and dressed.

So much for our romantic stay at Hawley Lake. *Thanks to you, stupid car,* I thought, wanting to kick its tire for good measure.

Our goal when we'd mapped our trip was to visit at least three mountain ranges in Southern Arizona. The next one was a good four-hour drive away, taking us back into the low desert before climbing high again. So far this trip had been nothing like I'd thought it would be. I'd expected more romance. I wanted impromptu kissing, love-making, fun, campfire-side conversations, and for us to spend time exploring scenic mountain trails. However, we hardly talked, and the hike I'd hoped for in the White Mountains hadn't happened. Because we'd left early, I hoped that at least we'd have time to go for a hike at our next destination.

At the large—by Arizona standards—busy Riggs Lake in the Pinaleño Mountains, we pitched our tent in a stunning Alpine forest. Who knew Blue Spruce grew in Southern Arizona? Not me.

I waited for Scott to suggest a hike or at least a walk around the lake, but instead, he kept to himself, propping up against a Douglas fir tree with a book in hand. I frowned. *This is no fun.* Then I decided that I'd been negligent about writing in my journal thus far, and figured I could catch up on my entries. An hour later, Scott was still engrossed in his book.

"I'm going for a walk," I said, standing up and stretching. "Want to come?"

"Hmm? No, you go ahead."

I walked away, deeply disappointed. This reminded me of an old married couple, comfortable and complacent, no longer feeling the need to spend time with each other. I mulled over a big question: *Is this what I want in a relationship?*

The drive home was quiet and thoughtful for me. I didn't know how to place my feelings for Scott, especially when our trip hadn't gone the way I'd envisioned. Not willing to give up just yet, I thought about the big picture. Scott said he loved me—and I believed that he did. I also thought that he loved me too much. What was too much? At that point, probably where it included exclusivity . . . something I did not feel prepared to give. I liked my freedom. I didn't like the idea of being tied down to him, or anyone. How I wished Scott and I could stay good friends . . . maybe things between us could work. But we were not just friends, and there was no backing-up.

Chapter 23

WHAT A PAIN to return to the working world of never-ending dull pencils, ringing phones, and timesheets. To make it all worse, McKelsey was in a foul mood, and it seemed like everything I did pissed him off. Late morning, when he sent me off to fill in for Wilma, I fumed. *Well isn't this just great. I'm gonna be stuck in the tower, bored and alone.* I cursed him as I tackled the seventy-five-foot tall structure, my eyes following the steep, metal, switchback stairs to the small square building on top.

I'd always marveled at Wilma's ability to stay in the tiny cubicle all day without going stir-crazy. Granted, she spotted a fire once in a while, which was the whole point of her being up there. No doubt that added some excitement to her day. Now that I'd be up there all afternoon, I wondered what in the heck I'd do with no one to talk to and nothing to do. Not that I'd miss paperwork, but at least it was something to keep my mind occupied.

Once I reached the hatch in the floor, Wilma gave me a hand up.

"I'll give you a quick overview," she said, walking me over to the equipment in the middle of the room. The Firefinder resembled a Lazy Susan of sorts, but with a ring for the turntable and a map underneath. She explained how I could locate a fire fairly accurately this way. "You'd need another lookout for triangulation and a more accurate reading, though. But don't worry, if you can give an approximate location to the dispatcher, our fire crew shouldn't have a problem."

I had no idea I'd have this much responsibility today. Not that I didn't think I could handle it, but I worried that with one minor screw-up, McKelsey would be even madder at me. Then I noticed something I'd not noticed before.

"Um . . . where's the bathroom?"

Wilma smiled. "The outhouse is down below."

Based on that new information and the long climb, I'd not be drinking much water.

Wilma raised a finger. "Oh, and most importantly, during a thunderstorm, you *must* sit on the stool until it's over. The glass feet will protect you from electrocution by lightning."

Electrocution? Maybe McKelsey really *was* trying to get rid of me—permanently.

Wilma left me to my duties, which included radio check-in, something I'd heard Inez do each morning. I decided to practice before the real thing. After a few attempts, I thought I had it down pat, but when the dispatcher began his query of all seven lookouts on the Coronado, he caught me off-guard by hailing Bigelow second. Jittery, I pressed the button on the microphone and squeaked out a feeble and far-from-confident-sounding "in-service" response: "Ten-eight?"

The dispatcher paused.

I cringed. *I sounded awful.*

"Ten-four, Bigelow," he said, moving on to the next lookout.

Mortified, I prayed McKelsey hadn't heard that, or any of the hot shots I knew, for two completely different reasons.

I'd brought a book up with me because Wilma said I could, but I didn't really want to read. The 360-degree view was something I could look at all day. The mounded form of the Rincon Mountains edged Tucson's eastern boundary, and even farther on the horizon there were other ranges, purple and hazy, one of which I figured were the Pinaleños, where Scott and I had just visited. I checked the map to identify the mountains to the south. They were the Santa Rita Mountains, a range I'd not yet visited.

At noon, I ate my cheese sandwich on the catwalk, watching white woolly clouds quickly turn dark and ominous, dropping the tower into a false night. Thunder rumbled. *Okay, time to go inside and get on the stool.*

Perched with my feet poised on the rungs, I waited.

Lightning streaked across the sky. Thunder boomed and rumbled. Electricity danced from cloud-to-cloud, followed by a brief explosion of pulsating light, illuminating a silver lining inside the towering thunderhead. A sizzling bolt hit the ground, hard, and my stomach lurched. *Geez! That was too close!* All at once there came an ear-shattering clap accompanied by a loud pop—as though the sky had fractured open. The tower shook, rattling the windows. Rumblings rolled off into the distance, reverberating for miles. I stayed planted firmly on the stool, my hands gripping the edge. Rain turned into marble-sized hail, pelting the windows, almost deafening as it drummed on the tin roof. I squeezed my hands over my ears. *Enough already!*

After a mere forty-five minutes, which felt like much longer, the sun peeked through breaks in the clouds, sending out silvery rays. Daring to step down off my stool, I grabbed the binoculars—time to look for smoke.

Once outside, I shivered, rubbing my hands on my upper arms. I'd not thought to bring a jacket. An aromatic mixture of wet pine needles and soaked earth permeated the brisk air. A few drops of cold rainwater dripped off the edges of the tin roof onto my hair, and I swept them off. At the railing of the catwalk, I peered through the lenses, scanning the forest. I zeroed-in on a smoke-like entity suspended between the pines, motionless, like a giant, white, floating comma.

Wilma had explained the different kinds of smoke I might see. Wood made white smoke, but so did those pesky water dogs, which weren't smoke, but an anomaly that formed when cold rain hit warm soil. *Is this a water dog?* I sure didn't want to get into trouble for reporting a false alarm—or worse yet, not reporting a fire. The hazy form didn't move, and because smoke would have, I decided it was just a water dog.

After I was told I could go home, I made my way down the steep steps, and drove to my trailer. What a day. And here I'd thought Wilma had a cushy job. *She has more guts than I'll ever have,* I thought, climbing into bed.

ON A SATURDAY in late August, with my summer job over, I packed up my belongings. My parents would be picking me up soon. In the meantime, I had something important to do. I snatched the blank timesheet I'd swiped from work, a book of matches from the kitchen, and went outside to my gravel driveway. After scoping-out the trailer park and not seeing a soul, I tore the timesheet into pieces, held a lit match to the heap, and joyfully watched the paper catch into brief flames, leaving behind fluttery black ashes.

Good riddance and never again!

Next summer would be different. I planned to apply with the Forest Service, but for an outdoor job. I admired Wilma's fire lookout position, but most of the time it had to be pretty boring. Maybe I could be a fire prevention technician, like Kathy, but that required a considerable amount of windshield time. The hot shots had an exciting line of work.

Plus, they traveled a lot. I'd always wanted to see the West, and what better way to do so while getting paid? I was open to possibilities, but one thing for sure: No more office work.

With still a few more hours to wait, I sat on my front step, reflecting. It was hard to leave, not only because I hated the thought of being unemployed again, but I'd miss the friends I'd made here. I also wondered what would happen with Scott. Would the distance between us help me define our relationship, or should I forget the whole thing and chalk it up to a summer romance and nothing more? Despite all that had happened between us, I'd not forgotten him saying just such a thing not that long ago. Did he still feel that way?

I'D MADE ENOUGH money to open my first savings account, and had accumulated a modest sum. I figured that until I returned to the Forest Service in the spring, enrolling in classes at Yavapai College would be good for me. First off, I'd take music theory, the subject I'd been denied at Prescott High because only band members were allowed. I thought a class in watercolor painting would be fun to explore, and the one in architectural drafting might improve my perspective drawing skills.

When I took a seat in Mr. Longfield's music theory class, I couldn't help but notice I was the only girl out of the ten students. Not that it bothered me, but I did think it odd. My class in architectural drafting had only one other girl out of twenty, and that also struck me as odd. Did only guys want to learn such skills?

Scott called daily, saying he wanted to come visit me. I didn't quite believe him, which is why he surprised me by doing just that the very next weekend. We went hiking amidst one of my favorite boulder-hopping places at Watson Lake. I had fun—taking in Scott's rapt attention, the breeze at the just right temperature, and the clearest-of-blue sky above. We sat on top of one of the "big guys" for a break. Scott put his arm around me.

"Have you seen Roy?" he asked.

I stopped breathing. That sure caught me off guard—but it probably shouldn't have. Shortly after we'd met, I'd filled Scott in a bit about the tumultuous relationship with Roy.

"Why, no, I haven't . . ." I said casually, despite the fact that the mere mention of Roy's name made my heart jump out of my chest. *Damn it all.* Why did hearing Roy's name throw me like that? What to say? What to admit to?

A few seconds passed before he spoke again. "It's just that I can't help but have concerns that you'll reconnect with him now that you're back in Prescott."

"I have no lingering feelings for him," I said, knowing it was an out-and-out lie. Roy *did* still occupy a place in my heart. No matter what he thought of me, or hated of me, I'd always be able to say, "Sure Roy, let's be friends," should he ever ask me if we could be. But how ridiculous. The chance he'd ever speak to me again was beyond remote—it was an unrealistic fantasy.

Scott ended up staying longer than he'd planned, thanks to his unreliable, always broken, car. This extended stay worked out okay for the most part, except that I longed to be alone to think without him around, especially when Scott's concerns were confirmed after I saw a guy in the Cornet store parking lot who resembled Roy; so much so, that my hands shook, and beads of perspiration formed on my upper lip. Why in Heaven's name did I think about Roy so much? He'd brought me so much pain. I was sick of thinking about him—sick of torturing myself over him.

Car repair made, Scott returned to Tucson, and I sat glumly in my bedroom wondering what would happen next. My soul felt empty. My life felt empty. I had Scott, even though I had doubts about our relationship, and Chuck, who was a good, close friend. However, so far, nothing had filled the huge void residing inside of me. And I didn't even know what or who would, or could, fill it.

I'd been thinking about what kind of relationship I wanted for a lifetime thing. Scott fit in many ways, but in other ways he didn't. For one, I considered myself a music freak. Simply put: I lived and breathed music. Music had to be present in some form every day. And I needed to be around someone who felt the same way. Otherwise, I worried that I'd lose the desire to keep playing guitar. It was okay with me if he wasn't into art . . . but if he didn't like music—that was another matter. It wasn't like I could keep this important part of my life silent. I knew I'd be lost without it.

Needing advice, I called Chuck.

"I don't know what to do," I said, after we'd caught up with what was new. "I fear Scott is too hung up on me, and I don't want that."

"Well . . ." he said softly, "I can see why he would be."

Caught off guard by this unexpected compliment, I went speechless for a moment. I smiled. *How nice* . . . and then forged on with my dilemma. "I . . . umm . . . was thinking of maybe writing Scott a letter, expressing my concerns and doubts. What do you think?"

After a thoughtful pause, Chuck said, "I think that's a good plan."

We said goodbye, and I opened my desk drawer for stationary, and stayed up late composing just such a letter. Out it went in the morning to our mailbox with the red flag raised.

When Scott called days later, he didn't mention the letter. After about ten minutes, I asked if he'd received it, and if so, what he thought.

"I'm not going to worry about it," he said. "First off, I'm not as serious about you as you think I am."

Really? I had reservations about believing that line; the one I'd heard before—which always turned out to be a lie. Well, maybe not a lie, but a definitely a cover-up of true feelings. Weary of trying to keep guys from tying me down, I guessed I'd have to keep untying those ties, for if I didn't, I'd end up in a big unworkable *knot*. I decided not to lose sleep over it. I would let things fall where they may.

With Scott in Tucson, my thoughts continued to drift to Roy. Everything reminded me of him: Places, songs, other people, movies. I recognized the problems associated with spending too much time thinking of him, but I didn't know how to stop. For all I knew, he had that girl with him now, and he'd erased me from his memory. Somehow I knew I'd never lose all the hurt and disappointment that we'd not worked out. I'd always keep the memories of the great times we'd had together in my heart. I'd never forget him. Ever. The magic I felt around him was still, and probably always would be, present. I never understood why things between us happened the way they did, but after much reflection I knew—that if I went back in time, somehow things would have still worked out exactly the same. Sure, there would have been a few left turns instead of rights, but it was obvious we weren't meant to be together. However, as philosophical, logical, and mature as that sounded—I missed him. I still loved him.

Chapter 24

WHAT A DISAPPOINTMENT that the architectural drafting class turned out to be too technical for my purposes, and quite boring. But the watercolor class was another story.

Betty Jean sat next to me the first day. She offered a warm, friendly smile, to which I responded in kind. The connection between us was mutual and instantaneous. With the class lasting three hours, we had plenty of time to talk. When the instructor arranged for a class field trip to the towns of Jerome and Sedona, Betty Jean and I agreed to sit together on the bus. Such a great time we had! Jerome, that old mining town where I'd gone to Spook Night with Roy and Chuck, had a completely different personality when visited for artistic inspirations. As a shadow of its former self, with caved-in roofs, crooked walls, and autumn-tinged plants reclaiming ground, it made for fascinating subject matter. Sedona, in what is known as Red Rock Country, had its own unique artistic qualities. Here, tall, red sandstone spires and golden aspens pierced a cobalt-blue sky. Betty Jean and I had such a great time together that we made plans for just the two of us to go camping and painting there another weekend. Our connection fit with just what I needed in the friendship department. Betty Jean and I were the same age, single, loved the outdoors and art—which made all the difference in the world to our fast-forming friendship.

The next Sunday I joined my parents, and my sister, Elaine, on an outing. As usual, my dad picked a route out of town and drove until a side road inspired us to turn. This day, we'd chosen Iron Springs Road, which led us into more of the unique granite boulders found in the much of the Prescott area. Once parked, we collected canteens, donned jackets, and started down a sandy arroyo to explore, with our little beagle-mix, Peanuts, leading the way.

A steady, strong wind in advance of an approaching storm whipped up wispy, horsetail clouds, and whooshed past my ears. Carried within the wind, an eerie, high-pitched and almost haunting sound raised goose bumps on my arms. *What in the world is that?* It took me a moment to realize that it was the wind making the wires on distant power poles sing. I stared at those wires for a moment, wondering why I couldn't see what I could hear. *How weird . . .*

We did more walking, mostly in comfortable silence, with my mom and me picking up sparkly rocks, and slipping them into our pockets. When we came upon the scattered bones of a cow, I gave it a quick, curious, but I-don't-really-want-to-know glance, like you do when you see a dead animal on the side of the road. A short time later we found another carcass, this time with its hide stretched over a sun-bleached skeleton. That, added to the spooky singing wires, unsettled me even more. Seeing those dead cows reaffirmed my conviction that when I died, I wanted to be cremated. In part because of the horrible shock of seeing the poor creature on display like that, but also because I'd never forgotten watching the news about a major flood back East, in which caskets popped out of the ground like corks. No doubt about it—cremation was the way to go.

After dinner, I stayed up late to watch a movie. As a huge fan of science fiction and extraterrestrials—*Star Trek, My Favorite Martian, Lost in Space*—all fascinated me. This was a topic Roy and I could talk about nonstop for hours. *At one time*, I thought sadly.

Purported to be based on a true event, this movie followed the UFO abduction of a middle-aged couple. Glued to the TV, it had me convinced that this had happened to them, and I couldn't help but wonder what I'd do if such a thing happened to me. I'd probably be so terrified that I'd never recover or be the same—but then again, why must I think that aliens would be out to inflict harm? Surely if they are intelligent enough to fly around in spaceships for many light-years they would not harm us. Why must I fear the unknown? What I worried more about was the rage we perpetuated against ourselves. I mean, look at what mankind did to mankind. Kill, destroy, hate, fight. So violent. Why was man so violent? Where did we come from? Why are we here? Did people in other worlds wonder the same thing? Would I ever talk to, see, or know for sure, of a living being from another world? How I wished I could share the movie with Roy, and ask him those questions. No doubt we would have discussed this movie for hours.

A phone call from Chuck the next night shook my world.

"I've got some bad news," he said. "Roy's mother told me that Roy lost his thumb and badly fractured his hand in a sawmill accident."

I almost dropped the phone. "Oh my God, no! Is he okay?"

"I guess so. Haven't talked to him yet."

After Chuck and I hung up, I sat there with my hand on the telephone, unable to move. More than anything, I wanted to call Roy— but what could I possibly say? How was he doing? Would he be able to play guitar again? He must be devastated. But I couldn't call him. The last I'd heard he was living with a girl in Northern Arizona. There was no way he'd want to hear from me.

In the morning I again hovered near the phone. The darned thing insisted: *"Call him. You must call him. Tell him how you feel. Tell him you care."*

What to do? I needed to know how he was doing. Calling him was not an option; but calling his mother was. I'd always gotten along with Roy's mom. Such a sweet lady. I wondered what she thought of her son's relationship (or lack thereof) with me. But, she'd never questioned me, and was always delighted to hear from me whether Roy and I were seeing each other or not.

"He's doing okay, and will be coming home this weekend," she said after I explained the reason for my call. "I'll let him know you called."

Oh. No. At that moment, I realized I'd set myself up to be let down when he did not respond. I stumbled for words, and ending up saying something lame. "Oh, gee, thanks . . ." instead of telling her that I doubted he'd care, so to please not say anything.

LITTLE BY LITTLE, my persistent intuition that Scott was not right for me became too strong to ignore. How to tell him? I practiced what to say for when he came up to see me the next weekend. This would be tough to pull-off, because when he visited, he stayed in the spare bedroom that doubled as my dad's office. Awkward, to say the least, once I told him how I felt.

Scott arrived late Saturday morning, and we spent the day not doing much. My feelings were all over the place. Could he tell? Probably. I knew I was terrible company.

After dinner with my family, Scott and I sat outside at the picnic table under the pines in our backyard. We struggled to make conversation, starting and stopping, still not finding anything to land on. The air held a chill, but that's not why my body trembled. Despite knowing I would be telling the truth, I dreaded saying what had to be said. I found the courage anyway. "This is hard for me to say, but I don't see a future for us."

"Okay," he said, way more casually than I'd expected. "Just how positive are you, really?"

That's when he took me into his arms and kissed me. Every nerve ending sparked, my body weakened with desire. We ended up making out for over an hour, with me getting totally lost in the sensations taking over my body and my mind. My intent to break up evaporated.

"Let's go someplace and make love," he whispered in my ear.

Although tempting, I just couldn't. What sense did that make?

"No, I don't think that's a good idea," I said. "Let's call it a night."

He sighed deeply. "Okay. I'm gonna sit here a bit longer."

After saying goodnight, I climbed the back steps, and went inside. When I shut the door and saw his silhouette at the table through the window, I paused. What was wrong with me? Why couldn't I make up my mind?

Once I crawled under the covers, my mind raced. I couldn't deny that I did have feelings for him, that I still felt the chemistry, but at the same time I knew this had nothing to do with love. And if this wasn't love, what was it? How could I know I didn't love him, and that he was not a good match for me, and yet have such a strong physical response? You'd think your brain should be in charge.

While I attended school the next day, Scott said he would hang out at the town plaza to wait for me. During a long break between classes, rather than go straight to the plaza, I drove around town in circles. *What am I going to do?* Finally, I parked, and set off to find him. It didn't take long. Studying him from a distance, where he leaned against a stately elm with a book in hand, a wave of desire stirred inside of me, making my heart pound. There was no denying he was a good-looking guy: a medium—but strong—build, expressive eyes, and a contagious laugh. And he loved me. How could I break up with someone who loved me?

Scott raised his head when I approached, set the book down, and stood up. Once in his arms, my heartbeat and breathing calmed. But I knew at that moment I'd not lied to myself, nor cheated on him by still harboring feelings for Roy. I did feel some kind of love for Scott, but this would not be the only love I'd ever know. Of that, I was sure.

Scott left the next day, and I spent a considerable amount of time contemplating the meaning of love. Each time I thought I was in love, it felt different. How was that possible? Could that mean that I'd never really been in love? Or did it mean I could love many people, but in different ways, levels, and intensities?

Chapter 25

THE FOREST SERVICE'S main office in Tucson called mid-November to inform me that they'd changed the hiring process. Unlike prior years, they would not hold a position until the end of the semester to accommodate college students.

I frowned. *Well, that just figures.* That meant if I was lucky enough to even get a job (no job is ever guaranteed), I'd have to drop out of school altogether. Although I enjoyed my classes, and would hate to quit in the middle of the term, I wanted, and needed, a job more. Then they dropped another bomb. The application deadline was next week, not the end of December as it had been in years past. In a panic, I rushed around madly all the next day, getting all of the proper forms collected, filled out, and in the mail. Afterwards, I flopped down on the couch, exhausted. Now all I needed were a million prayers and bundles of luck to get a job I wanted.

When Scott returned to Tucson, he had been promptly dispatched to a huge fire in California. The last I'd heard it'd hit over 57,000 acres. I didn't expect to hear from him for a while. This was okay by me . . . I'd let him leave believing we were fine, and felt guilty for doing so.

A nice distraction from Chuck came when he called me the day before Thanksgiving.

"Let's go out to the house in the Dells," he said.

Always game to visit that spooky old place with him, I agreed to go.

Chuck had come prepared with firewood in the back of his truck, and a bottle of wine. We chatted companionably as he built a fire, adding welcome warmth and ambiance to the room, something that probably hadn't happened since his family moved out many years ago. We snuggled on the dusty couch with questionable springs, when he surprised me with a quick kiss on the lips and a squeeze from his arm around my shoulder. A warm feeling of deep friendship swelled in my chest, no doubt enhanced by the wine. The wine buzz also made me want to share that feeling.

"I've always wanted to tell you I love you," I said. Which was true: I loved him as a good friend. There'd never been a doubt in my mind that this was the case.

He smiled at me. "I've wanted to tell you that I love you for a long time now." He kissed me lightly on my mouth. "There's something else I've always wanted to tell you."

I smiled. "There is?"

"You are beautiful. Absolutely beautiful."

This blew me away. I'd no idea he'd ever thought so, and frankly couldn't believe what I was hearing. What else had I missed? I snuggled against his shoulder. "Tell me what you're thinking about."

An eyebrow raised, and again he squeezed me close.

"I'd like to make love to you," he said.

Whoa! I'd never thought about having sex with him. Ever. Not once did it ever occur to me that he would want to have sex with me. What did this all mean? Talk about being caught off guard . . . I scrambled to respond. Did I want that? Could we make love and still stay friends? Now I questioned everything about our relationship all the way back to day one. Had he been in love with me all of this time? Was the friendship I'd felt for him all of this time love in disguise? This was completely overwhelming.

I tripped over words, trying to find the right ones to say when I had no idea what the right words would be. "Um, maybe someday . . ."

He took my wine glass from my hand and set it on the floor with his. That's when I realized "someday" was going to be right now.

When the most unromantic love-making I'd ever had was over, I did not immediately regret what I'd done. I didn't want our relationship to change, but it just had. Were we still friends? That's all I'd ever wanted. We weren't meant to be anything more. A little late for that reminder. There would be no turning back.

On the way to my house, Chuck's voice brought me back to the moment like a blasting car horn. "You know, I don't know what's going on with Roy. He's so unbearable to be around lately. I don't feel like I know him anymore."

This comment floored me. If Chuck felt that way about his lifelong friend, what would *I* think if I spent time with Roy?

"Maybe it's just me, but I don't like his girlfriend," he said, parking at the curb in front of my house. "It's weird 'cause I don't think Roy likes her much either. He treats her like shit. I just don't get it."

Okay, I had to admit that Chuck not liking Roy's girlfriend, and Roy's treatment of said girlfriend, screamed vindication on my part. If Roy treated someone he supposedly loved in that way, it shouldn't have been a surprise that he would treat me badly, too. It was a good thing we weren't together.

When I walked into the kitchen, I found a note on the counter saying that Scott had called from fire camp in California, and to call him back, collect. That message slapped me with reality, hard, by dealing me a full deck of guilt. He answered on the first ring. *Oh, God, he's been sitting by the payphone all of this time.* My heart melted at the sound of his voice. "I love you, Scott."

After I spoke, I began to tremble uncontrollably. I knew what I'd done with Chuck was wrong on every conceivable level. Not to mention the fact that we'd had unprotected sex. How much more stupid could I get? What if I'd just gotten myself pregnant? Guilt closed my throat. Despite my fear of confessing, I knew I had to tell Scott what had happened with Chuck. Once I did, he'd stop loving me. And I'd deserve it.

I sucked in a deep breath. "I don't know how to tell you this . . ."

After a few moments of post-confession silence, he said, "I'll have to admit this surprises me. My guess is you were drunk. However, I love you very much, and the fact that you and Chuck made love once doesn't bother me, but if you ever do it again, it will."

The trembling stopped, and I held in a sob. *He still loves me.*

We talked a bit more, and then he said he'd call again when he could.

I hung up. *I do not deserve his compassion or love. I don't deserve him at all, period.*

Chapter 26

AS IT NEARED the end of the semester, I had to make a decision on whether or not to complete the full year of music theory, or give up. Granted, if I landed the Forest Service job, it wouldn't matter, but that may not happen. I loved music, but this class made me feel inferior. While my classmates showed innate musical abilities, I had to work ten times harder than they did. With painful acceptance, I concluded that I was not good enough, and needed to stop pretending that I ever would be.

When I sat down in Mr. Longfield's office before class, his brow creased after I delivered the news. He removed his reading glasses, and set them on his desk.

"Why don't you want to finish?" he asked.

I hesitated. "Well, I just don't think I'm doing very well, and I've heard the second semester is tougher."

"Nonsense!" he said. "You have a solid B. There's nothing wrong with that."

His reaction made me smile, and a smidge of confidence returned. I registered for the spring semester.

With Christmas only two weeks away, after class I ran errands. My mood lighter and full of holiday spirit, I delighted in finding some perfect gifts. I was also buoyant with the knowledge that I finally had direction in my life. Confident I'd get that Forest Service job, even if it meant dropping out of school early to take it, I decided that all would be good, if not great.

Scott's call after dinner added to my decent day.

After we'd been talking for nearly fifteen minutes, he said, "I'm calling from your Greyhound Bus Station."

Shocked, I sputtered, "You *are?*"

Like a maniac, I sped to pick him up, thrilled by the impromptu visit. Instead of bringing him home right away, we parked on a forested road. There, I lost myself in his embrace, holding him as tight as I could, burying my face in his neck, not wanting to let go. He responded by clinging to me just as tightly.

After a good three-hour talk, later we sat in Sambo's over beverages with even more to say. It was there my exuberance shifted. One minute, I felt deep affection for him, another, less than that. I just didn't understand why this shift happened. Was it me? Was it us?

When Scott departed for Tucson, I wanted to be honest with him, tell him we would not work out, but the words just would not come. Although I didn't believe we would get married, I couldn't, or rather didn't yet want to, end whatever it was that we had.

A few days later, Scott called to tell me the Forest Service had offered him another round on the Catalina Hot Shots. He would start in February.

"Why don't you come to Tucson?" Scott said. "You can stay at my house and bug the Forest Service about your application status."

While this conflicted in every way with my indecision about us, I decided to go. "My sister is here visiting. I can come down with her tomorrow."

"Great," he said. "I'm housesitting this week; I'll tell my mom you're coming."

That plan fell apart when Cindy said I couldn't ride with her. I marched into my bedroom and slammed the door. *Well, fine. I'm not going.*

Funny how quickly things could change. As it turned out, some friends were heading to Phoenix that very night. A call to Scott had him ready to hit the road to pick me up in Phoenix. What a long night, though. We didn't get into Tucson until five-thirty a.m., crashing for a few hours where Scott was housesitting. For the rest of my visit, I would be a guest at his parents' home.

After not nearly enough sleep, Scott drove me to the Forest Service office where I hoped to catch McKelsey for an update on the job situation. Not as easy as I thought it would be. With the woman at the front desk about as friendly as a doorknob (maybe less so), I had to pry out of her that McKelsey was on leave until mid-January. I'd planned to stay two weeks, and decided four more days wouldn't be a too much of a problem. I'd miss a music theory class, requiring hours of make-up time, but my priority was a job.

Scott had things to do, so I hung out with his mom for the afternoon. I adored petite, plump Mrs. Carlson. Even though in age we were two decades apart, we could girl-talk nonstop.

Mrs. Carlson baked special occasion cakes. I sat at the kitchen table, leafing through her portfolio, impressed by the creativity and loving detail of her creations. They were simply too pretty to eat. She flitted around the kitchen, gathering ingredients and greasing pans for a wedding cake.

"I've noticed a significant change in Scott since he met you," she said with a warm smile over the noise of the Sunbeam mixer. "He radiates when he talks about you."

He does? This made me feel . . . well . . . special. But it also made my insides squirm.

What I saw coming, especially after hearing his mom's observations of how I affected him, was that when I did what needed to be done, his heart would be broken. I didn't want to hurt Scott. I wished I knew myself better. I wished I *understood* myself better.

After watching the late showing of *American Graffiti*, Scott and I drove out to a remote place in the desert to talk. Summoning up considerable courage, I decided to broach my qualms about us yet again. "I think we've changed."

"I agree," he said. "I'm getting used to you, and you aren't quite as 'extra special' to have around anymore."

What? If that was what it was like after only six and a half months— what would it be like after six and a half *years*? The foggy confusion lifted. I didn't want a serious relationship with him, and that's what we had. I would have to end this.

HANGING AROUND TUCSON the extra four days didn't accomplish a darned thing. McKelsey had no answers. It was time to go home. After saying goodbye to Scott—but still not ending us—I hopped on a bus to Prescott the next day.

Two days later, a letter from the Forest Service arrived to say that I didn't qualify. *I don't qualify? Unbelievable.* Here I thought I had an "in" with them. Disheartened, this news ruined the entire day. I couldn't seem to channel my thoughts into anything constructive. I stared at my bedroom walls with the stereo turned up loud to tune out a world bent on making sure that nothing I wanted would ever happen.

Later that night, still out of it, I switched on my portable TV and propped myself against the headboard. The 1930s movie, *Dark Victory*, played. After it ended, I took out my journal to write down my impressions before they were influenced by sleep.

> *. . . the movie brought on a wave of nostalgia for the way Scott and I were last summer—the love and the warmth between us, the fact that we never worried about losing one another, or becoming too serious. I still think about Ben off and on. It would have been so easy to love him forever—except that he wasn't who I thought he was. He didn't love me, he just liked the idea of loving me, I guess. I am still looking. I am looking for someone I will be with forever. I don't want to settle for anyone. I want to know that we'll last. I want to know we'll always be crazy and madly in love. That's what I want from life, and I have to learn to let it come to me. If it so desires to.*

Deep in thought, I chewed the end of my pen, and then wrote: *Scott is not the one. He is not.*

Chapter 27

KIM'S FRIEND, ROBERT, called me Saturday morning to invite me to his birthday party that night. I didn't particularly want to go, but I let him talk me into it. It wasn't like I had anything else to do.

The living room held a surprising number of guests—I'd no idea geeky Robert had that many friends. After accepting a soda, I noticed most of the girls were clustered around a guy visiting from England. Yes, his charming accent affected me, but I refused to swoon over him like the female crowd he'd drawn in. Their behavior was downright embarrassing. For me, it was his heart-stopping resemblance to Roy that stirred my emotions more than the way he spoke. I had to sit on my hands to keep them from trembling and force myself not to stare.

I stayed up quite late, not going to bed until three a.m. Unable to sleep, I mulled over Roy, and the guy who made me think of him. When I slept, my dreams desperately tried to sort out why Roy could still get to me, even when he wasn't physically present in my life.

Tuesday's mail brought more forms from the Forest Service. Baffled, as I thought they were done with me, I flipped through them, and tried to decipher what the heck they wanted now. There were more hoops to jump through, it seemed. Frustrated, but undeterred, I put on my bounciest sneakers, and jumped through them all.

At breakfast the next day, I sat at the table, pouring cereal into my bowl. My mom bustled around the kitchen, and then paused to say, "Oh, I forgot to tell you. Roy called yesterday."

I snapped my head to look at her. "He did?"

"Yes," she said, nonchalantly. "He asked me if maybe you might want to buy his guitar. I told you you didn't have the money, and he said, 'Okay, thanks,' and hung up."

The door in my heart that had opened for a second, closed. He would not be calling back. Sure, I realized it was probably better if he didn't ever call me again, but I wanted to talk to him, hear his voice . . . but what good would that ever do? I'd have to put him out of my head. It would be hard, but I'd done harder.

Sadly, that resolve didn't last long. What kept bothering me was that I could not remember our parting terms the last time we were together. Not surprising, considering from one day to the next we were either friends, not friends, heading toward being lovers, not being lovers, or someplace in between. The last time I saw him was . . . I had to think . . . December of 1974. Almost a year ago. Had he forgotten everything we'd been through? I wanted to talk to him—but I did not want to be the one to call him. Let him contact me if he wanted to. My friends didn't understand why Roy continued to haunt me.

"Let him go," they all said. "What's done is done," they said, "it's all in the past."

They were partly right, but mostly wrong. I needed someone to listen while I tried to solve a problem of the past that was affecting today. But I recognized that the only "talking" I'd ever be doing about Roy would be in my journal. I feared my fixation with him would drive what few friends I had away. How I wished that I could exclude the past, and believe that calling Roy would do no harm, that we could ask each other how we were doing. But I couldn't. I had to know *first* that he wanted to hear from me. But why would he? Chuck told me that he was now living with a girl named Jerri. The thought of her made my stomach twist into a knot. I pulled the blanket over my head and turned my face into the pillow, tears stinging my eyes. *What does she look like? She must be prettier than me.*

WAITING FOR A call from the Forest Service for days on end added to my down mood. What would I do if they didn't call? I decided to bum a ride to Tucson and talk to McKelsey in person. Maybe that would help. Even though my doubts about Scott hadn't changed, I accepted his offer to stay with him while I once again looked for work: Forest Service, or no Forest Service.

The night I arrived, Scott took me to a going-away party for Al, the guy who'd hired me to cook for the Helitack crew last summer. We pulled into the Forest Service recreation facility, and followed the music and voices to the group picnic area. Despite all of these familiar faces, I felt self-conscious. Would anyone remember me? Or care that I came?

"Hey, Linda," Al said. "Good to see you."

More heads turned my way with more greetings. They did remember me, and they did care that I came. Soon, I relaxed into conversation, laughter, and long games of silly volleyball. Silly, because the volleyball had gone AWOL, requiring us to use a basketball, with hilarious results.

Taking a break, I sat on the sidelines to watch another team play. Heartbreak Harry walked up to me.

"Hey, Linda. I saw you arrive. What a pleasant surprise," he said, giving me one of his soul-melting smiles.

We talked a while about music, and what we'd been up to. And then, out of the corner of my eye, I saw Scott. A deluge of memories swept in. I remembered last summer in one complete sweeping flash followed by a sharp pang—he loved me and I didn't love him. But doing something about it at that particular moment did not make sense, mostly for selfish reasons. I wanted to socialize, not deal with the mess I'd created and didn't have the guts to end. I continued to talk to Harry, coaxing him into playing his guitar for me. The song he picked was an old folk song that I adored. I sat quietly listening to his impressive chord skills and enjoying the sound of his voice.

After he finished, he handed the guitar to me. The wine quelled the jitters that always materialized when playing in front of most anyone who wasn't family. I played a song I'd written not too long ago, something I typically reserved for my ears only.

"That's really nice, Linda," he said, when I'd strummed the last chord. "The lyrics are good, and I like the melody."

"Thanks," I said, lowering my eyes. I figured he was just being polite. But it made me think: In all the time Scott and I had been together, not once had he ever shown any interest in my guitar playing. Sure, I'd known that this was the case all along, but at this moment his lack of enthusiasm over something that was important to me sunk in. *Is this someone I want to be with?*

The night's festivities wound down, and people started to leave. Someone offered to continue the party at their home. Scott asked me if I wanted to go, and I did.

Once there, Scott and I went our separate ways. I accepted a glass of wine from the host, and sat down in the kitchen, listening to the conversations around me. Music played on the stereo, and I tapped my foot to the rhythm of the dance-inducing Country-Western. Al, dressed to kill in his western attire and fancy cowboy boots, two-stepped his way over to me with a big smile. I laughed when he extended his hand.

"May I have this dance?" he said, bowing.

I laughed again. "But I don't know how."

"I'll teach you."

Breathless from the whirling, twirling and fancy steps interspersed with silliness over my goof-ups, I suddenly noticed Scott, leaning against a wall, alone, looking completely miserable. Dancing had never been his thing. Guilt rained on my good mood. But it didn't last long. *Hadn't I tried to end our relationship?* What failed to register at the moment was that not only did I need Scott to give me a ride, I needed him to give me a ride to *his* house.

About midnight, in his car, Scott hit me with, "I love you, but I can never, ever, bear to put up with another summer like last year."

I knew damned well what he was getting at. He'd hated all of the attention I got last year, making me now feel guilty—as though I'd done something wrong tonight by simply having a good time. We were up the entire night, arguing, crying, and eventually lying in his bed, silent. I hated myself for being in a relationship I didn't want anymore and couldn't summon up the strength to end.

I dozed for a half-hour just before daybreak, and when I opened my eyes, Scott was sitting upright next to me, staring into space. I rolled over to look at his clock: 8:10. I guessed he had no intention of going to work.

I slipped out of bed, put on my robe, and padded into the guest bathroom. The reflection in the mirror was not a pretty picture. My eyes were red and swollen, my hair a rat's nest. I splashed my face with cold water, and returned to Scott's room. He was still in bed, nonreactive. I dressed, and walked out to the kitchen, where his mom was making pancakes.

"Good morning," she said, in her always cheerful voice.

I must have faked a good enough smile, because she didn't catch on that everything was wrong. I also passed on food, which made her frown, but she didn't say anything. The entire morning, Scott wouldn't talk to me. I read, napped, talked with his mom . . . a dreadfully long day where my stomach had that overall sick feeling that Scott and I would break up that day. Maybe I waited for him to do what I couldn't seem to. A hole burned in my stomach as though I'd swallowed Drano.

I am such a Goddamned RAT.

The next day, with Scott back to speaking to me, albeit in simple sentences, he dropped me off at the bus station.

LATE MARCH, AND no word from the Forest Service. Discouraging. I thought for sure I would've heard something by now.

Scott called every day. Neither of us brought up that awful night at his house. At least for me, our relationship had shifted into friendship mode—or maybe I finally recognized that's where I'd been for a long time. How long would that last? Not long, I surmised. Throughout the whole week, I felt so rotten inside, that it hurt to smile.

With way too much time to dwell, I analyzed past relationships, and noticed a pattern. Once I knew guys had an interest in me, or told me they loved me, I ran away, or rather, I ran away *emotionally*. Why did I do this? Was it a fear? Of what? Of having to give instead of take? But how could that be when I loved to give—or maybe there was a certain kind of love that I couldn't give—real love. The kind I thought I wanted. The kind that eluded me. Maybe my fear of being rejected had prevented me from finding it. Had I already found real love with Ben, Roy, Tom, or Scott, but let it go? I did believe they all loved me. I just didn't know if what I felt for them constituted love. Sadly, I realized that if I *had* let real love go, there was no bringing it back.

AN OUTING WAS just what I needed to lift my spirits. I joined my parents and their friends on an excursion to the Verde River—the placid, meandering, watery artery of the Verde Valley, with the quaint town of Cottonwood, population of maybe two hundred, and Camp Verde, population of maybe less, bordering its banks. With the bright sun warm on my back—I couldn't have asked for a better day. The river shimmered in the most gorgeous turquoise blue. The lush fragrance of grass and water filled my senses. Horses grazed in fields, and homes were few and far between. The two-story with a large porch and a swing that hung from a majestic cottonwood could have been my dream home. A quaint Mom-and-Pop country market served as a grocery-hardware-drug store. I'd never gone inside to browse, but should have. It all reminded me of rural Upstate New York more than a place in Arizona. It also spurred the travel bug in me . . . to see new places, explore the West . . . the urge tugged at me, saying: *Let's go!* Then I sighed a deep sigh. I didn't want to go alone. I wanted to find the right person to see those places with me. Would it ever happen? My heart ached with emptiness that it might not.

On Tuesday, my watercolor class embarked on a field trip to visit the Tucson Museum of Art. On the road by five-thirty a.m., we arrived in the city mid-morning. First thing, I snagged a payphone to call the Forest Service to check on my application status. They delivered the most depressing news: "We haven't even gotten to the summer applications yet, and if all the positions are filled before we get to them, you're out of luck."

I hung up the receiver, and frowned. *Well, that's just great.* But I refused to let this ruin my day. They'd jerked me around so often in the past, I never knew what to believe anyway.

My classmates and I had a great time hanging out together, walking through the museum, commenting on styles and painting techniques. We all agreed that we had much to learn.

The bus didn't return to Prescott until after nine that night, and when I walked in the door my mom had news: "The Forest Service in Nogales called today."

Although tired when I walked in, I wasn't any longer. "They did?"

She smiled. "They want to offer you a job."

My questions came out in rapid succession without a breath in between. "They do? What kind of job? Where? When would I start? Do they want me to call back?"

She shook her head. "I don't know . . . the man didn't give me any details. He said he'd call you in the morning."

Morning? How in the world could I wait until morning?

I stayed up late, my mind whirling with the excitement of having a pending job offer. The thrill lasted for an hour or two—then I began to wonder what kind of job they were offering. What if it wasn't what I wanted? Plus, the location worried me. I didn't want a Forest Service job where there wasn't a forest. Was there a forest in Nogales? I didn't know. I mean, seriously—who would want to work for the Forest Service where there weren't any trees? I also didn't want another desk job, much less another timekeeping job.

After breakfast, I hung out next to the phone. What time would they call? I didn't dare even walk outside for a minute for fear I'd miss them.

At nine-fifteen, the phone rang.

"Hello?" I asked, both tentative and hopeful.

"Hello, my name is Ralph, and I'm with the Nogales Ranger District," he said. "I would like to speak to Linda Strader."

"This is she," I replied, trying to sound composed and in control, which I was not.

"I've got a firefighter position to offer you at Florida Ranger Station," he said, pronouncing the station's name as Flor-ee-da, "in the Santa Rita Mountains, about thirty miles north of Nogales."

This is great! Yes, yes, yes, I want it! But then I thought: *Wait. Don't rush into this.* The "Nogales" part still made me nervous. I didn't want to find myself fighting grass or brush fires like they have in Southern California.

"Ummm . . . are there any trees?" I asked, feeling a bit foolish, but dammit, I wanted . . . no, I *needed* to know.

He chuckled. "Oh, yes, there are trees."

Maybe I'd better be more specific. "I mean, are there *pine* trees?"

He outright laughed. "Yes, there are pine trees."

That worked for me. I accepted the offer.

"First you have to pass a physical fitness 'step-test.' You'll also need a doctor's exam," he said, next explaining how I would go about getting those accomplished.

I pressed my ear to the phone, my hands now quivering with excitement. *Oh my God! I have a job! With the Forest Service!*

"If you pass all the preliminaries, this is what you need to bring . . ." He began reading a list.

This list was familiar. One of my tasks at Palisades had been to offer jobs over the phone to potential hot shots. I gave them the very same list. Work clothes had to be cotton—synthetics had a nasty habit of melting to your skin near open flame. I already owned Levi's, the only jeans I ever wore, and a couple of cotton chambray work shirts, quite fashionable at the time even if you didn't "work" in them. Leather boots with eight-inch tops and Vibram™ soles were required, but not the kind with steel toes. I'd been told that steel got pretty darned hot if you happened to step into a bed of hot coals, and you'd get serious burns before you had a chance to unlace and shuck them off.

"Report to the Nogales District office on Wednesday, May twelfth, at eight," Ralph said. "You can come the night before and stay in a motel. Call the station in the morning, and I'll send someone to pick you up."

The rest of the day, I floated around the house thinking: *Wow, I guess I'm going to be a firefighter.*

Scott called that night. With significant exuberance, I delivered the spectacular news: "You'll never believe this! I got a firefighting job, and I'll be working at Florida Ranger Station in the Santa Rita Mountains and I need to take the step test first and make an appointment for a physical, but oh my God isn't this great?"

A long pause and a bit of static came from his end of the receiver. "You've made a big mistake taking that job," he said. "That's a horrible place to work."

I flinched. A few seconds passed before I could think of how to respond. "Well, it's too late. I took the job. I want the job."

"You'll hate it."

"*No* I won't."

After hanging up, I fumed. Not only was I annoyed that he wasn't happy for me, but even worse was that he criticized *where* I'd be working—as though the only place I *should* be working was where he could keep tabs on my social life. Fifteen minutes later, I calmed down.

The heck with his opinion. The heck with working on Mount Lemmon. I want this job.

Tentatively hired, I made arrangements with the Prescott National Forest office to take the step-test the next day. Early morning, the clerk escorted me to the back of the complex, where I watched two guys in Forest Service uniforms load chainsaws into the back of a green government pickup.

"Sam, we have a step-test candidate," the clerk said to a trim, fit, uniformed man engaged in conversation with another employee.

Sam glanced at us. "Yeah. Just a sec."

The guy he was talking to studied me curiously, his eyes shaded by his Forest Service cap. Self-conscious about being an outsider here, I wished I could become invisible until they figured out what to do with me.

"This way," Sam said, with a wave of his arm.

We entered a room in back of the workshop. Nervous, my eyes darted around the new surroundings, assessing various items on the walls, including a Smokey Bear poster, and photos of crews posing in front of the station.

"Hang tight a minute while I get the equipment." Sam pointed to a chair, and I sat down, anxious. My eyes continued to scan the room while he set up.

Sam placed a wooden bench in front of me. Then he opened a cabinet, and removed a metronome, stopwatch, and pad of forms. He must have noticed my wide-eyed apprehensive expression, because he smiled and asked, "First time?"

I smiled meekly, and nodded.

"You'll do fine. All you need to do is step up and down the bench for five minutes to the beat of the metronome. Any questions?"

I couldn't think of a thing to ask. I stood in front of the bench, palms sweaty, but ready.

"Okay. Ready. Set. Begin." He clicked the stopwatch.

The metronome ticked steadily at thirty beats per minute while I stepped up and down the bench, matching its rhythm. At first, this felt silly, but that changed once it became hard work, making my heart thump and my breathing labored.

Sam clicked the stopwatch off at the same time he said, "Stop. Sit tight—you get to rest one minute."

I sat down to wait. When the minute was up, he knelt next to me and pressed two fingers on the inside of my wrist. He clicked the stopwatch once, checked my pulse for sixty seconds, and snapped it off.

"Close," he said, standing up to put away the equipment. "You can try again tomorrow."

I tried to swallow, but the bulge in my throat wouldn't let me. *I didn't pass.* I drove home in a trance. Awake most of the night, my thoughts churned. *What if I don't pass? Then what will I do?* The thought of not getting this job felt like the end of the world.

First thing the next morning, I drove straight to the ranger station, hands gripping the wheel, jaw set.

A different person would administer the test this time.

"The key to acing this is to stay calm," he said as he set up the equipment. "Being nervous raises your heart rate, skewing your score. Take a deep breath, and let it out slowly before I check your pulse. That works for a lot of people."

Not anywhere near as nervous as yesterday, I nodded, both focused and ready. I did exactly as he said, and to my overwhelming relief, I passed.

"So you got a job on the Coronado?" he asked, as he filled out the government form.

"Yes!" I said, beaming like I'd just won a marathon.

"Heck, if I'd known you were looking, I could've gotten you a job here."

I stared at him in disbelief. *Now* you tell me.

SCOTT CONTINUED TO call, and our conversations grew more strained. I was still mad at him for belittling my new job, and for trying to make me believe that I'd made a mistake. I also didn't like him acting as though we were still a couple, when we were not—at least not in my world. I decided I had to write him a letter and spell it out: *We. Are. Done.*

After I did just that, I spent two days walking around in a daze, wondering how he'd react, dreading the inevitable phone call. I feared he would plead with me to *not* break up with him, and that I'd find some excuse to agree. Why couldn't I make a firm commitment to end our relationship? I knew I was taking the chicken-shit way out . . . putting the burden on him. My horrible insecurities were at also at play, taunting me, telling me that I was making a huge mistake. At a loss to find the right word that fit how I was feeling, I landed on "untogether." It was as though I was living in a fantasy world—floating around, waiting . . . waiting for what? Maybe for the universe to make the tough decision for me.

Chapter 28

AFTER MUSIC THEORY class, I tore off home, pedaling my bike as though on a mission. Because it was a perfect day, warm and sunny with that spring tinge in the air, I couldn't wait to spend time outdoors. I peeled off my school clothes, put on my cutoffs and halter top. Next, I spread a towel on the redwood lounge chair, and spent a luxurious hour sunbathing and studying for the final next week.

Betty Jean pulled into the driveway about four-thirty to pick me up for dinner at her house. After we ate, we visited an art show, and whispered to each other about the winners—one of which completely puzzled us. *That won?* It was discouraging in a way that I couldn't fathom how to fix.

Later, she drove us out into the forest, chatting nonstop. Watching her shift gears, I mentioned that I wanted to learn how to drive a manual transmission one day, as it might come in handy, especially working for the Forest Service.

"No time like the present," she said, pulling over to the side of the road.

The first time I pushed in the clutch and shifted into first, the car stalled. I turned to Betty Jean in a panic. "Did I break anything?"

She laughed. "No, you just need to get the gas and the clutch in sync, that's all."

I continued to stall the car multiple times. Frustrated, I realized that this would take lots of practice . . . difficult to do considering my parents drove automatics.

We ended up at Sambo's for tea, and hung out until eleven p.m. Betty Jean glanced at her watch. "My sister Julie is arriving from Nogales, Mexico tonight. I have to go pick her up at the bus station. Want to come?"

"Okay, sure."

Julie stepped off the bus shortly after we arrived at the Greyhound terminal. The two sisters hugged. Betty Jean introduced us, and we talked while heading to her car.

"How was your trip?" Betty Jean asked Julie.

"Not so good," Julie said. "Nogales, Arizona was just as bad of an experience as Nogales, Mexico." She wrinkled her nose. "Nasty old men poked at me."

I went into a complete panic. My first night in Nogales I'd be alone in a motel. After Betty Jean took her sister home, she spent three hours trying to calm me down. Despite her efforts, all night I did an excellent job of envisioning the multitudes of horrible things that could happen to me on this trip:

Vulgar, poking men.

Rape.

Robbery.

Kidnapping.

By morning I had myself quite worked up.

With my new job starting on a Wednesday, my parents wouldn't be able to take me to Nogales. I'd have to take a bus. I'd always had a vivid imagination for both bad and good . . . but I was especially adept at imagining the bad. Would I be safe? What if someone broke into the motel room? How would I *get* to the motel room from the bus station without being accosted?

Scott called later, which did and didn't surprise me. He didn't say anything right away about the letter. After we talked a bit, he said, "Your letter really upset me, and I immediately burned it. My first instinct was to call you that night, but I decided to wait until I got myself together. I want to change your mind about breaking up. I want you to give me a second chance."

Oh God, no. I gathered my wits. What good would a second chance do? "We aren't working out, Scott."

"That's not true," he said. "I love you. You can't deny that you are still attracted to me. I can feel it. Please give me a second chance. You owe me that."

Did I? I didn't respond right away—I didn't know how to. Should I give him another chance? As I'd feared I would, I began to waver. After all, I did care for him. I did still have a physical attraction to him. I just didn't think he was "the one." Did that mean I should stay with him, or go?

"I want you to listen to a song on the album I gave you last year. You know which one," he said.

It was by my favorite Tucson band that he and I often went to hear.

After we hung up, I pulled the record out of its sleeve, and placed it on my turntable, setting the needle on the track. In the heartfelt lyrics, the singer laments about living in sorrow because he fears he and his lover are through, and pleads for her to give him another chance. Once my tears started, I couldn't stop them for over an hour.

When I awoke in the morning, my emotions had numbed. I needed a nature fix. I convinced my parents that a hike to my spot at Wolf Creek was in order. Before the creek even came into sight, I heard the sound of gushing whitewater. Eager to get to the source, I out-hiked everyone. Granted, a similar feature back East wouldn't have impressed me much, but here, where water is not as plentiful, pure splendor. The creek, which normally played a lazy game of hopscotch over rocks, now tumbled with great exuberance in celebration of a wet spring. I carefully inched to the top of the twenty-five-foot waterfall. For the first time since I'd found this place, the plunge-pool was deep enough to wade into—I guessed five-feet—and I would have, if it hadn't been snow-melt. Water hurtled around me, filling my senses with the sounds of turbulence, and the scent of crisp, cold water. Finding a spot to sit, I contemplated what it would be like to break up with Scott. *Who would I talk to? What would it be like to not have a guy around that loved me? Would love ever come around again?* In high school I'd desperately longed for a boyfriend. For sure I'd never envisioned I would end up with more than one since then. But I also knew it wasn't fair to hang onto Scott knowing that I didn't want to marry him. Maybe with us working in different places this coming summer, the distance would make it easier to let our relationship fade away. Closing my eyes, I released my heartache and confusion, letting it flow and follow the currents downstream.

A WEEK BEFORE my start date, the Forest Service called with more particulars. At least now I knew where I'd be living, which was *not* in Nogales, thank goodness. I'd be living in the government quarters at Florida Ranger Station, at the incredibly cheap rate of sixty dollars a month. What would my accommodations be like this time? Hopefully better than the trailer on Mount Lemmon.

After my mom's traditional French toast breakfast the next morning, family friends joined us for yet another hike to Wolf Creek. We just couldn't get enough of the water show this spring.

Exhausted after the all-day trek, compounded by the lack of sleep the night before, I staggered into my bedroom after dinner to prepare for the next day's exams—and promptly fell asleep. At seven p.m., I awoke to light tapping on my door. Blurry-eyed and groggy, I opened it. The hall light blinded me for a moment before I recognized my mom and a figure next to her.

"Betty Jean is here," my mom said.

How unusual for Betty Jean to pop-in like that, but I didn't mind. We got comfortable on my bed and talked for a while, before deciding to head into the living room to watch TV.

When I reached the end of the hallway, I came to an abrupt stop. The living room was filled with my friends. A surprise party. My eyes swelled with tears . . . *everyone truly cares that I'm leaving.*

Two hours later, after closing the door behind the last person, I realized how much I would miss everyone—especially Betty Jean and Chuck, who would not be here when I returned in the fall. Betty Jean was moving to California, and Chuck would move to Northern Arizona with his girlfriend soon. What in the world would I do without them?

EARLY IN THE morning, I pedaled my bike to Yavapai College, carefully negotiating the narrow, winding streets where cars always promised a scare or two. I'd studied until I felt like my head would explode. The music theory final would take over two hours. I hoped for the best.

At my desk, I read each question and answered with careful thought. I wanted a good grade. Part two of the exam, "sight-singing," required that I sing the notes from a sheet of music—in key, mind you. That would have been relatively easy had it been a song I knew, but no, the point of this exercise was to be able to do this when you didn't know the melody. When I found myself alone in the big empty classroom, the last person to go, tears began to fall. Not because I feared I'd fail, but because even though I knew I wasn't good enough to pursue a formal music education any further, I'd really miss the challenges of this class.

With the dreaded vocal exam over, Mr. Longfield and I had a nice, long talk in his office.

"You're a great student," he said, smiling. "I admire how you stuck it out."

Compliments always embarrassed me. My face warmed. I returned his smile.

Peddling home, I decided that, hands down, he was one of the best teachers and people I'd ever met. I'd miss school, but I had a good job ahead, and I'd make new friends. Life would sure be different from now on, and although this scared me, I was ready.

Chapter 29

WHEN I CALLED Greyhound Bus Lines to make reservations, a bored agent said that they could get me to Tucson, but not to Nogales. That both surprised and concerned me. Good grief, were *they* afraid to go to Nogales too? I had to pry options out of him, which resulted in a call to another bus service for the last leg of my trip. That done, I made reservations at the Nogales Motel 6.

Tuesday night, I packed the largest suitcase we owned with essentials. My parents would bring down the rest of my belongings on Saturday.

Early morning at the Prescott bus station, I waited in line to pick up my ticket. Once at the window, the cashier shrugged, saying, "Greyhound changed their schedule. Your bus already left."

My bus LEFT? Images of not getting to Tucson on time, missing my connection, and most likely not reporting to work on time, made my knees weak. *I don't believe this.*

"Continental has a bus leaving in five minutes," the cashier said. "There's a seat available . . ."

I sprinted to the idling bus, and handed my luggage to the driver seconds before he closed the cargo door. Once seated, I calmed down, and shook my head. *Unbelievable.* At least I lucked out with a window seat.

Prescott's pines disappeared when the scenery changed to open, high desert with no trees. The bus approached the familiar plunge into the Phoenix Basin, where the Interstate turned into a steep, winding road through a series of dramatic canyons dotted with saguaro cacti poised like exclamation points. This stretch wasn't scary as a passenger, but I'd never forget the first time my dad let me drive to Phoenix. Petrified by every curve, I had to pry my fingers off the steering wheel when he took over before we headed into the heavy, congested traffic of the largest city in the state.

It was always hard to tell where the line between Not Phoenix and Phoenix began.

As usual, haze hung in the sky like brown fog, the stench of air pollution working its way through the closed windows. Mid-afternoon, the driver pulled into the bus station. Inside, rambunctious air conditioning had turned the grungy waiting room into a refrigerator. I shivered while I waited-out the hour layover. Most of the people were travelers like me, but the vagrants sleeping in chairs kept me on guard.

Back on board, my trip continued south, where the landscape turns flat and desolate. Barren, parched ground, which rarely saw rainfall, looked foreboding and just plain hot. *It sure wouldn't be fun if the bus broke down*, I thought, adding a new worry to my list. Undulating, wavy lines of heated air blurred distant mountains. A pool of water appeared on the asphalt in front of the bus. Mystically it moved ahead of us—always out of reach. I remembered my dad explaining the mirage phenomenon after we'd encountered them on our first trip out West. It now made me think of Wile E. Coyote in the Road Runner cartoons. I recalled one where Wile E. assumed with relief that he'd found a concession stand in the middle of a desert wasteland. Just as he raised the glass of lemonade to his lips, the liquid turned into sand. A bit exaggerated, but still made me both laugh and cringe.

When we approached Tucson, I immediately recognized the Santa Catalina Mountains on the horizon. What would it have been like had I been hired there again? Passing the exit I used to take, a tug pulled at my heart. I'd miss my friends at Palisades.

In Tucson, I boarded a Continental Trailways bus. A short time later, I sat up and paid closer attention to new territory. We crossed a bridge over the Santa Cruz River, and I craned my neck to see if it held water, but the sandy bottom was dry. There were several distant mountain ranges—none of which looked tall enough to support trees. A twinge in my chest. Had Ralph tricked me into taking a job nobody else wanted?

After reaching the small retirement community of Green Valley, the Interstate ended. The bus made its way to the two-lane Nogales Highway, a backcountry road with less traffic, but few passing lanes. When a rickety pickup truck, bed stacked high with hay bales, held us up for what seemed like forever, I worried about how we were doing for time. A glance at my watch told me: *Not good.* The motel reservation clerk had said I needed to check in by five. Anxiety mounted when we encountered more slowpokes.

We pulled into Nogales after six. Frantic, I waited impatiently for my suitcase, grabbed it the second it appeared on the conveyor, and took off in a dead run to the motel office.

A Hispanic woman, with heavy-lidded dark eyes, turned from the black-and-white television screen when I pushed the door open. I rushed to the counter.

"Got reservations?" she asked languidly.

"Yes, yes, I do," I said, out of breath. I set my heavy bag down, and adjusted my purse back onto my shoulder. "Linda Strader."

She ran her finger down entries in the reservation book, and slapped it shut. "Sorry, we gave that room to someone else. You were supposed to be here by five."

All of my nightmares were about to come true: I'd be spending a terrifying night in the bus station. But then something clicked. *Wait a minute. This is ridiculous.* "But don't you have another room?"

After a pause she said, "Well, yes, I suppose we do."

"Oh! Great." *Why didn't she say so in the first place?*

She flipped pages back and forth. "Would you like one with a TV? It's only five dollars more."

I thought about it for a second, and then decided it would give me something to do. I handed over twenty-five dollars. Room paid for, I hauled my bag up two flights of stairs, and unlocked the door of number 12.

Once inside, I quickly secured the deadbolt and slid the chain in place. *I made it.* Exhausted, I launched onto the bed, positioning the pillows as a prop. The TV stared blankly at me. *Might as well, I paid for it.* I got up and turned it on, twisting the knob through the half-dozen channels. After settling on what looked to be a movie, I suffered through fifteen minutes of it, and turned the set off. *What a waste of five dollars.*

Not remotely hungry, and frankly too scared to venture out for something to eat, I changed into my nightgown, turned off the light, and crawled under the covers. Sleep came quickly, but then I awoke every single hour wondering if it was time to get up yet. This gave me a considerable amount of time to mull over new-job-jitters. Would I like it? Would my coworkers be nice? I hoped to make new friends, but wanted the freedom to spend time with whomever I wanted, without commitments. Having a good job would also give me freedom. The thought of being financially self-sufficient created a different kind of jitters. Pleasant ones. Maybe I'd have my own place. I could eat anything I wanted to. I could buy some new music. Heck, I could save up for my first car. I thought about all of the times I felt as though I was waiting for something. Maybe the wait was over.

In the morning I skipped breakfast, not only because I was still too nervous to eat, but because I feared leaving the room. Instead, I sat by the phone waiting for eight o'clock so I could call for my ride.

At eight-thirty I answered the knock on my motel room door to find a short, stocky Hispanic man regarding me through black-framed glasses. The Forest Service badge pinned above the pocket of his uniform assured me that neither robbery nor kidnapping were on his agenda.

Rudy drove us to the district office, where I completed the necessary paperwork—reams of it in the typical government way. With my right hand cramping from filling out all of the forms, I accepted my reward: a "Red Card." Slightly larger than a business card, it documented my step-test score, and my classification as "Firefighter." I stared at it for a moment. *Firefighter. Wow.*

Ralph and I climbed into a government pickup, and we drove north to Florida Ranger Station. Along the way, I studied the road construction parallel to our route that I'd not noticed on the way down.

"The remaining portion of I-19 is almost done," Ralph said. "Looking forward to it. It'll make the trip between Nogales and Florida quicker."

Once leaving the highway, we headed up a two-lane paved road toward the Santa Rita Mountains. Ralph braked for a dozen reddish-brown cattle with blank white faces standing in the middle of the road.

"Damn cows," he said. "They've got to be the stupidest animal on the planet."

He tooted his horn. The bovines turned their heads, curious, but did not move. It always amazed me how cows had no fear of a shiny metal box ten times their size heading straight for them at a high rate of speed. Ralph laid on the horn again. A few moved, and gradually they all crossed the road, allowing us to continue.

Ralph drove silently while I stared out the window, frowning. The scrubby trees out there were definitely *not* pines. The road climbed steadily and the mountains loomed closer. The tallest peak did look intriguing—resembling Thumb Butte in Prescott somewhat, but on a much larger scale. Was the dark green vegetation up there what I hoped it was? I couldn't tell.

The luxury of smooth pavement ended, and we hit a washboard dirt road, truck fenders rattling, and tires flailing dirt and stones out behind us. Ralph answered a call on the radio, and I focused on the change of scenery. The scrubby tree variety I saw earlier grew taller here.

After a few miles of bouncing on the backcountry road, it narrowed, and Ralph let off the gas pedal. The road dipped, and we splashed through a shallow creek. Hand-laid rock pillars acted as sentries on each side of a cattle guard, the metal rails clattering as we crossed. Massive oaks shaded the way up the steep gravel road. Okay, oaks weren't conifers, but this was encouraging. Ralph veered right to climb up a steep driveway edged by a rock retaining wall. We parked in front of a small building where an American flag on a tall pole rippled in the late morning breeze.

"Glenn is in charge of Florida. I told him I'd be bringing you up today. Let's see if anyone's here," Ralph said.

The screen door squeaked on rusty hinges when we entered the office, our footsteps sounding hollow on the wooden floor. Cool, damp air blew from a noisy machine mounted outside one of the windows, enhancing the musty telltale odor of "very old building." With a quick scan of the room, I catalogued the mish-mash of furnishings gathered for function, not aesthetics: an industrial-gray metal desk, an antique wooden desk, two tall green metal file cabinets, and a few gray metal chairs against the walls. On top of a sturdy wooden dresser sat a large aluminum percolator, with assorted stained ceramic mugs neatly stacked around it. A canister of powdered creamer, plastic stir-sticks, and a diner-style sugar dispenser rounded out the coffee station. The aroma of stale coffee lingered.

"Guess they're over at the fire cache," Ralph said.

Instead of driving, we walked, passing a few of Florida's structures. On my left, an apricot tree bloomed in the front yard of a house with no signs of occupancy. I freely stared into the windows. *Oh, I hope that one will be mine!* The first building to my right also appeared vacant, but the next one, with a faded blue van parked in front, had music drifting from the open windows, and laundry on the clothesline. A cluster of buildings at the center of the complex formed a circle, where a group of men stood under a large oak. My gaze moved from them to landing on exactly what I needed to see—honest-to-goodness conifers! Tall, stately, and downright perfect.

A lean, darkly tanned man noticed us, and walked our way, taking long strides. He squinted at me from beneath the brim of his Stetson cowboy hat, and extended his hand.

"Hello, I'm Glenn."

After we shook hands, he held onto mine for a moment, and turned it palm up to give it closer inspection. He raised an eyebrow. Then he reached out and squeezed my right bicep, shooting Ralph a half-smile. Was he teasing, or questioning my ability to handle the tough job ahead? I decided he must be teasing, and smiled.

He released my arm.

Glenn next introduced me to the others. Most greetings and handshakes were friendly enough, but one guy raised an eyebrow as though thinking: *Who is this girl and why is she here?* Quite different from when I'd met the hot shots, who had flirted with me right away. I brushed it off, figuring it was probably because now I was the new gal, and by the looks of things, the *only* gal, with not one other girl in sight. No big deal. My thoughts were more focused on being a perfect Forest Service employee.

To my delight, the cute house with the apricot tree would be mine. Once inside, I wandered around, impressed by all of the furnished rooms: a combination living and dining area, a decent kitchen (although the fridge resembled the evil one at Palisades), a walk-in pantry—something I'd never seen before—two bedrooms, a deep, narrow bathroom, and *three* screened-in porches. Three! The porches thrilled me more than anything else about the place. I even thought about moving my bed into one in order to enjoy the night breezes. *Maybe later* . . .

I chose the larger bedroom, and tossed my suitcase on the bed. I hung workshirts in the closet, and stored the rest of my clothes in dresser drawers. How to make this place feel homier? My colorful bedspread would help. So would my modest kitchen essentials, my records and stereo, my guitar, and my watercolor paints—all of which my parents would bring down on Saturday. What else? Curtains would be nice. Nothing turns a house into a home like music and your own bedding, though.

"Linda?" Glenn called from the front door. "Fire training starts in ten minutes."

"Be right there!"

After a quick glance in the bathroom mirror to check my hair, I stepped out of my new summer home, closing the door behind me.

Originally from Syracuse, New York, Ms. Strader moved to Prescott, Arizona with her family in 1972. In 1976, she became one of the first women hired on a U.S. Forest Service fire crew.

Summers of Fire: A Memoir of Adventure, Love and Courage, was released on May 1st, 2018 by Bedazzled Ink Publishing. Her publishing history includes many web articles about writing memoir, her publishing and marketing experiences, and wildland firefighting. She has given talks on these topics to many clubs, including the American Association of University Women. *Parade Magazine* published an excerpt in 2018, and the PBS show *Arizona Illustrated* featured her segment "Wildland Firefighter," in the fall of 2019.

Ms. Strader holds two degrees: a Bachelor of Landscape Architecture, and a Masters in planning, from the University of Arizona. In addition to writing, she is a landscape architect, certified arborist, and watercolor artist. She currently lives in the same area where her Forest Service career began.

Visit Linda's website: https://summersoffirebook.blogspot.com

Just aim your phone camera at the QR Code

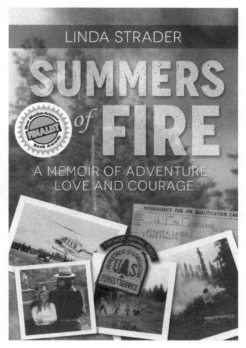

Summers of Fire
Linda Strader

Linda Strader is one of the first women hired on a fire crew with the U.S. Forest Service. A naïve twenty-year-old in the mid 1970s, she discovers fighting wildfires is challenging—but in a man's world, they became only one of the challenges she would face. Battling fire is exhilarating, yet exhausting; the discrimination real and sometimes in her face. Summers of Fire is an adventure story that honestly recounts the seven years she ventures into the heart of fires that scorch the land, vibrant friendships that fire the soul, and deep love that ends in devastating heartbreak.

978-1-945805-66-0
$14.95 (pb) ● $8.99 (eb)

Available at your favorite booksellers.